ARISTOTLE'S

PHILOSOPHY OF FRIENDSHIP

SUNY SERIES IN ANCIENT GREEK PHILOSOPHY
ANTHONY PREUS, EDITOR

ARISTOTLE'S

PHILOSOPHY OF FRIENDSHIP

Suzanne Stern-Gillet

STATE UNIVERSITY OF NEW YORK PRESS

Published by
State University of New York Press, Albany

For information, address State University of New York
Press, State University Plaza, Albany, N.Y., 12246

Production by Diane Ganeles
Marketing by Theresa Abad Swierzowski

Library of Congress Cataloging-in-Publication Data

Stern-Gillet, Suzanne
    Aristotle's philosophy of friendship / Suzanne Stern-Gillet.
        p.   cm. — (SUNY series in ancient Greek philosophy)
    Includes bibliographical references and index.
    ISBN 0-7914-2341-7 (alk. paper). — ISBN 0-7914-2342-5 (pbk. :
alk. paper)
    1. Aristotle—Views on friendship. 2. Friendship. I. Title.
II. Series.
    B491.F7S74 1995
    177'.6—dc20   94-10399
                                                                CIP

10 9 8 7 6 5 4 3 2 1

For Axel

ἐν παρ' ἐσλὸν πήματα σύνδυο δαίονται βροτοῖς
ἀθάνατοι. τὰ μὲν ὦν
    οὐ δύνανται νήπιοι κόσμῳ φέρειν,
ἀλλ' ἀγαθοί, τὰ καλὰ τρέψαντες ἔξω.

Pindar, *Pythian* 3.81-83

and for Bertrand

Ὄρσο, τέκνον,
δεῦρο πάγκοινον ἐς χώραν ἵμεν φάμας ὄπισθεν.'

Pindar, *Olympian* 6.62-63

CONTENTS

Abbreviations   1

Introduction   3

1. Selfhood   11

2. Selves and Other Selves   37

3. For the Sake of the Other   59

4. Self-Love   79

5. Self-Love and Egoism   103

6. Self-Sufficiency   123

7. Friendship, Justice, and the State   147

Conclusion   171

Notes   179

Select Bibliography   211

Author Index   221

Subject Index   223

Index Locorum   227

ABBREVIATIONS

D.A.   De Anima

E.E.   Eudemian Ethics

M.M.   Magna Moralia

Met.   Metaphysics

N.E.   Nicomachean Ethics

Pol.   Politics

Rhet.   Rhetoric

INTRODUCTION

I.

The topic of friendship figures prominently in Aristotle's ethical writings; one-fifth of the *Nicomachean Ethics* and one of the four books that are specifically *Eudemian* are devoted to an exploration of the moral aspects of this personal relationship. Yet, until recently, commentators have largely departed from Aristotle's lead in the matter, choosing instead to concentrate on what they must have considered to be more weighty matters in the master's ethics. Moral philosophers, too, long tended to ignore friendship, though they lavished much attention on the moral obligations incurred by humans in their relationships with one another. Friendship thus remained in a penumbra, traditionally considered to be a philosophical topic in virtue of the ancients' interest in the matter, yet rarely since systematically explored.

It would be interesting to speculate as to the reasons which led scholars, and philosophers generally, to relegate friendship to the fringe of ethics. Yet such is not my purpose in this study. The task that I set myself is to contribute to the analysis and interpretation of the texts in which Aristotle treats of friendship. Although I have proceeded on the assumption that the study of most ancient Greek texts does not stand in need of utilitarian apology, I should justify the present endeavour on two counts. Aristotle's conception

3

of friendship, far from being a mere appendix to his ethics, constitutes an integral and crucial part of it. As I shall argue, Aristotelian fully-fledged friendship effects a harmonization between the self-centred notion of *eudaimonia* (usually translated as happiness) and the altruism that many a later philosopher claims to be central to the moral life. Motivating humans to feel for and with others, as well as to act in their interest, complete friendship also uniquely contributes to the cognitive self-actualization of virtuous persons.

Aristotle's ideas on friendship, however, hold more than a narrowly scholarly interest. The incredulity, annoyance, possibly even shock, that readers new to Aristotle will experience when first confronted with books VII and VIII of the *Nicomachean Ethics* and book VII of the *Eudemian Ethics*, should usefully shake their complacent modernity. Because Aristotle's views on friendship are often in sharp contrast with corresponding modern notions, his present-day readers will be prompted to articulate and refine their own ideas, often all the more fiercely held for being imprecise, on the matter of interpersonal relationships. As a result, their own lives, as well as current debates on the nature of affective ties and of the moral problems that they pose, are likely to benefit.

It will here be argued that Aristotle's disquisitions on primary friendship cannot be fully understood unless they are related to his distinctive and complex, but only implicitly formulated, concept of selfhood. In chapter 1 this concept will be uncovered, investigated, and contrasted with corresponding modern notions. Chapter 2 will be devoted to the clarification of the complex claim that primary friends are other selves to one another, in the light of Aristotle's views on selfhood. Further implications of these views for the reflexive relations of self-love and self-sufficiency will be discussed in chapters 4 and 6. In chapters 3 and 5 a number of arguments will be presented to show that not only is Aristotelian primary friendship disinterested, but a reliance on the dichotomy of egoism and altruism seriously impedes the exegesis of Aristotle's treatment of primary friendship.

Lastly, chapter 7 will be devoted to an examination of the relations between civic and primary friendship.

All exegesis presents significant risks insofar as it cannot totally avoid reading the past in terms of the present and thus disregarding the fact that the past contained many seeds which never came to fruition. Not only is the past richer than we can ever hope to realize, but the mirror we hold to it is, to some extent, distorting. No exegesis should therefore aim at reconstructing a past philosophy "as it truly was,"[1] and differing interpretations of the same texts can and should be able peacefully to co-exist. The particular claims I make for my exegesis are, firstly, that it presents Aristotle's texts on friendship as a unified, coherent, systematic whole and, secondly, that it ties the views they express to central topics in his political philosophy and philosophical psychology. Together with book VII of the *Eudemian Ethics*, books VIII and IX of the *Nicomachean Ethics* constitute a veritable philosophy of friendship.

II.

The usual translations of φιλία by *friendship, amitié, Freundshaft*, etc., raise problems of interpretation insofar as the Greek word φίλος and its cognates (φιλία, φιλεῖν, φιλότης, φιλικός etc.) neither denote nor connote exactly the same relationships as their modern counterparts. Further, the Greek concepts themselves had already undergone a significant semantic evolution by the time Aristotle came to put them to philosophical use. The rich and unclear semantic history of φιλία weighed heavily on Aristotle as he attempted both to describe its nature and to systematize the moral norms it entails. Commentators must therefore be wary either of Homerizing or of modernizing a philosopher who, in fact, bore witness to the past of his culture while articulating some of the central ideas that were to shape its future.

Great scholars have traced the history of the concept of *philia*, and there is no call for me here to add to or challenge the claims of R.-A. Gauthier,[2] A.W.H. Adkins,[3] E. Benveniste[4] *et al*. Even less do I feel competent or called upon to settle their disagreements. A brief summary of their findings is nevertheless in order.[5] In Homeric usage *philos* functions both as a possessive reflexive (e.g., in *phila gounata, one's knees*)[6] and as an adjective which can designate either the members of one's household, or those one 'loves' (as used, e.g., by Achilles and Patroclus to refer to each other), or, lastly, those individuals who are linked by the bond of guest friendship (as alluded to, e.g., in the famous fight between Diomedes and Glaucus the Lycian[7]). In the first of its adjectival uses the concept mirrors the Latin *sui*, the French 'les siens' or the German 'die Seinen'. It designates those individuals whom blood, law, or custom have made one's 'nearest and dearest'. The meaning of *philos* in the second sense is very close to that of the modern concept of friendship. In the third sense the word refers to the socially well-established custom of offering hospitality and protection to travellers of similar rank and status (*xenoi*) to oneself who chanced to pass through one's land. A reciprocal relationship, guest-friendship provided men of substance and high lineage, to whom it was mostly confined, with a range of private and political benefits which considerably reduced the hazards of travel. The bond was usually trans-generational and of a non-affective nature. The nature of this relationship is ideally and famously exemplified in the encounter between Oedipus and Theseus in Sophocles' *Oedipus at Colonus*. In the main, pre-Classical Greek friendship is thus a social institution which has little to do with the inner lives of individuals. Homeric characters are born into particular networks of friendship, and they inherit claims to the guest-friendship of the descendants of their forebears' guest-friends.

So much have the complexities of Homeric usage absorbed scholarly attention that they have tended to overshadow later authors and contexts, and non-classicists could well be forgiven for thinking that, between Homer and Plato-Aristotle, the concept of *philia* underwent a somewhat abrupt semantic change. Those who have challenged this assumption have done so on the ground that Aristotle's *philia* is much closer to Homer's than is generally recognized.[8] A detailed study comparable to those already undertaken in Attic tragedy[9] of, e.g., Herodotus' and Xenophon's conceptions of friendship, would usefully document the evolution of that concept from the heroic to the classical period.

Herodotus, for instance, continues to use *philia* to refer to guest-friendship as well as to private mutual affection. Most frequently, though, in his usage, it serves to designate the mutual bond existing between allies, political or diplomatic, and between companions in arms, as well as between those who have concluded reciprocal arrangements to help, or refrain from harming, one another.[10] Herodotus' use of *philia* and its cognates contributes to accounting for Aristotle's preoccupation with the nature and casuistry of utility friendship and for the contrast he draws between it and what he calls virtue or primary friendship.

Xenophon's *Memorabilia*, on the other hand, written after the death of Socrates in 399, contains unmistakable signs of the evolution of the concept of *philia*, as the following example indicates. Advising Critobulus on the attributes that "make a man's friendship worth winning," Socrates lists[11] some of the qualities which will figure prominently in Aristotle's characterization of primary friendship, viz. generosity, moderation, benevolence, and disinterestedness. Although Xenophon's Socrates has no compunction to say that a man's virtue partly consists in "outdoing his enemies in mischief," his conception of friendship is nevertheless that of a tie which centrally engages the inner emotional life of the partners and makes serious moral demands on their character.

III.

In ancient Greek usage the concept of *philia* thus encompasses a wide and diverse field of personal and social relationships compared to which the extension of the modern concept of friendship is bound to appear very restricted.

Although the modern concept does not permit the drawing of neat distinctions between friends, on the one hand, and relations, associates, pals, cronies, and companions, on the other, it generally supports a definition of friendship in terms of "elective affinities." The adjective 'elective' is all-important in this context; unlike relatives and relations, friends are not imposed by external circumstances. Although they recognize that merely chance encounters often stand at the origin of their friendship, modern friends ascribe its development to a process of continuous choice. They tend, further, to view their respective personalities as akin in crucial, though sometimes disappointingly minor, ways. In short, they love each other in and for their unique-ness. It is not surprising, therefore, that the parties are generally content to leave their bond unexamined on the assumption that the grounds of love and friendship are not fit matters for close analytical scrutiny. Being capricious in origin and spontaneous in their development, modern friendships are fundamentally non-rational, though it is generally recognized that they involve some definite moral commitments.

Aristotle by contrast offers a very detailed analysis of the varieties of friendship, of their grounds, likely developments, moral implications, and general casuistry. What he describes as friendship's purest form, viz., virtue or primary friendship, differs significantly from modern friendship. Above all it is essentially a rational association which encompasses what is seen as the essential selves of the friends. As such, it evades the contingency and capriciousness which may well have caused the topic of friendship later to drop out of the philosophical agenda.

IV.

The following translations have mostly been used: of the *Nicomachean Ethics*, T.H. Irwin, of the *Eudemian Ethics*, H. Rackham, of the *Politics*, B. Jowett, revised by J. Barnes, of the *De Anima*, D.W. Hamlyn, and of the

Metaphysics, W.D. Ross, revised by J. Barnes. All departures from these translations are flagged in footnotes.

No knowledge of ancient Greek is presupposed. The few passages quoted in the original are so for the purpose of discussing points of syntax or terminology. The translations and comments that accompany these quotations should make them readily intelligible to Greekless readers. Furthermore, I have tried to be economical with Greek-English terminology. If Aristotle is worth studying now, he must, for the most part, be translatable into modern vernaculars. This notwithstanding, it has to be said that some of his key moral concepts, e.g., *eudaimonia* and *autarkeia*, do not have quite the same meaning or associations, as 'happiness' and 'self-sufficiency.' In those cases, I have followed the widespread custom of using the Greek words in transliteration.

V.

It is now common practice amongst philosophers to use the feminine pronoun to refer to the moral agent. For reasons which I hope will not be deemed to proceed from misguided historical fastidiousness, I have here departed from this practice. As is well known, Aristotle argued explicitly that women were incapable of the highest and best kind of friendship. I take the view that it does not behove commentators to gloss over or attempt to correct such bias of their authors. In this particular matter we must be content with the confidence that, had he lived today, Aristotle would most probably have revised his views on the nature of women. He was, after all, not only mindful of the opinions of the many but also sought to incorporate the views of the wise in his moral philosophy.

VI.

Even wise men, Aristotle wrote, derive benefit from intellectual companionship.[12] Less-than-wise persons, one infers, not only need to consort with their intellectual equals but also to learn from their betters. The following deserve special thanks: Gordon Neal, whose critical faculties remained alert through several readings of my manuscript, Anthony Preus, who offered perceptive comments and timely advice, Trevor Quinn, who kindly helped me to recover some of my lost Greek, Stephen Clark and Harry Lesser, who prompted me to clarify my thinking on a number of issues, Aurora Plomer, who offered constructive criticisms of my first chapter, and SUNY Press' anonymous readers, who have mastered the art of being incisive and urbane at the same time. The mistakes and misguided assumptions that are bound to remain are mine alone. Thanks are also due to Bolton Institute for easing off my teaching load while I was working on this book, and to Amanda Herod, whose command of the CD-ROM facilities transformed my untidy print-outs into a presentable text. Most of all, thanks are due to Axel Stern whose moral support never failed me and from whose philosophical acumen I have long benefited. Lastly, it is a matter of great satisfaction to me that my son Bertrand decided to learn ancient Greek while I was engaged in this project.

1

SELFHOOD

To receive enlightenment and instruction from Aristotle's disquisitions on friendship we must first appreciate how striking they are and how deeply they challenge some of our modern notions. This is not so easy as it appears since his pedantic style is apt to scatter a fine, almost imperceptible, dust on such familiar themes. "Down-to-earth"[1] though his treatment of the subject may appear to be, it is in fact both profound and contentious.

Aristotle's most arresting pronouncement on friendship is that, in the friendship of virtue, friends are "other selves" (ἄλλοι αὐτοί) to each other. Our first question should not be "What does Aristotle mean by 'another self'?" but rather "Why does a philosopher so generally sensitive to the workings of ordinary linguistic usage as Aristotle use, and keep using, this—to us—most provocative phrase?"[2] Such an investigation will detain us for two chapters. In the present chapter it will be argued that Aristotle's concept of selfhood differs significantly from ours. Historical remarks on this contrast will be followed by a detour through some arid landscapes of Aristotelian noetic in order to explore the background of his pronouncement that virtuous friendship involves 'other selfhood'. Chapter 2 will be devoted to unravelling the complexities of the phrase itself.

The statement that a friend, in the full sense of the word, is his friend's other self appears in both *Ethics* and is repeated in the *Magna Moralia*.[3] In the *Eudemian* version

Aristotle adapts popular wisdom to his own purposes when he invokes the proverb according to which: "'friend' really denotes, in the language of the proverb, 'another Hercules'— another self."[4] Commentators agree that originally this proverb did not apply to friendship but, in Rachkam's words, meant "as strong as Hercules."[5] In the same way as some other person can be as Herculean as Hercules, my friend can be as much myself as I am. Be it noted that in the *Eudemian* passage Aristotle shows himself aware of the paradoxical nature of this claim since he hastens to specify that a friend, though another (ἄλλος or ἕτερος) self, is also a separate (διαίρετος) being: ". . . none the less a friend means, as it were, a separate self."[6] In the *Nicomachean* version, on the other hand, Aristotle shows no such reservation. Not only does he there speak in his own name, but, on four occasions, as we shall see, he blithely reiterates, without attempting to substantiate, the contention that "a friend is another self."[7]

On the face of it, the phrase *allos autos* is a very confusing oxymoron which raises a number of issues. It poses a grammatical problem in so far as lexicographers and grammarians of classical Greek do not appear to have recorded other, similar, cases of the pronoun αὐτός being used substantivally. Since αὐτός in this case is not preceded by the article and cannot therefore mean 'the same' (*idem*), it cannot but mean 'self' (*ipse*). This would appear to justify the traditional rendering of *allos autos* by 'another self.' The possibility that, notwithstanding the exegetical tradition, *allos autos* actually means 'the other *qua* self' and thus serves to underline the separate identity of the friend, cannot be seriously entertained. As will soon become apparent, the coherence of several key Aristotelian texts on virtuous or primary friendship depends on the traditional rendering of *allos autos* as 'another self' being upheld.

Even by Aristotle's standards this constitutes marked stylistic insouciance, and the stylistic oddity of the phrase was not lost on subsequent writers and commentators. Though Cicero coined the expression *'alter ego'* in his private correspondence, he displayed greater caution in his academic writings: "the real friend . . . is, as it were, another self,"[8] he wrote in the *De Amicitia*. Be it noted both that Cicero writes *'alter idem'* (not *'alter ipse'*) and introduces an 'as it were' to mitigate the strangeness of the definition of friendship that is being propounded.

Aquinas, on the other hand, has no qualms about using the expression *'alter ipse'* to render the Aristotelian *allos autos*, but, more explicitly than Cicero, he cautions the reader against a literal interpretation of the phrase. Thus, commenting on *N.E.* 1170b5 sqq., where it is stated, in his rendering of Aristotle, that "The virtuous man is related to his friend as he is to himself because the friend is in a certain way another self," St. Thomas writes: "Therefore in the same way as his own being is choiceworthy and delightful to any virtuous person, so is for him the being of his friend. *And if not the same, yet very nearly so. Indeed, the natural oneness that characterizes the relationship that a person has to himself is closer than the oneness of disposition that prevails towards a friend.*"[9] This interesting gloss alerts us to the distance that separates medieval concepts of personhood from ancient ones. Not only does Aquinas here take it for granted that the self is "by nature" unitary, but he also deems the presence of the self to itself to be unlike other forms of awareness. As we shall have ample opportunity to note, these assumptions are un-Aristotelian.

Although Cicero's and Aquinas' demurrings seem more likely to have been prompted by the philosophical implications of the phrase than by its stylistic clumsiness, the question nevertheless arises as to whether the Aristotelian corpus provides other examples of a similar substantival use of the pronoun *autos*. Bonitz adduces a series of examples as evidence that "Not infrequently αὐτός or αὐτό is used absolutely, without the referring noun that it serves to stress, either because it can be understood from the context or, generally, because a universal notion is implied."[10] Since *allos autos* is not a "universal notion," Bonitz presumably intends one to conclude that in Aristotle's usage the referent of the phrase can be inferred from its context. Unfortunately this explanation leaves one problem unsolved: in the expression *allos autos* not only does the pronoun *autos* do duty as a noun but it also functions as itself the referent of the adjective *allos*. In the examples enumerated by Bonitz this is the only case where the substantivization of *autos* has been pushed that far.

On the philosophical front, the view that full friendship involves each friend in becoming his friend's other self is bound to appear almost perverse. Three particular questions will need to be raised, *viz*: (1) What conception of selfhood does Aristotle operate with? (2) Could friendship survive the conflation of the friends' selves? Indeed does not the very concept of friendship presuppose that the friends remain separate individuals? (3) Supposing that the symbiosis implied by the *allos autos* phrase be possible, would it even be morally desirable? To our modern sensibilities at least, appreciation of and respect for the otherness of the partner are vital components of friendship, as they are of love. The more the other is cherished in his/her otherness, it is generally held, the purer the friendship, and attempts to align another's dispositions, values, or tastes to one's own are mostly deemed misguided. Being personal relations, friendship and love, it is generally intimated, should endeavour to accommodate the personalities of individuals who are, by definition, unique. If it turns out that none of these claims fits easily into Aristotle's extensive and detailed analysis of friendship, we need to account for such significant differences in outlook between him and ourselves.

It is important to note that the contention that virtuous friends are other selves to each other mostly appears as a premiss in Aristotle's arguments; it is never itself fully argued for. This would seem to indicate that Aristotle did not consider it to be either obscure or especially contentious. Mentions of this premiss are generally to be found in discussions of the moral ideal of self-sufficiency (*autarkeia*). Since Aristotle viewed self-sufficiency as greatly desirable, he needed to argue that the good of friendship, which, *prima facie*, increases the virtuous person's dependence upon others, is in fact compatible with self-sufficiency. Clearly, the description of virtuous friends as other selves to each other is invoked partly to counteract the conclusion that friendship increases the virtuous person's dependence upon external factors.[11] If accepted, the 'other self' premiss would contribute to keeping *eudaimonia* (happiness, well-being) within the virtuous person's reach by internalizing what initially appears to be the irreducible alterity of the friend. To that effect it fulfills a crucial strategic function in Aristotle's argument. This in itself rules out the possibility that the phrase be no more than a pious platitude.

In order to be serviceable as a premiss, though, a statement needs to be correct or, at least, generally acceptable. Clearly Aristotle assumes that his description of virtuous friendship as other selfhood meets this condition. To explain why he could reasonably make this assumption, two brief historical comments need to be made; the first pertains to Homeric and tragic usage, the second pertains to shifting conceptions of selfhood.

Unfortunately, attempts to establish the precise nature of pre-Classical Greek views on such topics as human agency, the will, and the self have mostly come to grief. At present their authors either stand accused of importing unjustified assumptions into the endeavour or of going beyond the evidence.[12] Accordingly, one should be wary of building much on so shaky a foundation. Nevertheless, over the years a considerable body of evidence and analysis has accumulated which points to certain distinct features of Greek conceptions of selfhood and accounts for a number of highly charged and otherwise enigmatic metaphors in the poetry of the time.

Adapting a classification first introduced by Foucault,[13] Vernant injected much needed conceptual clarity into the matter by distinguishing between the concepts of *individual* (as contradistinguished from the group), *subject* (as source of his/her decisions and actions), and *I* (as object of reflexive awareness).[14] Only in this third sense, Vernant intimates, can it be claimed, not that "the Greeks" lacked a concept of self, but that their experience of the self was "differently organized from our own."[15] More precisely, in their view, he continues, "The subject does not constitute a closed internal world, which he must enter in order to find or, rather, to discover himself. The subject is turned to the outside. In the same way as the eye does not see itself, the individual looks elsewhere, outwards, before apprehending himself. His consciousness of self is not a reflexive process, a retreat into himself, an internal enclosing, face to face with his own person: it is existential."[16]

The hypothesis that pre-Classical Greek selfhood only carries minimal intimations of privacy, uniqueness, and reflexivity would contribute to explaining the relative frequency, in the *Iliad*, of phrases such as *'hena thumon echontes'* (having one spirit) and *'ison thumon echontes'* (having the same spirit)[17] to denote not only the coordinated action, on specific occasions, of comrades at arms but also the trans-subjective planning or resolutions of close friends. The psychological unity that, within the context of the *Iliad*, prevails between Achilles and Patroclus is an example in point. In his lamentations over the death of Patroclus, Achilles proclaims to have regarded his friend *ison emēi kephalēi* ('as myself', literally 'equal to my head').[18] The metonymical value of *kephalē* (head) makes the tribute significant, especially when it is placed in context. In the XVIth *Iliad* Patroclus had dressed for battle in Achilles' own suit of armour and found that it fitted him perfectly. Achilles' spears, too, were well adapted to Patroclus' hand.[19] Since Homer frequently resorts to bodily metaphors to convey mental states, we must take the friends' physical similarity to indicate the psychological state of unison that prevails between them. This view receives further confirmation in the XVIIth *Iliad* when we are told that Hector, though the equal of Achilles in valour, requires a divine intervention to make the armour, wrenched from Patroclus' dead body, fit him. Not only is Patroclus described as physically the same as Achilles, but also, throughout the poem, he appears to represent his friend's gentler, softer side. Indeed it is only after Patroclus' death that Achilles comes to exhibit some of the qualities of mercy and humanity that he had so conspicuously lacked before. So striking is the symbiosis between the friends that it might be suggested that in the Homeric text Achilles and Patroclus are implicitly presented as 'other selves' to one another.

If, as Arthur Adkins has argued, "the effects of Homeric usage persist to a considerable degree in the moral philosophy of Aristotle,"[20] we should at the very least keep in mind Homer's poignant account of the friendship between Achilles and Patroclus when attempting to interpret Aristotle's intricate and sophisticated pronouncements on the subject of friendship. More specifically, we may care to note that Aristotle's reliance on the other self premiss strikes a Homeric echo.

Though the extant intervening literature does not yield a rich crop of similar expressions, it is worth mentioning the enigmatic opening words of Antigone's appeal to Ismene in Sophocles' play: ὦ κοινὸν αὐτάδελφον Ἰσμήνης κάρα· Since no translation can fully convey the dark potentness of the Greek, it seems best here to rely on a pedantically literal translation, i.e., "O, common, own-sisterly head[21] of Ismene." In these words, Antigone is in effect claiming that the relationship of blood *philia*, whose claims she is to uphold throughout the play, effectively overrides individual separateness.[22] Euripides, too, alludes to this kind of unity when, in the *Orestes*, he has Elektra tell her brother that he has 'one soul' with her[23] and that those who are friends are 'one.'[24] Aristotle, who could rely on his audience's familiarity with these passages, even quotes Electra's first remark in both the *Eudemian*[25] and the *Nicomachean Ethics*.[26] In pre-Classical times, therefore, rhetorical claims about friendship occasionally included allusions to psychic symbiosis, and a number of writers appear to have assumed that *philia* could transcend the limitations later associated with bodily separateness and individual self-awareness.

These desultory literary allusions do not, of course, of themselves, license any firm conclusion on the vexed matter of archaic and classical Greek conceptions of selfhood. They are offered here merely as pointers, modest additions to recent discussions of the topic.[27] In any case, far from it being my intention here to contribute to these investigations, I only refer to them in so far as they provide useful background for my exegesis of Aristotle's views on friendship. More specifically, I shall now argue that, unlike modern readers, Aristotle's contemporaries were unlikely to be perplexed by his description of virtuous friendship as other selfhood. Indeed if, in their outlook, the self, as Vernant and others have claimed, appears to be "neither delimited nor unified,"[28] they could not be expected to appreciate some of the philosophical implications of Aristotle's contention that friendship at its best enlarges what we would call the natural boundaries of the self.

As for Aristotle himself, he did not, as we saw, consider that his views on other selfhood required much philosophical buttressing. Although he devoted much attention to the conditions of individuation of conspecific particulars, he did not investigate the criteria of personal identity. As I shall argue presently, the cluster of philosophical problems which the concept of selfhood generates for post-Cartesians could not even be fully formulated in Aristotle's terminology. This alone would appear to confirm the view that the conception of selfhood then embedded in Greek mentality differed from ours. Aristotle's commitment to the dialectical method, especially in ethics, would in any case make him reluctant to depart from commonly held beliefs (*endoxa*). For these reasons we can assume that his claim that a virtuous person is his friend's other self was meant literally.

As for a *theory* of the self, Aristotle had none that could even remotely be compared with modern ones. Nowhere does he systematically set out to address explicitly formulated and related questions on the issues of self-identity, personhood, and individuality. Nowhere does he attempt to uncover, formulate, and critically examine the structure of his predecessors' or his contemporaries' concepts of selfhood. Further, as we shall see presently, his theory of perception assigns only a minimal role to self-awareness. On the other hand, however, in the ethical treatises, Aristotle repeatedly advises us to nurture the part of our being that can most properly be called "our own." Only in so doing, he intimates, will we be truly at one with ourselves. I shall take these

pronouncements as evidence of the presence in his moral
thought of a concept of selfhood of sorts. Although it embodies a moral goal which may well turn out to be the direct
ancestor of our ideal of moral integrity, Aristotle's notion of
the self differs significantly from later, more purely cognitive
and descriptive, concepts of selfhood.

In order to vindicate these contentions, I shall now turn
to Aristotle's account of the genesis of reflexive awareness in
perception. Since my main interest in the matter lies in the
notion of self there presupposed, I shall leave unexamined a
great many of the complexities of Aristotle's theory of perception. This excursus will perhaps contribute to justifying the
considerations that I shall offer later in this chapter on some
differences between ancient and modern views of selfhood.

In the *De Anima* we are told that perception, of which
all animals are capable, consists in the apprehension by
each sense organ of the corresponding perceptible and individuated forms (as opposed to the matter) of particular
objects.[29] Perception further includes awareness of its proper
object.[30] Since such perceptual awareness could not come
about through the agency of a sense different from the particular sense organ concerned without generating an infinite
regress,[31] Aristotle concludes that it must be brought about
through the agency of the sense organ itself. This leads him
to claim that perceiving is not a single thing,[32] and that
"Each sense, therefore, is concerned with the subject perceived by it, being present in the sense organ, *qua* sense
organ, and it judges the varieties of the subject perceived by
it, e.g., sight for white and black, and taste for sweet and bitter; and similarly for the other senses too."[33] Let it be noted
that this account of perceptual awareness, although it
ascribes a discriminatory power to each sense, is conducted
without explicit reference to self-awareness. In itself this
does not signal a gap in Aristotle's account since, as is evident in the case of infants and animals, unity of perception
can obtain in the absence of self-awareness. Perception need
not presuppose apperception.

Before long, however, the absence of a unitary faculty
guaranteeing the unity of perception will adversely affect

Aristotle's argument. Indeed, since each sense organ generates both sensation and awareness of sensation, Aristotle
must account for the agency through which animals can,
as they do, discriminate between the data of different
senses, e.g., the visual sensation of whiteness and the gus-
tatory sensation of sweetness. He puts the problem suc-
cinctly: "Nor indeed is it possible to judge by separate means
that sweet is different from white, but both must be evident to *one thing*—for otherwise, even if I perceived one
thing and you another, it would be evident that they were
different from each other. Rather *one thing* must assert that
they are different; for sweet is different from white. *The
same thing* then asserts this; hence, as it asserts so it both
thinks and perceives. That, therefore, it is not possible to
judge separate things by separate means is clear."[34]

What is this "one thing" (*heis tis*), this faculty, which
Aristotle soon proceeds to describe as undivided (*achōris-
ton*)?[35] It is generally assumed to be the *koinē aisthēsis* (*sensus cummunis*)[36] or *koinē dunamis* (common power), i.e., the
sense whose main function is mostly described as the apprehension of the "common sensibles" (i.e. movement, rest,
number, figure, and size),[37] as opposed to the "proper objects"
of each sense. Amongst the other functions which he
ascribes to that sense, Aristotle appears to include the ability to collate and compare the information emanating from
the different senses.[38] In so far as it judges, the judging element is "both numerically indivisible and undivided";[39] in
so far as it senses several different objects (e.g., sweet and
white), it is several. Indeed if it were not indivisible *qua*
judging element, there would be no way of distinguishing
between the situation where Smith perceives both sweet
and white and the situation where Smith perceives sweet
while Jones perceives white.[40] In other words, Aristotle
needs here to postulate a single indivisible judging element
to account for the fact that perceptions are organized in different individual series. To that extent the unitary judging
element or *sensus communis* is the Aristotelian counterpart
of Kant's synthetic unity of apperception. The long and tor-
tuous argument in *De Anima* III,2 represents Aristotle's

attempt to formulate a concept corresponding to the modern notion of unity of consciousness.

In the *De Somno et Vigilia* Aristotle goes one step further in the characterization of the 'common element': ". . . all [senses] are accompanied by a common power, in virtue whereof a person perceives that he sees or hears."[41] Although, as this text indicates, Aristotle extended the role of the *sensus communis* to include second-order perceptual awareness, it should nevertheless be stressed that consciousness of self *qua* self is not explicitly listed as one of its several functions. Multi-faceted as the common power is described to be, it does not, in that treatise, include the apprehension of a unitary subject of consciousness.

Only in the *Nicomachean Ethics* are second-order perceptual awareness and awareness of self *qua* such brought together. Interestingly enough, the context is a discussion of the benefits uniquely brought about by virtue friendship. "If we are perceiving," Aristotle notes, "we perceive that we are perceiving; and if we are understanding, we perceive that we are understanding. Now perceiving that we are perceiving or understanding is the same as perceiving that we are, since we agreed that being is perceiving and understanding."[42] This passage licenses two inferences. Firstly, Aristotle considers that self-awareness is consequent upon a number of sensory activities; it neither precedes them nor is presupposed by them. The use of a verb of perception (*aisthanometha*) to describe the genesis of self-awareness shows how derivative the latter is. Secondly and more importantly, the seat of perception and cognition, which is both the agent and the object of self-awareness, remains nameless throughout this key passage. Though Aristotle considers that there is a single entity which apprehends itself apprehending the world, he neither has a word for it nor feels the need to coin one. To denote what later philosophers will call the self Aristotle has to resort to a subordinate clause 'that we are' (*hoti esmen*).[43] Although correct, remarks such as Hamlyn's that ". . . he [Aristotle] gives little attention to the role of the concepts of a person, the subject of consciousness and personal identity"[44] nevertheless strike an anachronistic note. Since the Greek of Aristotle's time did not have concepts for any of these things, the only conclusion that we can draw in the matter is that Aristotle did not coin technical terms for them. Was this because he had no philosophical use for such notions as personhood and self-identity? As we have seen, the evidence from his theory of perception points the other way. We shall return to this question.

Aristotle's inchoate concept of selfhood is in sharp contrast with the Cartesian self as the primary and unshakable datum of experience. Though various Cartesian texts could be invoked, the well-known wax example in the second *Meditation* illustrates the point adequately. Having established the certainty of his own existence, Descartes proceeds to investigate the nature of this 'I' who necessarily is whenever he, Descartes, thinks. His phrasing of the problem is characteristic: "I know that I exist; the question is, what is this 'I' that I know?"[45] In other words, the entity in question is assumed to be correctly referred to as 'I' prior to being investigated and defined. Together with cognition and will, sense is ultimately characterized with reference to the mind's reflexive awareness. By contrast it is only contingently that the 'I' depends on the occurrence of particular experiences. This is one of the lessons of the wax example. While in Aristotle's reasoning it is sense perception which ultimately leads to a budding concept of self-awareness, in Descartes' scheme of things awareness of self is the first foundation upon which the reliability of sense experience is eventually to be established.[46] Indeed Descartes goes as far as using sensory experience as contributory support for the view that the mind is better known than the body: "if my perception of the wax seemed more distinct after it was established not just by sight or touch but by many other considerations, it must be admitted that I now know myself even more distinctly. This is because every consideration whatsoever which contributes to my perception of the wax, or of any other body, cannot but establish even more effectively the nature of my own mind."[47] Not only does Descartes maintain that mind can exist independently of body and be better known than it, but he sets his whole philosophical quest in terms of an entity which he never feels the need to introduce, let alone justify, i.e., his own directly accessible and transparent self.[48] The autobiographical tenor of his major works, his rejection of any didacticism, his distrust of the senses, and his reliance on introspection all point to Descartes' fundamental assumption that his irredeemably private mental life constitutes the vantage point from which the world external to it may be reached. For Aristotle, who never doubted the existence of the external world and the general trustworthiness of our senses, on the other hand, the idea that mental operations furnish conscious individuals with an awareness of their own selves is explicitly stated only in the *Nicomachean Ethics*, although it makes a timid appearance in the *De Anima* and the *Parva Naturalia*.

The relative paucity of Aristotle's vocabulary in this respect can be traced to his concept of *psychē* (soul). Whichever definition of soul appears to us to fit most of his pronouncements on the topic, it will not be of an entity which can be defined independently of the body. Though the active (*poiētic*) *nous* can survive the death of the body and is therefore capable of separate existence, Aristotle views it as operating in conjunction with the passive (*pathētic*) *nous* during the life of the human individual. For Aristotle *nous*, like *psychē*, is thus not something over and above its operations. While he considers that the operations of *nous*, both active and passive, are activities of which the human subject is conscious, there is no sign that he considers that such consciousness gives humans a direct and private access to the workings of their own mental processes. A sure sign that this is so emerges from the fact that problems raised in connection with 'other minds' seem never to surface in Aristotle's philosophical psychology. Since Aristotle defines *psychē* as the principle of organisation and functioning of a live body, knowledge of it cannot depend upon the private data of introspection. Not possessing a fully articulated concept of self-awareness of the Cartesian kind, Aristotle needs not address the cognitive difficulties that such dualism creates.

Such difficulties have been dogging post-Cartesian philosophy for so long that they circumscribe the very framework within which such fundamental problems as that of personhood are formulated. Even those successors of Descartes who have since professed to debunk the notion of self-identity could not help paying their tribute to him. When Hume, for example, writes that "For my part, when I enter most intimately into what I call *myself*, I always stumble on some particular perception or other,"[49] he still resorts to a philosophically potent metaphor, i.e., that of a chamber so dark that, although he enters it deliberately, he cannot but stumble once inside it. Later, having used the similarly loaded "comparison of the theatre," Hume is careful to note that it "must not mislead us."[50] The point, however, is that Hume failed to come up with an analogy that would further his own cause. In spite of his warning, the metaphor of the theatre cannot but strengthen the very conception that he is at pains to rebut. Gilbert Ryle's later, famous use of the same simile[51] to discredit what he calls the (Cartesian) "Official Doctrine" of the mind (or self) as private and separate from its diverse manifestations, shows just how loaded the simile is. Thus, one of the reasons why Hume's warning was not more generally heeded would seem to be that the concept of self he aimed at debunking had become enshrined in ordinary as well as in philosophical usage.

It is therefore unsurprising that modern readers of Aristotle's books on friendship should be puzzled by the *allos autos* premiss. They bring to its exegesis a host of un-Aristotelian assumptions and notions which, added to the considerable difficulty of the Greek texts, make the problem of ascertaining the meaning of the Aristotelian phrase well-nigh intractable. I am not proposing that we divest ourselves from the Cartesian tradition. That would be impossible. But we should keep in mind that the concept of self, *as we use it*, was not one of Aristotle's basic philosophical tools. As I hope to have shown, his analysis of perception indicates that he was endeavouring to account both for the unity of consciousness and for the genesis of self-awareness without the benefit of what some modern philosophers would be pleased to call appropriate terminology.

When, leaving historical considerations aside, we turn to Aristotle's moral works, we are confronted with an explicit concept of self that differs significantly from the inchoate concept of the *De Anima* and the *Parva Naturalia*: selfhood is now mostly presented as a moral construct. As is well-known, Aristotle held that all living things are ensouled. Human beings owe their place in the hierarchy of living entities neither to their nutritive soul (which they share with plants) nor to their sensitive soul (which they share with all other animals) but to a rational element which they are alone in possessing. It is upon this conception of humans as essentially rational beings that the famous *ergon* argument in *Nicomachean Ethics* I rests: ". . . we take the human function to be a certain kind of life, and take this life to be the soul's activity and actions that express reason. The excellent man's function is to do this finely and well. Each function is completed well when its completion expresses the proper virtue. Therefore the human good turns out to be the soul's activity that expresses virtue."[52] Moral virtue, which consists in habitually acting and feeling as reason directs, is the single most important aspect of the Aristotelian good life. This is the core of Aristotelian ethics and does not here need rehearsing. What is worth pointing out, however, is the conception of selfhood as integrated soul which emerges from the *Ethics*. Though this theme will be developed at some length in chapters IV and VI below, some anticipatory comments may usefully be made here.

Aristotle repeatedly indicates that reason's success in co-ordinating and harmonizing the affects ensures wholeness of soul, while its failure in this respect results in some form or other of psychic imbalance or even disintegration. In *N.E.* IX and X, Aristotle goes further and identifies human beings with their intellect or understanding (*nous*): ". . . someone is called continent or incontinent because his understanding is or is not the master, on the assumption that this is what each person is."[53] As the reference to continence indicates, the *nous* with which Aristotle here identifies the human agent is practical reason, i.e., the element whose role it is to bring about the realization of those ends which it has formulated. Earlier on, we had been told that "the excellent person is of one mind with himself, and desires the same things in his whole soul. Hence he wishes goods and apparent goods to himself, and does them in his actions since it is proper to the good person to achieve the good. He wishes and does them for his own sake, since he does them for the sake of his thinking part, and that is what each person seems to be."[54]

These claims raise a number of issues. Granted that *nous* is the proper object of the good man's regard, who (or what), we need to ask, has regard for it? Aristotle's identification of human beings with their *nous* would seem to lead to the conclusion that, in good men at least, it is *nous* that holds itself in high regard. Contrary to what Aristotle indicates in the above passage, however, such a criterion would only assist us in distinguishing good men from bad ones if we could be sure that self-respect is totally alien to the base. But we cannot rule out the possibility that the bad man's *nous*, puny though it be, nevertheless respects itself, like a just man at the court of a corrupt ruler. Aristotle's claim that the good man agrees with himself, once reformulated in terms of the identification between human beings and their *nous*, yields a similarly disappointing, because platitudinous, conclusion. Furthermore, one cannot help wondering, which is the part of the akratic man's soul that regrets the domination of the appetites over reason?

Such objections need only to be formulated to show that we have gone adrift. They all proceed from the modern, but un-Aristotelian, assumptions that there are as many selves as there are human beings and that the integrity of a self lies beyond the reach of both vice and *akrasia*.

In fact, Aristotle views psychic unity as the result of a slow process of integration which is broadly co-extensive with the acquisition of moral virtue. Practical reason, in his outlook, constitutes the hub around which the self is formed, since it alone can effect the integration of the various psychic elements into a whole. Whenever it fails to do so, either through *akrasia* or vice, the individual remains unfree, a mere bunch of unstable elements and discordant parts. Aristotle's choice of words reflects this view of the self. Morally weak persons, he writes, *"abandon* themselves"[55] to pleasure, they are *"overcome"*[56] by it, and even suffer from some kind of *"madness."*[57] As for the base, they are described as *"at odds* with themselves."[58] Divided from their reason, i.e., the distinctively human part in them, the base are, according to Aristotle, effectively divided from themselves. While good men are those who value, desire, and plan with their "whole soul," bad ones are beleaguered and unsteady, since one part of their soul desires that which will harm, enfeeble, or distress another. In the *Eudemian Ethics* Aristotle expresses this idea by means of the traditional Greek dichotomy of the one and the manifold: ". . . the good is simple, whereas the bad is multiform; and also the good man is always alike and does not change in character, whereas the wicked and the foolish are quite different in the evening from that they were in the morning."[59]

These considerations help us to resolve the difficulties regarding reflexivity that were raised earlier. Rather than, in the strict sense of the term, identifying human beings with their *nous* at the exclusion of anything else in the Soul, which would effectively leave the wicked without central powers of agency, Aristotle assigns to *nous* the exercise of a regulating and predominating influence over the other elements in the human soul. In human beings *nous, qua* such, cannot, therefore, exist independently of the rest of the soul; just as rulers cannot rule in the absence of subjects, *nous* needs irrational or imperfectly rational drives and wants over which to exert its stewardship. Only when *nous* is unimpeded in the discharge of this function can human beings, in Aristotle's outlook, be said to be "at one" with themselves. In this sense *nous* is the *sine qua non* of an integrated personality. But it is also a *sine qua non* in so far as it constitutes the one specifically human element in the soul, upon whose recognition as such moral virtue depends. Good men are those who value most what is most valuable in themselves, i.e., the element that makes them beings of their kind, and who enable it to exert its natural authority over the appetitive and emotive parts which have long been trained in the habit of ready compliance. Bearing in mind the distinctive aura of Aristotle's concept of selfhood should help us to understand how and why he could, in effect, restrict a full measure of it to those who are morally virtuous and, by implication, hold that selfhood admits of degrees.

In the *Nicomachean Ethics* the self-concurrence of *nous* is, unsurprisingly, expressed by means of reflexive personal pronouns. Furthermore, in its four *Nicomachean* occurrences the phrase *allos autos* is itself unambiguously linked to a third person (singular or plural) reflexive pronoun whose referent is clear from the context. How significant is this construction? Might it assist our understanding of the puzzling claim that friends of virtue can be each other's selves? The passages are as follows: (1) γονεῖς μὲν οὖν τέκνα φιλοῦσιν ὡς ἑαυτούς (τὰ γὰρ ἐξ αὐτῶν οἷον ἕτεροι αὐτοὶ τῶ κεχωρίσθαι) ("A parent loves his children as he loves himself. For what has come from him is a sort of other himself");[60] (2) τῷ δὴ πρὸς αὐτὸν ἕκαστα τούτων ὑπάρχειν τῷ ἐπιεικεῖ, πρὸς δὲ τὸν φίλον ἔχειν ὥσπερ πρὸς αὐτόν (ἔστι γὰρ ὁ φίλος ἄλλος αὐτός) ("The decent person, then, has each of these features in relation to himself, and is related to his friend as he is to himself, since the friend is another himself");[61] (3) αὐτάρκεις οὖν ὄντας οὐδενὸς προσδεῖσθαι, τὸν δὲ φίλον, ἕτερον αὐτὸν ὄντα, πορίξειν ἃ δι᾽ αὐτοῦ ἀδυνατεῖ (". . . being self-sufficient, they need nothing added. But your friend, since he is another yourself, supplies what your own efforts cannot supply");[62] (4) ὡς δὲ πρὸς ἑαυτὸν ἔχει ὁ σπουδαῖος, καὶ πρὸς τὸν φίλον (ἕτερος γὰρ αὐτὸς ὁ φίλος ἐστίν) ("The excellent person is related to his friend in the same way as he is related to himself, since a friend is another himself").[63]

Each of the above passages features a noun, viz., οἱ γονεῖς, ὁ ἐπιεικής, οἱ αὐτάρκεις[64] and ὁ σπουδαῖος, to which a reflexive pronoun, directly, and ἄλλος αὐτός, by extension, refer. We are told that a person can have the same relation to a friend as he has to himself (1, 2, and 4) and that the friend, being another self, extends the range of goods available to the virtuous (3). The Homeric assumption that friends could be "of one mind" has, in these passages, been refined and provided with some theoretical underpinning. In virtue friendship, Aristotle in effect tells us, the reflexive relation that individuals have to themselves is extended to encompass another individual, i.e., the friend. In order to express this arresting suggestion, Aristotle needs a concept of selfhood which is not only reflexive but also symmetrical. While the reflexive pronoun expresses the first condition, the phrase *allos autos* arguably represents an attempt to embody the second. As for the substantivization of *autos* in the phrase *allos autos*, it points to the emergence, in Aristotle's thought, of an entity to which such properties can be ascribed.

To resume the argument so far: in Aristotle's scheme of things the notion of 'self' appears to be an achievement word, since it denotes a state of equilibrium between the various parts of the soul and constitutes an ideal towards which we should strive but which we may not reach. According to such a conception akratic and vicious people are not 'selves'; not only do their passions and appetites pull in different directions, but they rebel against and weaken the part that ought to direct them. Thus to the extent that Aristotelian selfhood is an evaluative, commendatory notion, it differs significantly from modern, purely descriptive conceptions of selfhood.[65] While a descriptive concept of self, in the modern sense, can at most be argued to emerge in Aristotle's text, an explicitly normative concept of self plays an important role in his ethics.

Before moving to a consideration of selfhood in book X of the *Nicomachean Ethics*, a last point on the morally virtuous self needs to be made. In so far as the mean characteristic of moral virtue is to be determined "with reference to us" (*pros hēmas*)[66] it would seem that selfhood, as emerging from psychic harmony, is always individual. The proverbial widow's generosity, for example, which is proportionate to her gender and circumstances, has little in common with a Gulbenkian's liberality. Practical reason must work on the material at hand, and that material will differ from individual to individual. The assimilation of the moral agent with his *nous*, for which Aristotle argues in Book IX of the *Nicomachean Ethics*, is thus compatible with the uniqueness of human agents. To that extent, it does not run counter to, though it does not, of course, prefigure, the modern concept of selfhood.

Unfortunately for the present enquiry, the tenth book of this *Ethics* appears to convey a rather different message. It is now the theoretic intellect which is singled out to constitute the specifically human element in the human soul. The context of this passage is well-known. Not only is the life of theoretical contemplation said to possess incidental advantages (viz., it is eminently pleasurable, self-sufficient, and leisurely), but it is also presented as intrinsically superior, since "If happiness, then, is activity expressing virtue, it is reasonable for it to express the supreme virtue, which will be the virtue of the best thing. The best is understanding, or whatever else seems to be the natural ruler and leader, and to understand what is fine and divine, by being itself either divine or the most divine element in us. Hence complete happiness will be its activity expressing its proper virtue; and we have said that this activity is the activity of study."[67] Those who, albeit intermittently, lead the theoretic life do so not in so far as they are human but in so far as they succeed in cultivating what is divine in them, i.e., their dianoetic *nous*.[68] Aristotle expands on this view in an uncharacteristically eloquent passage: "We ought not to follow the proverb-writers, and 'think human, since you are human', or 'think mortal, since you are mortal'. Rather, as far as we can, we ought to make ourselves immortal, and go to all lengths to live a life that expresses our supreme element; for however much this element may lack in bulk, by much more it surpasses everything in power and value."[69] Why should we do so? Aristotle's answer is intriguing: ". . . each person seems to be his understanding, if he is his controlling and better element; it would be absurd, then, if he were to choose not his own life, but something else's."[70] While the human (*anthrōpinos*) life, i.e., the life of "the compound" (*to suntheton*) calls for the exercise of the moral virtues, the god-like life of contemplation has its own specific excellences. While moral virtues have a social aspect and pertain to the emotions, which in turn depend on the body, intellectual virtue (*sophia*) is separate (*kechōrismenē*).[71]

The various exegetical difficulties raised by these passages are awesome. Fortunately there is no need to address them all here. Like most commentators, I shall assume that Aristotle uses *to suntheton* to refer to the composite of matter and form that is the live body. As far as selfhood is concerned, *N.E.*, X.8 raises the following problem: if the characteristically human life is that of the compound and if that life is best organized around practical reason, why does Aristotle here recommend his (human) audience to lead the (god-like) life of contemplation, not only on the ground that it is the life of the best element in them, but also on the ground that it is the life that is most their own (*oikeios*)? If his readers are human and therefore compound, why does he advise them that it would be unseemly to lead the life of another entity (in this case the human life) in preference to their very own (i.e., the life of the dianoetic, divine element)?

The context of the argument makes it clear that in *N.E.*, X,8 *oikeios* refers not to what is unique in each individual (as is the case with the modern English idiom 'to do one's own thing') but to what is characteristic of the species concerned. In this case it picks out what distinguishes humankind from all other kinds. The identification of the theoretic element as the essentially human factor, by implication, excludes as peripheral whatever makes each person unique. So, as the *Nicomachean Ethics* draws to a close, Aristotle is increasingly relegating as trivial and unimportant those elements which make each person different from all others, i.e., those very elements for which modern debates on self-identity aim at accounting. Indeed, if humans are their dianoetic element, and if the activity proper to that element is pure contemplation, there is no way that, e.g., Coriscus' contemplation can differ from Callias'. Consisting in an effortless intellectual apprehension of essences and fully intelligible thoughts, contemplation is beyond both toil and particularity. To the extent that human beings succeed in leading the theoretic life, they transcend the boundaries of their own idiosyncrasies, individual circumstances, and private concerns. Unlike moral virtue, theoretic contemplation cannot be "with reference to us" (*pros hēmas*). As for the object of contemplation, it must not in any way resist full intelligibility, which is a way of saying that it must be abstracted from its individuating features and pared down to its essence. The impersonal conception of selfhood which is put forward in chapters 7 and 8 of book X of the *Nicomachean Ethics* thus appears to be seriously at variance with that defended in book IX. This discrepancy is, of course, but one facet of the larger problem posed by the presence, in the *Nicomachean Ethics*, of two seemingly rival conceptions of the good life, one practical and the other contemplative. Besides raising a great many exegetical problems, the displacement of moral activity from the centre of the good life in favour of contemplation constitutes a source of difficulty for all those who seek to ground their virtue ethics in Aristotle's ethical treatises. This by itself probably accounts for the vast amount of scholarly literature produced in English on this topic over the last twenty years. The cumulative effect of these exegeses appears at the present time to tip the balance in favour of an integrated reading of the *Nicomachean Ethics*, according to which Aristotle's claims on the nature of the good life are mutually consistent.[72]

In an attempt to explain this doctrinal discrepancy by the history of Aristotle's texts, Nuyens,[73] followed by Gauthier and Jolif,[74] had earlier famously argued that the composition of *N.E.* X predates that of the other books. These authors rest their case on the doctrinal closeness between *N.E.* X and an early work of Aristotle's, the *Protrepticus*. They claim that the text which now constitutes book X of the *Nicomachean Ethics* shows that its author was still under the influence of Plato's mind-body dualism and had yet to work out the conception of the soul as the life principle of the body, or entelechy, which forms the central argument of the *De Anima*. Thus, while the identification, in book IX, of the self with the practical intellect would tally with the monism of the *De Anima*, the claim, defended in *N.E.* X, that humans 'are' their theoretic intellect would bear witness to Aristotle's youthful dualism. Although this is not the place to proceed to a detailed examination of this, nowadays mostly rejected, interpretation, there appears to be a substantial body of evidence in favour of the argument[75] that *N.E.* X.8 should be read conjointly with *De Anima*, III.5. The following brief considerations can usefully be brought to bear on the issue.

In *De Anima* III.5, one of the most obscure passages in the Aristotelian corpus, a distinction is drawn between the passive (*pathētic*) intellect (*nous*) and the active (*poiētic*) intellect.[76] The passive intellect, which accounts for most of human cognition, is receptive of the individuated forms provided by perception and imagination. It differs from them insofar as its function is to apprehend essences as opposed to individual things.[77] Aristotle adds that the passive intellect can think all things, and, in the process, does become whatever it thinks; in that respect it is pure potentiality (*dunamis*). In contrast with the passive intellect, the active intellect is "in essence actuality" (*tēi ousiai ōn energeia*).[78] Aristotle's fundamental doctrines of the complementarity of potentiality and actuality, and of causation, in effect required him to posit something like the active intellect to account for the intermittent actualization of the passive intellect in and through the cognition of essences. But, as the vast amount of scholarly literature devoted to this distinction shows, the concept of the active intellect raises more problems than it solves. Indeed, if it is pure act, it is unaffected and unmixed, and if it is unmixed, it is immortal and eternal.[79] Not only does this last claim run counter to the *entelecheia* conception of the soul in Aristotle's late psychology, but it raises a host of unwelcome metaphysical problems. Is the active intellect to be identified with the unmoved mover whose activity is described in the *Metaphysics*?[80] And, since Aristotle cannot mean that each of us has a separate active intellect, must we assume, e.g., with Ross, that though the active intellect is "in the soul," it nevertheless "goes beyond the individual"?[81] If that is the case, we should have to conclude, with him, that "it is identical in all individuals."[82]

The fact that the problems raised by the distinction between passive and active *nous* are very far from being resolved need not, however, detract us from tentatively linking it to Aristotle's two different contentions in the *Nicomachean Ethics* on the nature, either practical or theoretic, of the good life. Indeed, the latter distinction can be viewed as the ethical version of the former. Firstly, while the self that Aristotle identifies with practical reason is, to some extent, individual, the self as theoretic reason cannot but be impersonal. There need be no contradiction here. Indeed, Aristotle's general concept of selfhood as an ideal allows him to urge his audience to make themselves, as it were, into tangents to the divine curve, even though he knows that their humanity will almost always pull them down. Secondly, as the active intellect is said to be "immortal and eternal,"[83] the life of contemplation is presented as "god-like."[84] Thirdly, it is in order to account for human knowledge that Aristotle was led to postulate the presence in humans of a purely active principle or *nous*. We should therefore not be surprised that he came to proffer the moral advice according to which, hard as it will be, we must try and reach out to the thinking actuality of the active *nous* which is in us, but which we arguably share with all other 'knowers'.

On this interpretation, the tension between book X and the rest of the *Nicomachean Ethics* corresponds fairly closely to the tension between the central doctrine of the *De Anima*, that the soul is the entelechy of the body, and the view expressed in III.5 of that same treatise that the soul comprises a separate and purely active element.[85] There is thus no need to invoke Plato's influence on Aristotle's earlier work to explain the panegyric of the theoretic life at the end of the *Nicomachean Ethics*.

Though one can try and explain how Aristotle came to express two different views on the nature of the specifically human element or self, and related topics, one cannot wholly explain away the discrepancy. The fact remains that at times he locates the human self in the practical intellect, and, at least one other time, he identifies human beings with their dianoetic element. Unsurprisingly the moral implications drawn from these identifications are at variance with each other, although they are not incompatible. What is clear is that Aristotle never wavered in his conviction both that the essential human self is noetic and that the moral life is second best to the life of contemplation. This latter type of life represents an ideal that he did not expect to be achieved by very many or very often. Most of us will not succeed in "immortalizing" ourselves in the way indicated, and the moral life will have to be our chosen way of becoming a 'self'. It is upon success in that endeavour that the formation of virtue friendship depends, since the formation of *other* selves presupposes that selfhood has been achieved.

2

SELVES
AND
OTHER
SELVES

Aristotle's noetic conception of selfhood and the moral implications he draws from it constitute the framework of reference of his further claim that virtuous friends are other selves to one another. In order fully to understand Aristotle's views on the matter of other selves, however, we should first appreciate how and why he came to restrict the application of this claim to the friendship of virtue.

In both the *Eudemian* and the *Nicomachean Ethics* Aristotle stresses the polymorphic nature of friendship. Not only can friendship proceed from diverse motivations (advantage, pleasure, or the desire for mental communion),[1] he held, but it can also bond persons of unequal moral worth, social standing, and intellectual status. What keeps such a wide spectrum together is the relatedness of each and every point on it to the primary form or paradigm of friendship. Only in so far as any given personal association sufficiently resembles the primary form is it justifiably called friendship. The reason is that ". . . the friendship of good people in so far as they are good is friendship in the primary way, and to the full extent; and the others are friendship by similarity."[2]

Primary friendship, he further specifies, presupposes, on the part of the partners, not only similarity in virtue but also awareness that their affectionate goodwill is both mutual and grounded in moral excellence.[3] Although lesser kinds of friendship inevitably fall short of the standard, they nevertheless succeed in lifting themselves up above purely instrumental, exploitative, or manipulative relations. They are, to a greater or lesser extent, friendships. Aristotle's discussion of these kinds of friendship and of their casuistry evidences his philosophical interest in the lives and the opinions of the many. It is a fact that less than fully virtuous people do not generally lack friends and companions; to deny the name of friendship to such associations would clearly not only do violence to the observed facts (*ta phainomena*)[4] but also reduce the status of primary friendship to that of a generally unattainable ideal. Indeed, the merit of such recent exegeses as J.M. Cooper's[5] and K.D. Alpern's[6] has been to lay emphasis on those aspects of the friendships of utility and of pleasure that entitle them to be called friendships, rather than on those which make them different from, and therefore inferior to, the primary form. To a certain extent, friendships of utility and of pleasure do exhibit various other-regarding qualities, such as cooperation, trust, and loyalty, and in Cooper's convincing argument: ". . . those who have enjoyed one another's company or have been mutually benefited through their common association, will, as a result of the benefits or pleasures they receive, tend to wish for and be willing to act in the interest of the other person's good, independently of consideration of their *own* welfare or pleasure."[7] Yet, though genuine, such benevolence is nevertheless circumscribed by those inevitably contingent aspects of the friend's personality that make him useful or pleasant. In the friendships of utility and of pleasure, as Aristotle himself had contended, "the beloved is loved not in so far as he is who he is, but in so far as he provides some good or pleasure."[8] Although friends of pleasure and of utility can, to a certain extent, be loved *for* themselves they are not loved *in* themselves. This can either be due to the fact that they have not yet achieved the moral excellence that alone can make a person lovable in himself or, alternatively, that they have undeservedly been befriended for some peripheral, i.e., non-essential, property that they happen to possess.

Friends of virtue, on the other hand, love their friends in, as well as for, themselves. As we shall argue in chapter 3 below, Aristotle's claim[9] that the virtuous person loves his friends for their own sakes means that he loves them 'qua good'[10] or—what comes to the same thing—in so far as they are 'selves'. By this, as we shall see, Aristotle does not simply mean that primary friendship is fully disinterested. This would be a platitude, since moral goodness cannot be either the object or the ground of egoistic desire. It will be argued that Aristotle should, more correctly, be taken to mean that primary friends love their friends for their (noetically defined) self rather than for their useful or pleasant traits. Of the three kinds of friendship only the friendship of virtue, therefore, establishes a relationship between whole persons, i.e., persons who have achieved the moral excellence required for being selves in Aristotle's normative sense. Whenever this condition is left unsatisfied, the relationship falls correspondingly short of primary friendship.

Equality of virtue between friends is thus presented as a necessary condition of friendship in the full sense of the word, and the implication of this condition is explicitly drawn: "In all friendships corresponding to superiority, the loving must also be proportional, e.g., the better person, and the more beneficial, and each of the others likewise, must be loved more than he loves; for when the loving reflects the comparative worth of the friends, equality is achieved in a way, and this seems to be proper to friendship."[11] This is, in more ways than one, a strange passage. Firstly, it presupposes a conception of love that appears to be at odds with our modern sensibilities. In promoting the view that love can and should be carefully tailored to the worth of its object, Aristotle makes it a far more deliberate and active relation than most of us should like. Love is often assumed by us to be a spontaneous flow of reactive inclination which, as such, can neither be commanded nor trimmed at will. Philosophers, from Kant to Oswald Hanfling, who make a distinction between 'propensions of feeling',[12] on the one hand, and loving *behaviour* towards others,[13] on the other, are trying to articulate this conception while, at the same time, making conceptual room for the biblical injunction to love one's neighbour as oneself. Aristotle, for his part, could neither have endorsed the definition of love as pure inclination nor Jesus' moral command to love as oneself all those in need who chance to cross one's path. As we shall see presently, the love that Aristotle claimed to characterize primary friendship stems not only from affection but also, and more importantly, from a proper appreciation of the moral stature of the other. Emerson could well have had Aristotle in mind when he wrote that "In the last analysis, love is only the reflection of a man's own worthiness from other men."[14]

The counter-intuitive implications, on the subject of love and friendship, of Aristotle's description of fully-fledged *philia* can usefully lead us to identify and question some of our own assumptions. It could be argued, for instance, that it is more gratifying to be the object of primary friendship, as described by Aristotle, than of spontaneous and, therefore, possibly capricious and unsteady inclination. As for affection itself, why are we prone to balk at the idea that it is all the more fulfilling for being bestowed on a worthy object? After all, there is nothing intrinsically noble in initiating and sustaining a relationship, whose nature is to be mutual, with someone who, for one reason or another, cannot be fully respected. Prior to their change of heart, prodigal sons and other lost sheep[15] are not fit for mutual affective relationships, although they may well elicit loving concern on the part of their high-minded relatives and associates. As has often been remarked, modern concepts of love tend to differ significantly from ancient ones, and the question will have to be asked as to whether Aristotle's primary friendship can properly be described as love, in the modern sense of the word. Before it can be addressed, however, one needs to gain a fuller understanding of what this relationship entails.

To understand how Aristotle could advocate tailoring love to worth, we need to bear two points in mind. Firstly, his doctrine of the general primacy of (actualizing) activity over process and passivity leads him to pronounce loving to be more choiceworthy[16] than being loved.[17] For this reason the activity of loving (*to philein*) appears to be "the virtue of friends."[18] Secondly, unequal levels of love between the would-be partners in primary friendship would secure the equality required in this relationship. Indeed, fully-fledged friendship between unequals would require the less virtuous friend to be the more active of the two. Inferiority in virtue would have to be compensated by increased activity. Since, as we saw, the virtue of friendship consists in the activity of loving, the less virtuous but more active of the two friends would, *ipso facto*, proportionately increase his virtuous activity. Unequal in virtue though the friends initially were, they would thus end up as equals. This is not so unconvincing as might at first appear. Indeed, it might be argued that those who, being aware of their own moral deficiency, love their virtuous friend(s) all the more, show thereby that at least some of their affects are guided by a correct apprehension of the end of human life. To the extent that they direct their love to what is truly lovable, i.e., their friend's moral goodness, they can be deemed virtuous.

If the view that loving should reflect the worth of its object thus appears arguably to sanction greater activity on the part of the less virtuous partner, it must now be asked whether it can also justify the *prima facie* unpalatable conclusion that the more virtuous partner need not love his inferior friend as much as he is loved by him. Indeed, this conclusion is inescapable; not only does Aristotle make moral virtue the ground of friendship, but as we have seen, he also views it as a *sine qua non* of an integrated personality. He does not therefore contend that only the virtuous *deserve* to be loved in and for themselves; he claims that only the virtuous *can* be so loved. Since humans are to be identified with their *nous*, those who fail to be rational will correspondingly fail to be fully themselves. To that extent, they cannot be loved *in themselves*. Given the premises, the reasoning is unimpeachable. Yet one may well continue to wonder why, for instance, a temperate person cannot be friends of virtue with an alcoholic whose oft but sincerely reiterated good resolutions mostly remain unfulfilled. In this instance common-sense, which points to the instability of such friendships, yields the same answer as theory. The weak-willed partner is loved for what he aims at being rather than for what he is; being generally at variance with himself,[19] he forsakes his claim to be loved in himself. Aristotle's initially startling claim that friendship in the full sense of the word be restricted to those who are (moral) selves, i.e., those whose characters exhibit moral wholeness, does therefore not totally lack plausibility, even though it may shock those who would love sinners despite their sins.

The difference between fully-fledged friendship and its inferior varieties can usefully be expressed in terms of the distinction between activity (*energeia*) and process (*kinēsis*) as outlined in the *Metaphysics*.[20] An action is correctly classified as a process when it is transitive, i.e., when it is undertaken for the sake of a goal which both differs from the action itself and can be described independently of it. Considered on its own a process is therefore incomplete and, to that extent, imperfect. An activity, by contrast, is immanent, since it embodies its own end and is complete at any time it is pursued. Finally, it can be continuous. Since immanence, integrity, and continuity appear to be criteria of perfection, it can be concluded that agents derive greater actualization from activities than from processes. The examples of actualization through activities given in the *Metaphysics* show this to have been Aristotle's view: ". . . when there is no product apart from the actuality, the actuality is present in the agents, e.g., the act of seeing is in the seeing subject and that of theorizing in the theorizing subject and the life in the soul (and therefore well-being also; for it is a certain kind of life)."[21] Further evidence is provided by the ascription later in the *Metaphysics* of continuous immanent activity to the prime mover[22] or God.

The distinction between activity and process may be brought out clearly in the following example. It can correctly be said of the contemplative nun at any time during her contemplation both that she is contemplating and that she has contemplated. Contemplation is an activity. When the same nun is cooking the communal collation, on the other hand, it cannot be said at any one time both that she is cooking and that she has cooked. Cooking is a process. While it is engaged in for the sake of an end which is over and beyond it, contemplation is engaged in for its own sake. The former is instrumentally valued, while the latter is conceived of as intrinsically valuable.

Friendship is too multi-sided a phenomenon to be assimilated either to an activity or a process. It can be contended nonetheless that while primary friendship exhibits many traits characteristic of activities, the two inferior varieties of friendship are in several respects like processes. Primary friendship, which is initiated and cultivated for its own sake, is continuous and stable. It is intrinsically praiseworthy. Further, as we shall argue presently, it actualizes the very core of the personality of the moral agent, as opposed to peripheral aspects of his nature. By contrast, friendships of utility and of pleasure can be compared to processes. Being essentially instrumental, friendships of utility not infrequently fade out once their goal has been achieved, and their desirability depends on that of the ends they serve. The actualization they afford is correspondingly inferior. As for the friendships of pleasure, which are less easy to categorize, they are at the mercy of the partners' superficial and changing interests or tastes, and, as such, they are prone to ebb away whenever they cease to be a source of entertainment or diversion for them.[23] Aristotle likens this kind of friendship to the "seasoning on food"[24] which should not, of course, be either essential or plentiful. A detailed comparison between Aristotle's use of this culinary analogy, as a put-down, and Jesus' use of a similar expression, i.e., 'the salt of the earth',[25] to commend, can, lamentably, not be undertaken here.

A disregard of the distinction between activity and process mars the otherwise ingenious interpretation of the 'other self' tenet put forward by John Benson.[26] Friends of virtue, Benson claims, become other selves to each other by simultaneously actualizing themselves through the medium of their friendship. This process, which Benson likens to the actualization gained by a craftsman through the practice of his craft, consists in the joint "making of other selves." Benson grounds his interpretation in two short passages of the *Nicomachean Ethics*. In the first text Aristotle invokes the fact that "the father is the cause of his children's being, which seems to be the greatest benefit, and of their nurture and education"[27] to account for fatherly love. In the second passage Aristotle invokes a comparison in order to explain that benefactors love their beneficiaries more than they are loved in return: "This, then, is what the case of the benefactor resembles; here the beneficiary is his product, and hence he likes him more than the product likes its producer."[28] These texts authorise us to conclude, Benson claims, that "There is a sense in which what I put my work into is me, but existing apart from me. It is another self. It might seem rather farfetched to say this of a pot or a poem, and Aristotle does not actually use the phrase in that context, but he does say that 'the product is, in a way, the producer in his actualization'."[29] Unfortunately, neither of these two texts will bear the weight that Benson needs to place upon them to vindicate his interpretation of primary Aristotelian friendship as enlarged narcissism. As regards the love of parents for their children, it is not a relationship of equality; Aristotle himself states this explicitly.[30] To that extent it is not an adequate model for the 'other self' variety of friendship which, being friendship in the primary sense of the word, presupposes equality. The craftsman's analogy is similarly unhelpful since the practice of a craft is a process, not an activity. If the analogy were to apply to friendship at all, it would be to its inferior varieties where, as in a craft, the goal is different from and independent of the means. The friendship of virtue, whose very practice includes its end, cannot ever be a question of 'making'. If it were, we would have to conclude that once friendship is 'achieved' it comes to an end, just as an actually completed house terminates the process of building.

Benson is right, nevertheless, to interpret the 'other self' premise in terms of the mutual actualization that any ongoing primary friendship affords the partners, and it is to the precise nature of that actualization that we must now turn. I want to argue that primary friendship provides the virtuous with both moral and cognitive actualization. I shall further claim that while the moral fulfilment brought about by primary friendship could arguably also be achieved through active civic involvement, the cognitive benefits which it confers could not be obtained in any other way. The following remarks on the moral and social dimensions of friendship proper will inevitably be sketchy, since they are a mere anticipation of a fuller treatment of that theme in chapter 7.

In the *Politics* Aristotle famously claims that "man is by nature a political animal."[31] True, in that treatise, it is the state rather than inter-personal virtuous friendship which is presented as the end of human nature. Let us remember, however, that in both the *Politics* and the *Nicomachean Ethics* friendship is pronounced to be "the greatest good of states,"[32] and that its binding effect on communities is such, Aristotle claims, that "legislators would seem to be more concerned about it than about justice."[33] Unfortunately, these claims are unspecific and could be applied to all three kinds of friendship. In so far as the friendship of utility accustoms citizens to co-operate, albeit in the pursuit of mutually self-interested goals, it generates within the state centres of goodwill and even trust. In so far as the friendship of pleasure increases the enjoyment of leisure, it spreads companionableness and good fellowship, albeit on a super-ficial level, amongst the citizen body. As for the friendship of virtue, we shall see that the benefits it holds for the state are correspondingly higher. More than any other, the activities (*energeiai*) involved in primary friendship actualize the distinctively human potentialities of those citizens who are capable of it. Furthermore, since, in Aristotle's reasoning, "if the earlier forms of society are natural, so is the state, for it is the end of them, and the nature of a thing is its end. For what each thing is when fully developed, we call its nature,"[34] then we can conclude, on his behalf, that in con-tributing to the utmost actualization of individual citizens, primary friendship also generates and sustains the highest good of all, i.e., that of the city. In other words, friendship between select individual citizens is an enabling condition, since it at least facilitates the smooth running of a well-ordered city, and at best helps to ensure that the goals the city sets itself are worthy ones.

On the level of private morality it can easily be shown that virtuous friendship actively involves, or at least pre-supposes, a number of the moral virtues analyzed in the *Ethics*. We are told explicitly that it encapsulates justice, since ". . . if people are friends, they have no need of justice, but if they are just they need friendship in addition; and the justice that is most just seems to belong to friendship."[35] Friendship also requires courage, since, in Aristotle's esti-mation, friends of virtue must, if necessary, be ready to sac-rifice their lives for each other.[36] Insofar as virtuous friends love and value each other intrinsically, they will need to have overcome the tyranny of their pleasure drives and, to that extent, have achieved full temperance. Furthermore, true friends willingly share material possessions and sundry advantages that each may possess, and thereby display the virtue of generosity. In fact, their generosity will be espe-cially noble, since "it is finer to benefit friends than to ben-efit strangers."[37] More generally, let us note that friendship ensures that the performance of a whole range of virtuous actions will actually be pleasurable to the agent, since they are undertaken for the sake of his friend. One of the defin-ing criteria of virtue, viz., that the agent enjoys performing virtuous actions,[38] is thus met through primary friendship. It should finally be stated that friendship tells of the good condition of the affects, since it can joyfully direct them to what is truly loveworthy, viz., virtue. Considerations such as the above must be taken to justify Aristotle's terse state-ment that friendship is not so much a moral virtue as an activity that involves moral virtue.[39]

Being a mutual relation between virtuous individuals, primary friendship provides the friends not only with the opportunity of practicing a range of moral virtues, but also of apprehending, at particularly close range, the moral virtues of an other. Indeed, if, as Aristotle plausibly claims, the best friendships are both long-standing and *perforce* fairly exclusive, they cannot but entail intimate acquaintance with the character and the circumstances of, at most, a few others. Not only do primary friends know of each other's current views, interests, goals, sorrows, and successes, but they are also in a position empathetically to understand how these arise from earlier influences, achievements, traumas, difficulties, ambitions, etc. Each knows how the other became the virtuous individual he now is. Beyond communing "in conversation and thought,"[40] friends of virtue, it must be assumed, are furthermore engaged in common activities and enterprises whose outcome will depend upon individual contingent factors. Mindful of particularity, the bond of primary friendship thus shares with moral virtue the characteristic of being always "with reference to us,"[41] i.e., individuated. No two individuals' virtuous dispositions need be the same, nor should their virtuous actions have to be performed at a similar level or in comparable circumstances, to be deemed virtuous. Standing one's ground in battle and backing an unpopular measure in the assembly require different kinds of courage, and most lives will not provide the opportunity for performing either or both actions. Thus, for instance, if Callias is joined with Coriscus in primary friendship, it is Coriscus' particular courage that Callias apprehends and likes rather than courage *simpliciter*. Since each partner apprehends the other's individual virtuous actions and lovingly appreciates the particular excellent dispositions from which they stem, it is Coriscus that Callias loves even if he loves him for his virtue. Not only does primary friendship give each partner the opportunity of pleasurably practicing a number of moral virtues, we conclude, but its intimacy and reciprocity also provide them both with a unique experience of moral virtue incarnate. Involving as it does the witnessing as well as the performing of morally virtuous acts, primary friendship has a cognitive dimension. Such cognitive dimension, it will presently be argued, is further developed by the status of the friends as other selves to each other.

Before proceeding, however, a possible objection needs to be forestalled, i.e., that reliance on purely theoretical considerations in the study of friendship risks distorting what is, after all, an essentially practical relation. As Aristotle himself took care to note, the aim of moral philosophy "is not to know what courage is but to be courageous, not to know what justice is but to be just."[42] Such remarks as these, it might be argued, should be taken as a warning that too exclusive an interest in the cognitive or ethical dimensions of friendship may actually impede the realization of one's *telos* (end) as a social being.

Such objections would not be justified. Aristotle not only does draw parallels between the operation of the discursive intellect and that of practical judgement but also states explicitly that the two are interdependent to the extent of feeding each other. Thus in the *Nicomachean Ethics* "As assertion and denial are to thought, so pursuit and avoidance are to desire. If then, the decision is excellent, the reason must be true and the desire correct, so that what reason asserts is what desire pursues,"[43] and in the *De Anima* "To the thinking soul images serve as sense-perceptions. And when it asserts or denies good or bad, it avoids or pursues it."[44] Thus besides indicating that action is, *de facto*, informed by cognition, at however modest a level, Aristotle also maintains that morally excellent actions and activities are those that express true thoughts. Furthermore, his empiricism leads him to assert that "unless one perceived things one would not learn or understand anything and when one contemplates one must simultaneously contemplate an image."[45] In other words, the operation of the intellect depends upon the apprehension of the particulars which perception furnishes.[46] Even at a highly abstract level, moral reflection, we can infer, needs the sustenance of the close insight into individuated virtue that primary friendship alone can provide. Considerations such as these, one assumes, constitute the background of Aristotle's famous remark that only the virtuous can profitably embark on the study of moral philosophy.[47] Non-virtuous individuals cannot be relied upon to recognize virtue when they see it.

Unfortunately, nowhere in the *Ethics* does Aristotle explicitly analyze the cognitive dimension of primary friendship. Important pointers can nevertheless be gleaned from passages in which he draws two implications from his claim regarding the mediacy of self-awareness. Firstly, friendship supplies us with self-knowledge, which, like all knowledge, is, in Aristotle's estimation, a source of both pleasure and fulfilment. This point is vividly put in the *Magna Moralia*: ". . . we are not able to see what we are from ourselves (. . .) As then when we wish to see our own face, we do so by looking into the mirror, in the same way when we wish to know ourselves we can obtain that knowledge by looking at our friend."[48] Primary friendship, which opens up the essential self of each partner to the benevolent gaze of another, can be assumed to yield deeper and therefore more satisfying self-knowledge than any other form of friendship. How this can be so will presently be investigated. Secondly, primary friendship widens the virtuous person's acquaintance with virtue. Indeed, since "we are able to observe our neighbours more than ourselves, and to observe their actions more than our own,"[49] Aristotle avers, the virtuous person will take interest and pleasure in his friends' virtuous deeds, and all the more so as he is more closely associated with them.[50] There is thus a *prima facie* case for claiming that the relation of 'other selfhood' is a source of cognitive, as well as moral, actualization for those engaged in it.

To yield its full significance, however, Aristotle's premise that the friend is another self, together with its cognitive implications, will require a somewhat heavy interpretation, and the analysis of the noetic function in the *De Anima* will once more have to be invoked. In that treatise Aristotle maintains that, in the same manner as sense organs take on the form of their objects, each individual *nous* becomes that which it thinks. Unlike sense organs, however, *nous* cannot be anything prior to exercising its specific function,[51] since the fact that it is not located in a physical organ gives it the plasticity required to think *all* things.[52] This latter claim is crucial for the present inquiry. Only through individual acts of intellection, Aristotle indi-

cates, can the human *nous* at all overcome its purely potential state[53] and achieve the actualization to which it, in common with all living things, tends. Only through intellection
does *nous* realize its nature, since Aristotle identifies a
thing's nature with the actualization of its specific potentialities.[54] In other words, *nous* can only actualize itself
through becoming something else than itself, and it is only
in gaining awareness of this, its object, that it can gain
awareness of itself.

Let it be noted next that Aristotle refers to these views
on intellection and self-awareness in both the *Eudemian*
and the *Nicomachean Ethics*. Although in both treatises the
context is a discussion of the limits of human self-sufficiency,
only a modest exegetical extrapolation will be required to
ground the conclusion that, at its best, friendship is the
source of considerable cognitive benefits which could not
otherwise be secured. In the *Eudemian Ethics* he makes
the point that friendship yields some kind of self-cognition,
since "To perceive a friend, therefore, is necessarily in a
manner to perceive oneself, and to know a friend is in a
manner to know oneself."[55] A few lines earlier Aristotle had
indicated that the degree of noetic actualization that a person derives from knowledge directly reflects the worth of
the object known: ". . . we are not each of these things in ourselves but only by participating in these faculties in the process of perceiving and knowing (for when perceiving one
becomes perceived by means of what one previously perceives, *in the manner and in the respect in which one perceives it*, and when knowing one becomes known)."[56] As for
the *Nicomachean* passage, which has already been alluded
to in chapter 1 above,[57] it deserves here to be quoted in full:
"Someone who sees perceives that he sees; one who hears
perceives that he hears; and one who walks perceives that
he walks. Similarly in the other cases there is some element that perceives that we are active. Hence, if we are
perceiving, we perceive that we are perceiving; and if we
are understanding, we perceive that we are understanding.
Now perceiving that we are perceiving or understanding is
the same as perceiving that we are, since we agreed that

being is perceiving or understanding."[58] This claim is
directly followed by the statement that "The excellent person is related to his friend in the same way as he is related
to himself, since a friend is another himself."[59] Together
these contentions serve as premises for the conclusion that
the virtuous will value his friend's being as highly as his
own.[60] A detailed exegesis of these texts will, it is hoped,
justify the claim that friendship plays a unique and crucial
role in the noetic actualization of moral agents. More precisely, it will aim at showing that primary friendship
enables such agents to gain conscious awareness of their
own individual moral excellence, or selfhood, since
Aristotelian selfhood is a byword for virtue embodied.

In order fully to appreciate the extent of friendship's
contribution to self-realization, two Aristotelian theses need
to be borne in mind, viz., (1) that self-awareness is indirect,
and (2) that *nous'* actualization is directly proportional to
the intelligibility of the object that it apprehends.[61] Thus,
in sense perception, i.e., in the apprehension of enmattered
forms, humans gain awareness of themselves *qua* perceivers
of the external world. However, since sense organs take on
the form of the particulars that they perceive[62] and since
matter, as such, is unintelligible, perception causes the perceiver to grasp objects that resist full intelligibility.
Unsurprisingly, the actualization that humans derive from
knowledge is of a higher order. Being a "form of forms,"[63]
nous can apprehend objects that are "especially fit for
thought," viz., universals, and it receives sustenance from
them.[64] The fact that universals are "somehow in the soul
itself"[65] means that compared to perception thinking is relatively independent from external objects and to that extent
self-sufficient. This, in turn, enables humans to think whenever they wish.[66]

Although the above reasoning is the result of patch-
work on a number of claims scattered through the *De
Anima*, it is presented, albeit in a different context, as a
continuous argument in the *Metaphysics*. Outlining the
nature of the prime mover, Aristotle is there prompted to
state that

> ... thought in itself deals with that which is best in itself, and that which is thought in the fullest sense with that which is best in the fullest sense. And thought thinks itself because it shares the nature of the object of thought; for it becomes an object of thought in coming into contact with and thinking its objects, so that thought and object of thought are the same. For that which is capable of receiving the object of thought, i.e., the substance, is thought. And it is active when it possesses this object. Therefore the latter, rather than the former, is the divine element which thought seems to contain, and the act of contemplation is what is most pleasant and best.[67]

The implications for primary friendship of these noetic claims will now be investigated.

In common with all cognitive and practical activities, friendship relies on the particulars furnished by perception (*aisthēsis*), and, like all practical functions, it incorporates desire (*orexis*). In the case of the friendship of virtue we must assume that such desire is 'correct', i.e., that it is guided by the intellect (*orexis dianoētikē*[68] or *boulēsis*[69]). Furthermore, involving as it does a number of moral virtues, primary friendship will, like them, presuppose an awareness of what constitutes the best good for a human being *qua* agent.[70] This universal is the prime cognitive object of 'practical wisdom' (*phronēsis*), which Aristotle describes as the "eye of the soul."[71]

More importantly, primary friendship also involves the ability and the readiness to relate this universal to particular cases and circumstances. Through its characteristic features of intimacy, steadfastness, and mutuality, primary friendship, it was argued earlier, provides each partner with first-hand detailed acquaintance with moral virtue as individuated. Further, assuming, as we must, that primary friends are "practically wise" men (*phronimoi*) and bearing in mind the crucial role that Aristotle assigns to such persons in his definition of virtue,[72] we can infer that virtuous friends will generally widen each other's moral experience. This will be effected in a number of ways which will complement the individual self-awareness of which primary friendship is the occasion. For instance, not only can a friend provide his friend with insights into situations as yet unfamiliar or even effectively inaccessible to him, but he can also offer him a standard by which the appropriateness of different reactions to such situations may be assessed. To put the point differently: primary friendship supplies virtuous persons with such intelligibles (*noēta*) as are embodied in their friends' highly virtuous dispositions and actions. Although Aristotelian primary friendship deeply engages the affects of those concerned, it is nevertheless compatible with the measure of intellectual distance necessary for *understanding* its moral components. In C.H. Kahn's words, virtue friends "recognize in their common humanity and common rationality a unifying principle that makes their concern for one another possible."[73]

Like all forms of cognition, moral experience, even when it is vicariously induced, is a factor of noetic fulfilment. Indeed, the *nous* of the excellent man assumes the intelligibles embodied in, or generated by, his partner's virtuous dispositions, and thereby gains deeper actualization than could be obtained by an exclusive reliance on his own resources. Further, since the degree of actualization reflects the degree of intelligibility of the object of cognition, primary friendship is a factor of particularly high actualization.[74] Lastly, it causes virtuous persons to gain awareness of themselves *qua* actualized, i.e., *qua* apprehending a good that scores high in intelligibility and determinacy.[75] Such self-realization, which the intimacy of primary friendship renders possible on a fairly continuous basis, is a source of pleasure for the virtuous who by definition[76] delights in what is good in itself.

Together with Aristotle's noetic conception of the self, and the fact that primary friendship is by definition mutual, the foregoing considerations contribute to explaining how he could claim that a friend of virtue is another self. Indeed, the epistemic plasticity of *nous* ensures that in primary friendship it "becomes" the intelligibles embodied in the partner's rational activities. Since, as we saw in chapter 1, Aristotle identifies humans with their reason, we can now infer that those whom primary friendship binds together, "become" each other's self in the act of apprehending each other's moral excellence. Heightened individual self-awareness constitutes an additional benefit of this joint process in which each partner is both the source and the beneficiary of noetic enrichment. Primary friendship, it should be stressed, is the only personal relationship in which such process of intellectual symbiosis occurs. No other human bond meets the conditions of intimacy, mutuality, and equality of virtue[77] that are presupposed in any pair of primary friends' joint actualization and awareness of their own selves. Rather than banal rhetoric, the phrase 'other selfhood', as used in both *Ethics*, therefore represents Aristotle's attempt to bring some theses of his philosophical psychology to bear on the question of the best life for humans. Primary friendship not only safeguards the moral virtue of the partners and enriches their moral outlook, it also provides the mirror in which each may see himself. To that extent it constitutes the most complete moral experience of which a human being is capable.

Though the above argument is never explicitly clinched in the *Nicomachean Ethics*, we found that all its premises are either mentioned or at least presupposed in that treatise. The argument here presented is built from all Aristotelian blocks broadly contemporary with the *Nicomachean* texts. The question should now be raised as to whether the *Eudemian Ethics* contains similar claims. In fact, as we shall see presently, all the premises necessary to unravel the 'other selfhood' claim appear in the *Eudemian* treatise, too. It should further be noted that the context of occurrence is the same; both *Eudemian* VII,12 and *Nicomachean* IX,9 are devoted to a resolution of the *aporia* as to whether friendship is compatible with self-sufficiency. The poor state of the *Eudemian* manuscripts, however, should induce caution, and a detailed analysis of the passage must be undertaken.

In the *Eudemian Ethics* Aristotle begins by rehearsing his well-known thesis that life, in the active sense and as an end, consists in perceiving and knowing,[78] and therefore that friendship involves perceiving and knowing together. He then introduces, seemingly as a contrast (using a δέ for which there is no corresponding μέν), the view that ἔστι δὲ τὸ αὑτοῦ αἰσθάνεσθαι καὶ τὸ αὑτὸν γνωρίξειν αἱρετώτατον ἑκάστῳ.[79] Rackham, following Solomon, emends both τὸ αὑτὸ in the manuscripts into αὑτὸ τὸ. Bonitz, followed by Susemihl, Dirlmeier, Décarie, and Walzer and Mingay, on the other hand, emend the first τὸ αὑτὸ into τὸ αὑτοῦ, while they suggest reading the second as τὸ αὑτὸν. Thus, while Rackham translates the passage as "But perception and knowledge themselves are the things most desirable for each individual," Décarie, for instance, renders it as "Mais se connaître et se percevoir sont ce qu'il y a de plus désirables pour chacun de nous" (But to know and to perceive oneself is what is most desirable for each of us). Eight lines later we read that εὐλόγως δὲ τὸ ἑαυτοῦ αἰσθάνεσθαι καὶ γνωρίξειν αἱρετώτερον.[80] Although this sentence is virtually the same as that quoted above, it is interesting to note that Rackham does not suggest emending the pronoun, and that he resorts to an ambiguous translation, viz., ". . . perceiving and knowing oneself is reasonably more desirable." Later in the passage we read that τὸ αὑτοῦ βούλεσθαι αἰσθάνεσθαι τὸ αὑτὸν εἶναι τοιονδὶ βούλεσθαι ἐστίν (to wish to perceive oneself is to wish oneself to be of a certain character);[81] these reflexive pronouns, too, have been left unchallenged.

Bonitz's emendation is to be preferred on the grounds that it allows for a more unified interpretation of the whole passage, and that it yields a clear and ready solution to the aporia under discussion. Friendship poses no threat to self-sufficiency, would Aristotle here claim, since it enables each partner to gain awareness of himself *qua* perceiver and knower. That Aristotle is here thinking of self-knowledge rather than knowledge *simpliciter* seems to emerge from his later statement that "If therefore one were to abstract and posit absolute knowledge and its negation (. . .) there would be no difference between absolute knowledge and another person's knowing instead of oneself; but that is like another person's living instead of oneself."[82] Rackham's interpretation, on the other hand, leaves unclear why a reference to the desirability of knowledge in general could help resolve the problem as to whether friendship imperils the virtuous person's self-sufficiency. Lastly, Bonitz's reading tallies with the interpretation of the 'other self' doctrine propounded above. Although knowledge, as a good in itself, is choiceworthy, self-knowledge is even more desirable to each and every knower, Aristotle indicates in the passage. This prepares the ground for the view, which is expressed in the remainder of that chapter, that it is only in the intimacy of established primary friendship that virtuous individuals can gain awareness of their highly actualized moral and social selves.

It could, of course, be argued on Rackham's behalf that Aristotle's view of the mediacy of self-awareness makes all knowledge into a source of self-consciousness. Indeed, if life in the active sense consists in perceiving and knowing, Rackham could arguably maintain, any exercise of the cognitive faculties actualizes the knower. A reference to self-consciousness would therefore be uncalled for at this stage. Rackham's rendering, however, does not explain how and why this view is at all germane to a discussion of friendship. By contrast, if we accept Bonitz's reading of both τὸ αὐτὸ as reflexive pronouns, the lines 1244b27-1245a1 make a clear contribution to the main argument of the chapter. They specify that, far from it being the case that friendship threatens the virtuous person's self-sufficiency, it in fact affords him a good which he could not otherwise enjoy. Such good is the consciousness of himself *qua* apprehending through the intercourse of friendship the particular interpretation of the good life for man embodied in his friend's moral personality.

As far as the general argument presented in the *Eudemian Ethics* VII,12 is concerned, it, too, therefore supports the conclusion that primary friendship is a factor of unique self-actualization. The steps of the *Eudemian* reasoning are as follows:

Premise no. 1: Life, in the active sense and as an end, consists in knowing;[83]

Premise no. 2: "The known and the perceived are generally speaking constituted by their participation in the 'determined' nature";[84]

Premise no. 3: Self-knowledge is mediate.[85]

Premise no. 4: Self-knowledge is proportional to the intelligibility of the object apprehended either by sense or by the intellect.[86]

Aristotle concludes not only that "To perceive and to know a friend, therefore, is necessarily in a manner to perceive and in a manner to know oneself,"[87] but also that whenever the partnership is "preeminently in things included in the End,"[88] each friend beholds himself "enjoying the superior good."[89]

The above *Eudemian* reasoning licenses two inferences. Firstly, the actualization brought about by primary friendship is of a high order since it is obtained through the apprehension of the highly determinate object constituted by moral virtue embodied. Secondly, in primary friendship, where each is both lover and loved, knower and known, the partners become 'other selves' to each other through the process of jointly apprehending and thus becoming their practical excellence or selfhood. Being the happiest and the best,[90] such friendship includes joint reflection[91] and the sharing of such ends as each is capable of attaining.[92]

It can now finally and, I hope, justifiably be claimed that in his ethical works Aristotle is consistently ascribing to primary friendship, which combines the loving perception of individuals with the apprehension of their virtue, a crucial role in the achievement of the good life. Friendship derives its moral significance both from the choice that presides at its formation and from the virtues involved in its cultivation. To that extent it signals a concordance between reason, passion and desire. As far as friendship's cognitive dimension is concerned, it has been argued in this chapter that it lies in the self-actualization and self-awareness that each virtuous friend gains through his intimate acquaintance with his partner's moral virtue. Since the degree of intelligibility of an object of cognition determines the value of the above mentioned reflexive states, there appears to be a case for claiming that friendship's noetic benefits are unsurpassed in the moral life. Before that conclusion can be confidently asserted, however, a detailed examination of Aristotle's views on civic friendship will need to be undertaken. As for Aristotle's use of the 'other self' premise, it is grounded in both this identification of the self with practical reason and in his definition of *nous* as pure potentiality in its pre-cognition state. In Aristotle's scheme of things, therefore, the formation of primary friendship involves the joint becoming of each other's self, while its continuing practice ensures a form of noetic communion.

Concentration on the complexities of Aristotle's notion of 'other selfhood' has led us, so far, mostly to ignore the more narrowly moral aspects of primary friendship. To repair this omission, an investigation into the other-regarding and the self-regarding dimensions of primary friendship must now be undertaken. Although the Aristotelian texts concerned have recently benefited from a good deal of exegetical attention, they still suffer from past attempts to force them into either of the twin pigeon-holes of egoism and altruism. It will soon become apparent that these represent over-simplifications.

3

FOR
THE SAKE
OF
THE OTHER

In the *Nicomachean Ethics* Aristotle tells us that a friend, in the primary sense of the word, loves his friend for what he is (δι᾽ αὐτον) rather than because of pleasure or of utility,[1] and he cares for his friend for the friend's sake (ἐκείνου ἕνεκα) rather than for his own.[2] Although different turns of phrase are used in the *Eudemian Ethics*, the idea that primary friendship is other-regarding is stressed there, too.[3] As for the *Rhetoric*, which is more clinical in approach, it contains the similar definitional claim that desire for the friend's good be genuinely felt even when it is mistakenly aimed: "We may define friendly feeling towards anyone as wishing for him what you believe to be good things, not for your own sake but for his, and being inclined, so far as you can, to bring these things about (. . .) Those who think they feel thus towards each other think themselves friends."[4]

Like most of Aristotle's pronouncements on friendship, these claims, especially when placed in context, are less straightforward than might appear at first glance. What exactly does Aristotle pack into his assertion that a true friend loves his friend for the friend's sake? Does he mean, simply, that primary friendship is disinterested?[5] Or that it is directed at the essential self of the other? Either claim raises problems. One will wonder, firstly, whether the interpretation of the 'other self' premise presented in chapter 2 above can be squared with the contention that primary friendship is disinterested. Indeed, if its rewards include widened moral experience, deepened actualization, and heightened self-awareness, can the conclusion be avoided that primary friendship is mainly an occasion for securing benefits, albeit of a mutual and exalted kind? Secondly, if a primary friend loves his friend for his essential self, which, as we have seen, is not to be equated with his unique individuality, can we avoid inferring that, in Aristotle's view, friends are replaceable *qua* such?

Even in a modern context and notwithstanding the joint difficulties which they raise, the above two claims are best kept separate. Although 'love of another for him/herself' is mostly contrasted with 'love of another for one's own sake,' it can also be opposed to 'love of another for his/her peripheral properties.' It is the first opposition that we have in mind when we disparagingly refer to 'fair-weather friends' and 'cupboard love' or express bitterness at being befriended as, e.g., a purveyor of lifts to the station or a source of academic references. It is the second opposition that we uphold when we resist idealization or caricature and remind ourselves that beauty is only skin-deep. While the first contrast makes a broadly uncontroversial moral point, the second often generates puzzlement. If true friends, by definition, love their friends in themselves, the question arises as to which qualities, properties or characteristics constitute the essential self. Further, we sometimes wonder, are good qualities more fundamental to the self than bad ones?

These latter problems are well set up by Pascal in a passage that deserves to be better known:

> what about a person who loves someone for the sake of her beauty; does he love *her*? No, for smallpox, which will destroy beauty without destroying the person, will put an end to his love for her. And if someone loves me for my judgment or my memory, do they love me? *me*, myself? No, for I could lose these qualities without losing my self.

> Where then is this self, if it is neither in the body nor the
> soul? And how can one love the body or the soul except for
> the sake of such qualities, which are not what makes up
> the self, since they are perishable? Would we love the sub-
> stance of a person's soul, in the abstract, whatever quali-
> ties might be in it? That is not possible, and it would be
> wrong. Therefore we never love anyone, but only quali-
> ties. Let us then stop scoffing at those who win honour
> through their appointments and offices, for we never love
> anyone except for borrowed qualities.[6]

In this bleak and acerbic passage Pascal, who coined the
phrase 'the hateful self', not only reduces the self to a bun-
dle of qualities but also refuses to accept that some of these
qualities are more central to the self than others. Can we
construe what Aristotle's answer to Pascal would have been?

In order to come to a convincing interpretation of
Aristotle's dual claim that in primary friendship individuals
are loved in and for themselves, it will be helpful to identify
and describe not only the contrast that it implies in
Aristotle's usage but also the meaning of the equivalent
modern expressions. This will enable us better to resist
importing our own assumptions into the interpretation of
his texts. The modern view that friendship involves loving
one's friends in and for themselves can be broken down into
two separate claims: the first is normative and fairly
straightforward, while the second is descriptive and more
problematic.

The Normative Claim

We commonly distinguish genuine, i.e., disinterested,
friendship from relationships of utility. To love somebody
for her own sake amounts to loving her for what she is
rather than for what she has or what she could do for us.
This involves a concern for her welfare as well as a readiness to further her interests, even at the expense of our
own. It is in this connection that we agree that friendship
imposes moral obligations upon us. Such obligations can be
justified on consequentialist grounds centring on the notion

of the 'general good'. Thus Sidgwick: "It much promotes the general happiness that such services (i.e., counsel and assistance in the intimate perplexities of life, which one is only willing to receive from genuine friends) should be generally rendered. On this ground, as well as through the emotional pleasures which directly spring from it, we perceive Friendship to be an important means to the Utilitarian end."[7] In this passage Sidgwick provides not only an explicit Utilitarian vindication of friendship as a practice but also an implicit justification of the moral obligations that it entails. Alternatively, since a deontological justification of friendship and of its commitments would involve serious difficulties[8] in reconciling inclination and duty, direct altruism, presented as intrinsically valuable, is sometimes invoked[9] to account for the moral claims embodied in personal relationships. Lastly, in the wake of Epicurus and his modern-day successors, one might endeavour to argue that since individual fulfilment lies in the cultivation of intimate and disinterested friendships, the sacrifice that they require will not be perceived as such[10] and therefore that friendship is compatible with hedonism properly understood.

A strong normative overtone can also be detected in the claim, often heard, that affective relations in general should entail a willingness to accept the other as he/she is, warts and all. In *Sanctuary* Edith Wharton expresses this assumption when she has conformist Denis resentfully blurt out to high-principled Kate, "you're simply in love with my virtues. (. . .) I had an idea women loved men for themselves—through everything, I mean. But I wouldn't steal your love—I don't want it on false pretenses."[11] Philosophers, like İlham Dilman, who claim that "Where it has an interest in keeping its object lovable love is shallow,"[12] endorse this view.

The Descriptive Claim

A prominent feature of modern conceptions of friendship is that friends are loved for what makes them unique, i.e., different from all other individuals. In a formula that

suffers from over-exposure, Montaigne said of his friendship with La Boétie: "if you pressed me to tell why I loved
him, I feel that this cannot be expressed, except by answer-
ing: Because it was he, because it was I."[13] Montaigne
ascribes this to an "inexplicable and fateful force" and, even,
to "some ordinance from heaven," and we have come no
nearer than he did to explaining why, contingent factors
apart, it is X rather than Y whom we love, even when Y
has as many good and desirable qualities as X. It is perhaps because we ascribe intrinsic value to the unicity of the
love bond that we view dating agencies and 'singles clubs' as
a last, somewhat shameful, resort.

Among what she calls the "passions of friendship"
Elizabeth Telfer lists affection, which she defines as ". . . a
desire for another's welfare and happiness *as a particular
individual*."[14] Affection, she pursues, ". . . does not seem to
have any necessary connexion with the particular character
of him for whom it is felt. If asked to explain why we are
fond of someone, we *may* mention characteristics in him
which stimulate affection, but it makes equally good sense
to give an historical explanation—'I've known him a long
time' . . . or a biological one such as 'He's my brother, after
all'. Affection is in this sense *irrational*, and because of this
may survive radical changes in the character of its object.
Thus we often continue to be fond of someone when we no
longer like or respect him, and such a situation is not considered in any way odd."[15] Whether or not we agree with
Telfer that such a situation is "not odd," the fact remains
that she has articulated a view that is strongly held by
many. Yet it is altogether foreign to the spirit of Aristotle's
philosophy of friendship. More will need to be said on this
discrepancy.

In his *Love and Human Separateness* İlham Dilman
puts forward a more original interpretation of the assumptions built into the modern view that love attends to the very
particularity of individuals. Whenever uniqueness, *qua* such,
is reducible to the mere contingently determined conglom-
eration of properties, each of which is instantiated elsewhere,
he contends, it holds no fundamental relevance for love.

What does matter, on the other hand, is that those we love should think and act autonomously, and that their emotions or feelings should emanate from and express their own personality and character. Thus, in Dilman's argument, "to meet someone as an individual is to respond to him as someone who has the centre of his actions and passions within him, one who in his words and deeds does not merely reflect what is outside him. The will we come in contact with in his gratitude, forgiveness, anger, sorrow, determination, especially when we are its object, is something we cannot manipulate, and it stands out as such."[16] Although Dilman's view is couched in the terminology of Sartrean existentialism, we shall see that it is better attuned than Telfer's to Aristotle's *di' hauton* condition of primary friendship.

When we try and unravel the strands of Aristotle's own claim that virtuous agents love their primary friends in and for themselves, we find that it, too, embodies both a normative and a descriptive element. Although not easy to keep apart, these are best examined separately.

The Normative Element

Aristotle contrasts loving one's friend for his own sake with friendships that are mainly initiated and cultivated for the sake of future benefits, either mutual or one-sided. The clearest expression of this contrast is to be found in the *Nicomachean Ethics*. There Aristotle begins by formulating the general principle that the mutual well-wishing of friendship reflects the kind of affection that bonds the partners: "those who love each other wish goods to each other in so far as they love each other."[17] This means that: "Those who love each other for utility love the other not in himself, but in so far as they gain some good for themselves from him. The same is true of those who love for pleasure; for they like a witty person not because of his character, but because he is pleasant to themselves. And so those who love for utility or pleasure are fond of a friend because of what is good or pleasant for themselves, not in so far as the beloved is who he is, but in so far as he is useful or pleasant."[18] The same line of argument is pursued in the *Eudemian Ethics*: Aristotle castigates the base on the ground that, preferring things to people, "they are not, properly speaking, friends, for the proverbial 'common property as between friends' is not realized in this way—the friend is made an appendage of the things, not the things of the friends."[19]

In both *Ethics* the further point is made, at some length, that utility friends, who deal with each other in the expectation of gaining benefits, are prone to squabble and recriminate whenever they think themselves short-changed.[20] In these passages a tone of censorious high-mindedness can be detected; Aristotle appears to view with fastidious distaste some of the motives which prompt people to initiate and sustain such a friendship. Intimations of mean-spiritedness, manipulativeness, and pettifoggery surface here and there in his text. They have the effect of high-lighting, by contrast, the eulogious nature of his account of virtue friendship in which "one person is most a friend to another if he wishes goods to the other for the other's sake, *even if no one will know about it*."[21] The affection and benevolence of primary friends, Aristotle intimates, is attentive to the needs of the other, pure of ulterior motives, generous, and therefore unmarred by pettiness. As he says, primary friendship is 'fine'.[22] Presently, I shall explain why, notwithstanding the very real benefits that a virtuous person, *qua* such, stands to derive from primary friendship, his pursuit of them cannot be deemed self-serving.

In asserting that friends of virtue love each other *ekeinou heneka*, Aristotle therefore puts forward a normative claim. In perfect friendship, he indicates, each partner makes the other the end of his activities as a friend,[23] and any benefit that he himself stands to derive from the association is incidental to his motivation. Or, as Martha Nussbaum puts it, "the object of *philia* must be seen as a being with a separate good, not as simply a possession or extension of the *philos*; and the real *philos* will wish the other well for the sake of that separate good."[24]

Aristotle places further prescriptive requirements on friendship when he says not only that a real friend loves his friend for his friend's sake and is thus eager to benefit him,[25] but also that he will be prepared to die for him.[26] How does he justify such requirements? Aristotelian ethics being generally inimical to consequentialism, it is unlikely that the type of justification invoked by Sidgwick would fit the texts of either *Ethics*. True, Aristotle advises legislators to promote citizenly friendship, but, as we shall see presently, perfect friendship eschews justification in terms other than those of individual eudemonic autarky, or self-realization, and therefore cannot be justified in terms of the general good. How individual self-realization can, in turn, be reconciled with some of the extreme altruistic requirements that he builds into the very concept of friendship will be investigated in chapter 5 below. For now, it can be concluded that the normative claims embodied in Aristotle's analysis of virtue friendship are not unlike those discernible in modern theories.

The Descriptive Element

In both *Ethics* Aristotle makes a further crucial distinction between the object of primary friendship and that of the other two kinds. "Those who wish goods to their friend for the friend's own sake," he writes in the *Nicomachean* version, "are friends most of all; *for they have this attitude because of the friend himself*, not coincidentally."[27] Likewise in the *Eudemian Ethics*: "Since to love actively is to treat the loved object *qua* loved, and the friend *qua* dear to him but not *qua* musician or medical man, the pleasure of friendship is the pleasure derived from the person himself *qua* himself."[28] In these texts Aristotle distinguishes between the love which responds to the very being of another person and that which remains contentedly at the periphery of his personality. While friends of utility and of pleasure love their friends for some accidental (*kata symbebēkos*)[29] characteristic (such as wealth or political clout) or quality (such as musical ability or medical skill) that they happen to possess, virtuous persons love their friends in and for themselves. The former's self-interested motivation, as well as, presumably, their superficiality of character, causes them to love others for qualities which happen to suit them when they initiate or continue to cultivate the friendship. Accordingly, friendships of utility and of pleasure, which do not outlast the friend's useful or enjoyable qualities, lack the steadiness and permanence of virtue friendship.[30]

In this second contrast, where the object of love, rather than its motivation or its goals, is analysed, the expressions *ekeinou heneka* and *di' hauton* introduce the descriptive claim that a primary friend loves the essence of his friend's being rather than his accidental characteristics. In this context *kata sumbebēkos*, which should be understood in terms of the Aristotelian distinction between substance and accident,[31] designates those qualities which are extraneous to a person's being and whose loss would not therefore impair his identity. Indeed, not only are these qualities haphazardly distributed, generally reflecting neither merit nor effort, but they also tend to be prized, as Price,[32] following Buridan, has argued, for their social effects rather than intrinsically. They are marginal to the self. Since, as was established in chapter 1 above, Aristotle identifies persons with their *nous* or 'understanding part', we can conclude that the primary friend is he who loves and cares for his partner's true self. To love another *ekeinou heneka* entails wishing goods to him for the sake of his rational element and not for the sake of his accidental qualities which happen to be of transient benefit or pleasantness to ourselves.

Aristotle's descriptive claim that the object of true friendship is the essential self of another thus turns out to be interwoven with his normative claim that this friendship is disinterested. This is not surprising since descriptive and evaluative elements are not readily separable in his ethics. It is only because virtuous persons are selves, in Aristotle's normative sense of the word, that they can be loved in and for themselves. The love that their partners in primary friendship bear them is made the standard by which other forms of friendship are described and assessed. Although inferior kinds of friendship do have a role to play in most human lives, they fall short of the ideal because they place the contingent, the marginal, the changeable over the essential, the central, the permanent. In other words, they are most often informed by an inadequate notion of value.

Although the above interpretation has the benefit of strong textual support in both *Ethics*, it would not be accepted by all commentators. A.W.H. Adkins, most notably, criticizes Aristotle for here playing "a linguistic trick"[33] on his readers. By this he means that what I termed the second, descriptive, use of *ekeinou heneka* represents an equivocation on the part of Aristotle. According to Adkins, "Earlier, 1155b31, in a passage which is relevant to all three types of *philia, ekeinou heneka* is used in an 'ordinary Greek' sense, and must be intended to include wanting useful or pleasant things for a man 'for his own sake'. Here, however, 'for their own sake' is opposed to 'as a result of some accidental quality'; and this must refer back to the same phrase in 1156a16, and be intended to exclude the other two types of *philia.* . . ."[34] We should be wary of putting an altruistic interpretation on the latter passage, warns Adkins, since the text as a whole ". . . means that all men *philousin* [love] on account of the things which are or seem to them to be *agatha* [good] for themselves, but that in the case of *agathoi* [excellent men] the things which are *agatha* for them are also *haplōs agatha* [good unconditionally]. Quite late in the discussion we are informed that all three types of *philia* [friendship] are equally selfish."[35] In a footnote Adkins attempts to justify the arresting claim embodied in his last sentence: "For *haplōs agathon* does not mean '*agathon* for both A and B at the same time', but 'really *agathon* for A, who finds things which are really *agathon agathon* for him because he is *agathos*'."[36]

The above argument represents a move on the part of Adkins to justify his overall thesis that: "In essentials, the concept of *philia* [in Aristotle] remains as it was in Homer."[37] Aristotle's "linguistic trick" and "the curious nature of the arguments he is obliged to use"[38] are, in Adkins' interpretation, evidence of a growing tension in late Classical Greek society between competitive and cooperative values.

True, philosophers will use "curious arguments" to square their theories with their moral intuitions. But scholars and commentators with a general interpretative scheme of their own should also be wary of them. Bearing this warning in mind, I shall now proceed to argue for an alternative, less strained, interpretation than Adkins' of the *ekeinou heneka / di' hauton* condition that Aristotle ascribes to primary friendship. Before spelling it out, however, a closer examination of one of Adkins' arguments should prove useful.

Adkins does not appear to take note of an obvious but crucial distinction between that which can properly be called 'good unconditionally' and that which is only *'agathon* [good] for X'. While the former expression refers to what is good, both intrinsically and objectively, i.e., independently of individual preferences, wants, or needs, the latter phrase implies that some values are relational. As both Plato and Aristotle repeatedly point out, a diseased person will readily desire and seek things that are not intrinsically good.[39] It is characteristic of the healthy man, on the other hand, that he sees as good for him and desires what is good *per se*. Likewise it is the mark of the virtuous to seek what is good unconditionally rather than what he expects will gratify his (non rational) passions. From this we cannot but infer that the very point of describing a good as good *unconditionally* is to indicate that no reference to individual preferences, needs, and wants, is required to justify its goodness. To vindicate the goodness of what is good unconditionally, therefore, it is not necessary to invoke the fact that is is actually desired. Certain goods would still properly be described as good unconditionally even in the (unlikely) case of nobody desiring them in a particular society. The move from 'good for X' to 'good unconditionally' is the move from the scope of individual concern to that of intrinsic value, which is potentially a value for all.

Secondly, such goods as can properly be described as good unconditionally cannot be the objects of an individual's egoistic desires. Indeed, it only makes sense to call my desire selfish if my obtaining what I desire is likely to debar others from obtaining it. But whatever is good unconditionally tends not to be of such a nature that X's having more of it will result in Y's having less.[40] Knowledge, happiness, and the virtues are examples in point, while wealth, fame, or living space are not. *Pace* Adkins, the desire to possess goods that can properly be described as good unconditionally is not therefore a sign of selfishness, since no one suffers any loss or deprivation through another's enjoyment of such goods. One important difference between the friendship of utility and the friendship of virtue is thus that the good of the latter cannot be an object of competition. This may well be one of the reasons why Aristotle makes no reference to the reactive emotions of jealousy, envy, and covetousness in his account of primary friendship.

It might here be objected that in *N.E.*, IX,8 Aristotle argues as if 'the fine' (*to kalon*), which he normally claims to be an intrinsic good, could be an object of competition. "The excellent person," he there states, "will sacrifice money, honours, and contested goods in general, in achieving what is fine for himself."[41] A few lines later, he is even more explicit: "It is also possible . . . to sacrifice actions to his friend, since it may be finer to be responsible for one's friend's doing the action than to do it oneself. In everything praiseworthy, then, the excellent person awards himself what is fine."[42] These lines prompt Irwin to comment that: "Clearly the virtuous person's attitude to his friend's good is not entirely selfless and self-forgetful."[43] If correct, Irwin's interpretation would thus lend support to Adkins' claim that primary Aristotelian friendship has an ineradicable egoistic steak.

Although the above Aristotelian claim about friendship and the fine is somewhat ambiguously stated, there is no compelling reason to read in it the unpalatable view that the fine can be an object of barter. A virtuous friend who renders financial assistance to his friend both fulfils his friend's need and gains "what is fine" for himself. The motive of the gift, however, cannot just be the acquisition of "the fine" since in the terms of the *Eudemian Ethics*, the fine encompasses those ends (*telē*) ". . . which are both the motives of laudable actions and laudable themselves."[44] Not only can it

be argued, on Aristotle's behalf, that no one except a virtuous agent would value the fine over worldly goods, but it
must also be noted that in the above examples the fine is a
by-product of the sacrifice rather than its presiding motive.
If, as Adkins and Irwin seem to think, the actions had been
undertaken *in order to* obtain the hoped for "fine," they
would either not have represented a sacrifice or the sacrifice
would have been self-defeating. As D.J. Allan pointed out:
". . . a noble man may sacrifice wordly goods to another, but
not the fineness of virtuous action. The attempt to do so
would frustrate itself, and he would only secure 'the fine'
in a higher degree for himself."[45]
     He who forbears from acting heroically to allow his
friend the honour of doing so cannot but be disinterested
and act *ekeinou heneka*, even though such forbearance will
inevitably attract the bonus of an extra helping of the fine.
To pronounce this choice self-interested is tantamount to
mistaking the fine for some kind of after-life reward for the
sake of which one might be prompted to act decently in this
life. In fact, the virtuous friend whose forbearance Aristotle
describes in this passage desires *the* good rather than *his
own* private good. Having successfully educated his desires,
he has reached a stage where he aims at what is truly and
objectively good and where the tension between 'good for
me' and 'good *haplōs*' has therefore ceased to be. At such a
stage the fine has become its own motivating force. To
express this view in modern, non-Aristotelian terms, one
could say that to act for the sake of the fine is to subordinate
one's actions to the impersonal requirements of morality.
     Having established that the fine cannot be the object of
self-seeking motivation, we return to Aristotle's claim that a
true friend loves his friend *ekeinou heneka* (for his sake),
di' hauton (because of the friend himself), or *kath' hauton* (in
himself), and spell out its implications for the nature of primary friendship. We note, firstly, that Aristotle pays very little attention to such aspects of the genesis of friendship as
spontaneous, non-rational inclination. In one way this is
puzzling. Common experience, which Aristotle is usually
careful to integrate in his moral discussions, suggests that

friendship is often initiated by immediately unaccountable and contingent mutual attraction. Further, Plato had given a famously graphic account of this phenomenon.[46] Aristotle's neglect of the topic, one might be tempted to argue, shows the extent of his over-intellectualization of primary friendship. This conclusion, however, would be hasty. As we saw, there is clear evidence that Aristotle, for whom moral virtue cannot but be individuated, viewed primary friendship as the on-going affectionate communion encompassing most aspects of the lives of two (or more) individually excellent persons. One reason for Aristotle's reticence in the matter is more likely to have been that nothing much of significant philosophical, as contrasted with psychological, interest can be said about it. Further, although initial attraction and continuing mutual inclination do have a role to play in primary friendship, theirs is not the crucial one. What, according to Aristotle, distinguishes this kind of friendship from its inferior varieties is its concern with and care for the very core of the personality or self of the partner. Unless friends take pleasure in each other *qua* good, they "are not bonded in primary friendship."[47] In both *Ethics* Aristotle thus specifically grounds primary friendship in the preeminence, which is characteristic of all morally virtuous agents, of reason over passions which, being intractably individual, resist philosophical analysis.

Furthermore, since individual qualities (such as beauty, wit, business acumen, musical talent, or medical skill), which often prompt the affection or the interest of friends of pleasure and utility, are reduced to the status of accidents, they cannot ever form the basis of virtue friendship. While the loss of such characteristics may well entail the loss of fair-weather friends, it will not undermine the steady affection of primary friends who love each other for what they are in themselves. Indeed, the latter are unlikely ever to cease to be worthy of each other's respect and affection,[48] since virtue, in the proper sense of the word, is by definition stable and enduring. However, mistakes can occur, and it is to reduce their likelihood that Aristotle would submit friendship to the test of time.[49] When he at last confronts the problem as to how and when friendships of virtue may have to be dissolved, it is to claim that "what is bad is not lovable, and must not be loved."[50] Clearly, he thought, good people neither will nor ought to remain friends with those who are no longer worthy of respect. Having changed for the worse, the latter are no longer the ones with whom the former had made friends. The dissolution of a friendship of virtue can only be justified, therefore, by an (improbable) impairment or loss of selfhood. Nothing could be further from Telfer's claim that it is of the nature of affection to be irrational and, for that reason, to be able to "survive radical changes in the character of its object."[51]

Thus are we again driven to conclude that in Aristotle's usage the phrase 'what a person is in himself' does not pick out the contingent characteristics which serve to differentiate this person from all others, but refers instead to his essential nature. It is the actualization of that essential nature through the practice of moral virtue that in the main prepares individuals for primary friendship and enables them to become the 'other selves' of their virtuous partners. Though Aristotle's insistence on the individuated character of moral virtue allows him somehow to account for the uniqueness of the friend, the equation between selfhood, reason, and goodness nevertheless pushes such uniqueness off the centre of his analysis of primary friendship. Even Martha Nussbaum, who has done much to document the extent of Aristotle's ethical preoccupation with contingency and particularity, writes that: "We do not even love particular individuals in the Aristotelian way without loving, centrally, repeatable commitments and values which their lives exemplify."[52]

'What the friend is in himself', i.e., that which makes him truly lovable, thus turns out largely to lie in virtues and qualities that he possesses in common with all other good persons, although he may not possess them in exactly the same manner as they do. Whoever succeeds in becoming a self *ipso facto* becomes (truly) lovable, although contingent factors may well prevent him from being actually (truly) loved. Whoever is bound to another in primary friendship (truly) loves the essential self of that other and disinterestedly wants it to flourish. This, in turn, might appear to license the inference that virtuous friends are replaceable, *qua* friends. Only in inferior friendships, it might be thought, does Aristotle allow that friends are valued for clusters of properties which, having nothing or little to do with practical rationality, might well make them unique as individuals and to that extent irreplaceable.

The worry that Aristotle may unwittingly have presented primary friends as variables in an equation is, however, not justified. True, he does not appear to have considered that, in its initial stages, the formation of primary friendship was anything else than contingent. The virtuous man does not set out purposefully and deliberately to find a friend, as Diogenes is alleged to have looked for a man, and, to begin with, at least, all excellent persons are potential candidates for his (primary) friendship.[53] With whom he actually makes (primary) friends is more generally a matter of happenstance than of pre-existing complementarity. Further, Aristotle's identification of selfhood with a largely impersonal principle and his characterization of primary friendship by its cognitive and ethical aspects leave him little room for a philosophical account and justification of the role played in the formation of this personal relation by attraction, inclination, and affinity. However, if Aristotle plays down such psychological preconditions of primary friendship as the recognition by the would-be partners of their temperamental compatibility, this does not mean that he leaves non-rational affective factors altogether out of account. He neither says nor implies that, *once formed*, a friendship could survive the replacement of either party by just any other suitably virtuous person. On the contrary, friends are not like coats, he writes, and "you ought not in place of an old friend to choose one whom you do not know to be a better man."[54] In any case, only actual friendship could reveal the other to be a better man. Through the length of time necessary for its maturation, primary friendship provides both partners with a rich baggage of shared memories and experiences as well as with a detailed acquaintance with each other's character and temperament. Having eaten the proverbial peck of salt together, primary friends can count on each other's loyalty—which is but a way of saying that each has become one of his kind for the other and is not in any way to be replaced. Even a cursory glance at Aristotle's will reveals just how personal an experience he had of this kind of loyalty and how respectful he was of the individual needs of his dependants.[55] But he also expressed this point more philosophically when he remarked, in a somewhat anti-Platonic aside in the *Eudemian Ethics*, that "if a friend is really to be your friend, he must not only be good absolutely, but also good for you."[56] Although he used the distinction between 'good absolutely' and 'good for X'[57] to reiterate the point that in primary friendship these two goods are in harmony, the fact remains not only that he distinguishes them but also that, in this passage at least, he deems the relational good to be, of the two, the more relevant to friendship.[58]

If each primary friendship is made unique by the past that it carries within it, then Aristotle cannot stand accused of fostering the impression that friends of virtue are interchangeable and his views on the matter are close to modern intuitions. On the other hand, his contention that primary friendship entails a disinterested regard for the self or reason of another does mean that, unlike later writers on the subject, he did not consider personal singularity to be a fit object of wonder. Even though moral virtue, in his view, cannot but be individuated, the fact remains that it constitutes the single most important criterion of primary friendship.

Such a crucial difference between Aristotelian and modern views of friendship need not, of course, signal a failing on Aristotle's part. Though our conception of friendship gives pride of place to the unicity of friends and thus to their individual irreplaceability, it remains vague as to what such unicity consists in. In that respect it is unsatisfactory since we want to be loved *both* uniquely *and* for our good qualities. As Pascal pointed out, these two requirements are not easily combined. Aristotle's way of individuating primary friendship through time may paradoxically be more satisfactory.

The stage has now been reached at which the descriptive and the normative claims, which had been identified in the *ekeinou heneka* and the *di' hauton* conditions of primary friendship, can be drawn together again. As we have seen, the two claims are intertwined in both treatises, and it is only for clarity's sake that they have generally been kept separate so far. To love a person in himself is to love him for what he quintessentially is, i.e., a rational being and a virtuous agent. It follows that only good persons can be loved in themselves, since the wicked, the dull, the feeble-minded, the self-indulgent, and the akratic, being irrational, fail to be 'what is mostly themselves'. Primary friendship can only bond equals in virtue. Thus the motives for initiating and cultivating a primary friendship are bound to be disinterested, since the good pursued in the activity in question is not of a competitive nature. Indeed, one cannot love virtue and rationality for one's own exclusive sake. Not only is rationality non-personal by definition, but the Aristotelian notion of 'the fine' further rules out a purely instrumental reliance on it. Further, those who love their friends for their virtues show thereby that they are innocent of the temptation to reduce these others to the status of means to their own hedonistic or utilitarian goals. Whenever we love our friend primarily for what he essentially is, rather than for his contingent and ephemeral qualities, we therefore do like him for his own sake rather than for ours. The normative requirement that Aristotle places on primary friendship is therefore grounded in the descriptive claim that the essence of friendship lies in what makes a friend 'mostly himself', i.e., his virtue and his rationality.

To conclude: the formulae *ekeinou heneka* and *di' hauton* (in its descriptive sense) should be handled cautiously, since, as we have seen, they do not quite connote the very same values as their modern language equivalents. Aristotelian primary friendship is mostly justified in terms of abstract values (the good, the fine, the rational), while modern disinterested friendship centres around concrete values, i.e., values which are essentially rooted in particulars. This explains why virtues such as fidelity and solidarity, which play a central role in modern conceptions of friendship, play only a supportive role in Aristotle's analysis of primary friendship. The Aristotelian virtuous person's prime loyalty could in any case never be to particular individuals, however close they be to him, in preference to what is unconditionally good. Although goodness in the sublunary world cannot but be embodied in and related to particulars, the fact remains that it is identified with impersonal values which are capable of being variously instantiated. If this appears a strange view to hold for the philosopher who saw individuals as the most real things in the world, we may care to remember that Aristotle is also the philosopher who wrote that "Poetry is (. . .) of graver import than history, since its statements are of the nature of universals, whereas those of history are singulars."[59]

4

SELF-LOVE

Self-love, my liege, is not so vile a sin
as self-neglecting.

> —Shakespeare, *King Henry V*,
> Act II, Scene IV

If the Aristotelian notion of selfhood embodies rational and moral norms, as has been argued so far, it must be expected to carry specific implications for a number of reflexive relations. More particularly, it will affect the delicate and crucial issue of self-love and of its relation with the love of one's other selves. Though there have been philosophers, most notably Bishop Butler,[1] who have argued for the compatibility of self-love and altruism, most modern moral philosophers in the Western tradition present self-love as an obstacle to be surmounted in the achievement of the moral life. As Kant notoriously says in his discussion of the notion of reverence for the moral law,[2] "Reverence is properly awareness of a value which demolishes my self-love." According to this latter view, morality requires that each agent views herself as no more than one entity amongst others, all equally worthy of moral respect. In the Aristotelian scheme, on the other hand, if the achievement of selfhood constitutes a moral ideal, self-love could be both a condition and an expression of moral excellence. Aristotelian self-love, in other words, would not necessarily carry the unpalatable egoistic connotations that we

79

have come generally to associate with this notion, and it could also co-exist with or even ground disinterested love for others. Yet Aristotle is often classified as a 'moral egoist'. The exegesis of Aristotle's pronouncements on the complex issue of self-love and its relation to friendship, which is the purpose of this chapter and the next, aims at strengthening the case of those who have recently argued that the Aristotelian best human life includes some amount of disinterested concern for others.[3] More specifically, it will here be argued that Aristotle's assertions that "one is a friend to oneself most of all"[4] and "the good person must be a self-lover"[5] can effectively be squared with his view that friendship in the primary sense involves loving one's friends in and for themselves.

Although the notion of self-love appears in the *Eudemian Ethics*, the term itself (φιλαυτία) does not,[6] and it is in the *Nicomachean Ethics* that it occurs most frequently and prominently. The notion itself receives different though compatible treatments in the two *Ethics*. While the *Eudemian* discussion focuses on an examination of the paradoxical nature of self-love, the *Nicomachean* treatment gives pride of place to its moral significance. In the latter treatise Aristotle distinguishes two senses of *philautia*, one commendatory, the other pejorative.[7] While he enjoins the good man to be a friend to himself[8] and presents such a person's self-love as morally commendable in so far as it requires virtue,[9] he stresses that ". . . in the way the many are [self-lovers], we ought not to be."[10] Although this latter kind of relationship to self is natural (*phusikon*),[11] it does not deserve the appellation of *philautia* since it rests on an incorrect view of the self. Deluded as to what is truly to their own advantage, self-lovers in the popular sense of the word gratify the non-rational part of the soul at the expense of the dianoetic, specifically human, element. Basely they try to secure for themselves the biggest share of competitive goods.[12] This not only makes them prone to psychic tension, as we shall see, but it also, in turn, renders them unfit for genuine friendship.

To the extent that the concept of *philautia* appears to presuppose a division of the self into a part that loves and a part that is loved, it appears to hinge on a plural conception of *psychē*. Psychic pluralism would, in this instance, allow Aristotle to bypass the conceptual difficulties involved in concurrently assigning an active and a passive role to the self. But it also raises difficulties of which Aristotle is keenly aware.

In the *Eudemian Ethics* we read that friendship to self, like weakness of the will and injustice to self, can be explained in terms of a plural *psychē*. Aristotle's tone, be it noted, is cautious: "All these relations involve two separate factors; in so far as the soul is *in some sense* dual these relationships *somehow* belong to it, insofar as these parts cannot be separated these relationships do not belong to it."[13] The use of the adverb *pōs* (somehow) signals that Aristotle is less than fully committed to the thesis he is currently invoking. Although he makes the same point in the *Nicomachean Ethics*, it is in an even more cautious manner: "Is there friendship towards oneself, or is there not? Let us dismiss that question for the present. However, there seems to be friendship in so far as someone is two or more parts."[14] The reason for this noncommittal tone may be that he considered purely theoretical considerations to be out of place in ethics.[15] But it could also be that in both *Ethics* Aristotle already viewed psychic pluralism with the reservations which were to be most clearly expressed in *De Anima*.[16] That this might indeed be the case seems to emerge from the *Nicomachean* discussion of the putative notion of injustice to self. Such a notion, Aristotle writes, is problematic: ". . . if one could [be unjust to oneself], the same person could lose and get the same thing at the same time. But this is impossible; on the contrary, what is just or unjust must always involve more than one person."[17] Yet, a few lines later Aristotle adds, very much as an after-thought, that a dualistic psychology can ground by analogy (*kata metaphoran*) the notion of injustice to self.[18] In that passage he dissociates himself from such a psychology when he notes that "*in these discussions the part of the soul that has reason is distinguished from the non-rational part. People look at these and it seems to them* that there is injustice to oneself, because in these parts it is possible to suffer something against one's own desire."[19] What are those 'discussions' which, in Aristotle's view, had led people astray?

References such as the above to earlier discussions of the possibility of various reflexive relations raise the vexed question of the *exoterikoi logoi*, and commentators' attention has often focused on this. An unfortunate by-product of their industry, until recently, has been the unwarranted neglect of the more characteristically Aristotelian aspects of the notion of self-love. In the present chapter I shall contribute to redressing this bias of critical scrutiny and argue that *philautia* in the commending sense, which signals the smooth operation of practical reason, *is* nothing less than virtue experienced by the virtuous from within.

His explicit reservations about psychic pluralism notwithstanding, Aristotle's portrait of the virtuous self-lover bears witness to Plato's influence, and it is not unlikely that the problem of whether a person can be his own friend had been discussed in the Academy. This would explain why some of Aristotle's pronouncements on the matter sound an unmistakable Platonic echo. Firstly, a genuine *philautos*, Aristotle claims, ". . . awards himself what is finest and best of all, and gratifies the most controlling part of himself, obeying it in everything. And just as a city and every composite system seems to be above all its most controlling part, the same is true of a human being; hence someone loves himself most if he likes and gratifies this part. Similarly, someone is called continent or incontinent because his understanding is or is not the master, on the assumption that this is what each person is."[20] Further, since "the base person appears not to have a friendly attitude even towards himself,"[21] he cannot but be miserable, argues Aristotle, and "everyone should earnestly shun vice and try to be decent."[22] Socrates, of course, had argued this very point in support of his claim that justice benefits the just.[23] In Plato's *Republic*, it will be recalled, Socrates tells Glaucon: "Fashion me (. . .) one kind of multiform beast with many heads, a ring of both tame and wild animals"[24] coupled to both a smaller form of a lion and a still smaller form of a man. He who commits injustice in the hope of reaping benefits, says Socrates, "does not accustom one part to the other or make them *friendly*, but he leaves them alone to bite and fight and kill each other."[25] On the other hand, one who knows that justice is to the advantage of the just ". . . will care for all of them and rear them by making them all *friendly* with each other."[26] The self-love that Aristotle was later to present as the reflection of virtue is precisely the harmonization of the elements of the soul which results from a successful attempt to make them all friendly with one another. Alternatively, the self-love that Aristotle regards as a misnomer arises when the "multi-headed monster" is given free rein over the other parts and thus unpredictably goes hither and thither without consideration for them.

Likewise in the *Phaedrus* analogy, the task of the human charioteer is to control two steeds which are liable to pull in diverging directions. The divine chariots, on the contrary, "are well matched and tractable, and, as a result, go easily."[27] Reason, continues Socrates, is "the pilot of the soul,"[28] while the non-rational parts are compared to a prison-house, a tomb, or, less pejoratively, to the shell of an oyster.[29] More generally, Aristotle's self-lover (*ho philautos*) can be viewed as the fulfilment of Socrates' famous prayer to Pan in the same dialogue: "grant that I may become fair within."[30] Lastly, such a *philautos* is clearly one who has heeded the precept of the Athenian Stranger in the *Laws* to honour his soul as "his holiest (. . . .) most intimate possession."[31] Such unmistakable Platonic echoes in *N.E.* IX, 4 and 8, lead Jaeger, Gauthier, and Dirlmeier to conclude that in these passages Aristotle is arguing from a Platonic conception of the soul and hence that they are dialectical.[32] As mentioned earlier,[33] they had prompted Nuyens to conclude that the conception of *psychē* in the *Nicomachean Ethics* is intermediate as between the Platonism of the *Protrepticus* and the mature views expounded in the *De Anima*.

Such striking similarities between the two philosophers should not, however, obscure the different roles played by the ideal of inner concord in their respective moral systems. For Plato, psychic harmony is a healthy state of the soul which allows potential knowers to direct their gaze towards immutable reality. Aristotle, on the other hand, as we shall see, presents self-love as a reflection of the smooth operation of rational choice in the man of practical reason. It is symptomatic that, while in the *Symposium* the love of concrete individuals is but a stage to be overcome in the mind's ascent to the Form of Beauty, in the *Nicomachean Ethics* self-love constitutes a *sine qua non* for the achievement of primary friendship with other virtuous individuals. In Aristotle's usage of *philautia*, Platonic psychic harmony has been, as it were, brought down to earth or, in the well-known phrase, 'turned on its head'. Though the concept of *philautia* appears to have its roots in Platonic psychology, it has nevertheless received a characteristically Aristotelian definition. The substantiation of this claim, however, requires an exegesis of the complex argument presented in *N.E.*, IX,4. Although the passage is long, it deserves to be quoted in full:

> The many, base though they are, also appear to have these features. But perhaps they share in them only so far as they approve of themselves and suppose they are decent. For no one who is utterly bad and unscrupulous either has these features or appears to have them. Indeed even base people hardly have them. For they are at odds with themselves, and, like incontinent people, have an appetite for one thing and a wish for another. For they do not choose things that seem to be good for them, but instead choose pleasant things that are actually harmful. And cowardice or laziness causes others to shrink from doing what they think best for themselves. Those who have done many terrible actions hate and shun life because of their vice, and destroy themselves. Besides, vicious people seek others to pass their days with, and shun themselves. For when they are by themselves they remember many disagreeable actions, and expect to do others in the future; but they manage to forget these in other people's company. These people have nothing lovable about them, and so have no friendly feelings for themselves. Hence such a person does not share his own enjoyments and distresses. For his soul is in conflict, and

because he is vicious one part is distressed at being restrained, and another is pleased [by the intended action]; and so each part pulls in a different direction, as though they were tearing him apart. Even if he cannot be distressed and pleased at the same time, still he is soon distressed because he was pleased, and wishes these things had not become pleasant to him; for base people are full of regret.[34]

Not only do these lines make intriguing claims but they also raise exegetical problems which must now be considered.

In the chapter from which this passage is excerpted, Aristotle presents *philautia* as a state of inner serenity that is enjoyed by virtuous persons who have become true to their own selves. As for the passage itself, it clearly purports to show that self-love is inaccessible to those who are not virtuous. To that effect, as I understand him, Aristotle proceeds to contrast the inner peace of the virtuous with the self-reproach and discontent that are the inevitable accompaniments of the two dysfunctions of practical reason, viz., the venial form or weakness of the will (*akrasia*) and the more drastic form or wickedness (*mochtēria*). It is therefore essential to my interpretation that Aristotle be taken at his word when, in 1166b2-25, he claims to be referring to the state of mind of the wicked *as well as* to that of the akratic. This has been denied by some commentators, most notably Gauthier,[35] who take the passage to be exclusively a description of the akratic. While agreeing with Gauthier that the text makes some claims about *akrasia*, I shall contend that these claims are subsidiary to its main point, which is the incompatibility of wickedness (or baseness) and self-love in the proper sense of the word. In Aristotle's moral philosophy virtue and genuine self-love cannot but be concomitant.

Unfortunately, the exegesis of this and related passages raises a number of difficulties, two of which need to be discussed here. Firstly, Aristotle appears to have contradicted himself on the issue of remorse, regret, and wickedness. In book VII of the *Nicomachean Ethics*, he had identified the absence of regret as the main defining feature of the intemperate or vicious character,[36] thus leaving open the possibility that the wicked might be at peace with, and to that extent, love themselves. Although incontinence and intemperance may have similar objects (usually bodily pleasures), he there uncontentiously claimed, they nevertheless differ in so far as the incontinent, but not the intemperate, is prone to remorse or regret (*metameleia*). For this reason, the former is morally curable while the latter is not. In book IX of the same treatise, on the other hand, we are told that "base people are full of regret,"[37] and therefore they cannot love themselves. The contradiction appears blatant, and there is no easy way to iron it out. The second difficulty lies in the contentiousness of Aristotle's claim that friendship towards oneself is inaccessible to the wicked on account of his regretfulness. To a modern reader, at any rate, it seems a matter of definition that wickedness is characterized by the absence of remorse or regret and the phrase "contented scoundrel" is readily applied to a range of real-life and fictional characters. The fact that the view put forward in book IX, unlike that expressed in book VII, is counter-intuitive should make us wary of assuming that our concepts of regret, remorse, and wickedness fully match Aristotle's.

Any attempt to resolve the contradiction, if it can be resolved at all, calls, firstly, for a number of remarks on the Greek notion of *metameleia* which is central to the whole issue. To begin with, the words 'remorse', 'repentance', and even 'regret', by which English translators normally render *metameleia*, have their own connotative haze which may prove very difficult to dispel. More specifically, it is far from certain that the Greek concept carried as pronounced intimations of interiority and introspection as our corresponding notions. Further, it is worth bearing in mind that in classical Greek *metameleia* can refer to a change of purpose as well as to regret and to pangs of conscience.[38] These points will briefly be taken in turn.

Although modern common parlance often assimilates remorse and repentance, they should be distinguished. Remorse is directed at one's own past avoidable infringement(s) of one or several moral principles or rules that one has endorsed. It mostly centres on another being, human or not, whose entitlements one has flouted. As for repentance, it is a theological concept, linked to the notion of sin or offense committed against the deity whose forgiveness is then sought. Most often, it is induced by the realization of the extent of one's own moral lapses, although deficiency in the theological virtues of faith and hope can also constitute occasions for repentance. Unlike remorse and repentance, regret need not be directed at those lapses for which one considers oneself to be responsible, directly or indirectly, but generally consists in feeling despondency at the thought of one's past deeds, attitudes, and decisions in the light of their consequences, which may not have been foreseeable at the time. To that extent, regret is not always a moral emotion. Unlike remorse and repentance, it can also be felt on behalf of another with whom one is closely associated. On the assumption that these conceptual distinctions are broadly correct, I shall now offer some brief comments on the corresponding Greek notions.

If it is true that Classical Greece was a shame culture while ours is a guilt culture, then we should expect *metameleia*, in its moral sense, to carry connotations of dishonour, humiliation, or, at least, embarrassment. Rather than an emotion experienced within the privacy of one's own conscience, it would be generated by the cringing realization that one's own inferiority has been rendered manifest to another, who may be real or imagined. In fact, as we shall see, the Aristotelian notion of *metameleia* appears to be quite free of such connotations. On the other hand, while our 'guilt culture' tends to value remorse and repentance as commendable emotions, 'shame cultures' are likely to associate the best heroic life with the redundancy of shame. Nowhere is the celebration of remorse more clearly expressed than in Luke's Gospel: ". . . there shall be joy in heaven over one sinner that repenteth, more than over ninety and nine righteous persons, which need no repentance."[39] In his commentary on the *Nicomachean Ethics* Gauthier eloquently speaks of this crucial difference between the Judaeo-Christian and the Greek notion of remorse. After reminding us that in Scripture remorse is presented as the necessary condition of salvation, he adds, "the more saintly the saint, the more gnashing his remorse and the greater his penance."[40] By contrast, as we saw, Aristotle makes it a matter of definition that the virtuous should feel no remorse since he has done nothing to justify moral sorrow. As for shame, it is inappropriate in a man of mature years, he writes, "since we think it wrong for him to do any action that causes a feeling of disgrace."[41] Far from evidencing moral fastidiousness, therefore, remorse in Aristotle's outlook, can signal only moral failure. The akratic, forever deploring the rift between his deeds and his convictions, is the embodiment of such failure. But, as we shall argue presently, *pace* Gauthier, Aristotle holds that remorse or regret can also vitiate the life of the wicked and base person whose short-term and long-term goals are fundamentally flawed and at odds with each other. Furthermore, there is nothing admirable in akratic remorse or in vicious regret, according to Aristotle who, in this one respect though not in others, thought like a representative of a 'shame culture'.

In his *Greek Popular Morality in the Time of Plato and Aristotle*, Kenneth Dover's survey of the extant relevant literature indicates that Athenians of the Classical period tended to be more often motivated to act morally rightly by fear of untoward consequences than by the internal promptings of their consciences or inner moral sense. Although Dover has found allusions to morally upright individuals who, in the words of Lysias, acted ". . . in the belief that a good man should help his friends *even if no one was going to know about it*," such tributes tend to be the exception rather than the rule.[42] It may also be significant that the Greek verb for 'to repent', viz., *metamelei*, is impersonal, taking the dative of the person who 'repents'.[43] Although one should be very wary of overstressing the importance of such lexical data, the fact remains that remorse and repentance tended to be expressed as events happening to a person rather than as mental processes initiated by him. As for the deponent verb *metamelomai*, which also means 'to repent' or 'to regret', its frequency increased significantly after the Classical period. In the Classical age it not infrequently served to express a change of purpose or regret of a non-moral kind.

It is against this background, where *metameleia* can, but need not, be a moral concept (in the modern sense) that Aristotle's usage must be studied. Precluded by moral virtue, remorse, he implies, chides and goads the akratic and, in some cases, the young, onto the path of self-improvement. Although it may prove ineffectual, its presence in the soul is unsettling and sufficient to disturb the akratic's peace of mind. To that extent, it is the reverse of self-esteem. Aristotle does not describe *metameleia* in any great detail but indicates that it is a nagging and sorrowful awareness of one's failure to live up to one's own considered decisions and values.[44] In as much as it inevitably accompanies weakness of the will, *metameleia*, in the *Nicomachean Ethics* thus designates a moral emotion, self-present to the agent, which is generated by the consciousness of a gap between deeds and convictions. In this sense *metameleia* is properly translated by 'remorse'.[45]

The *metameleia* of the intemperate, on the other hand, appears to be altogether different. To start with, it cannot act as a spur, since, in respect to his appetites at least, the intemperate is literally single-minded. He does not realize or care that his character is fundamentally flawed. Indeed, while the akratic generally feels remorse at the very moment of action, the intemperate experiences no such painful dissociation at that point. These brief comments, which Aristotle makes in *N.E.* VII,8 are unexceptionable. How then can we explain his later, to us counter-intuitive, contention that the base is as full of regret as the akratic, and thus, like him, he can never truly love himself? Five considerations are brought to bear on the issue.

A. διαφέρονται γὰρ ἑαυτοῖς, καὶ ἑτέρων μὲν ἐπιθυμοῦσιν ἄλλα δὲ βούλονται, οἷον οἱ ἀκρατεῖς (". . . they are at odds with themselves, and like incontinent people, have an appetite for one thing and a wish for another.")[46] The subject of διαφέρονται, which can unmistakably be inferred from the clause preceding the present quotation, is οἱ φαῦλοι (the base or the wicked). Intemperate and incontinent persons, says Aristotle in this passage, both suffer from a lack of convergence between their (non-rational) desire and their (rational) wish. *Pace* Gauthier, Aristotle does nor here provide a definition of incontinence—he will do so presently—but states his general claim that psychic integration is unavailable to both the wicked and the akratic. Aristotle's identification of a common feature between intemperance and incontinence clearly shows that far from assimilating the former to the latter, he sees them as different. Otherwise, his comparison would be pointless.

B. αἰροῦνται γὰρ ἀντὶ τῶν δοκούντων ἑαυτοῖς ἀγαθῶν εἶναι τὰ ἡδέα βλαβερὰ ὄντα (". . . they do not choose things that seem to be good for them, but choose pleasant things that are actually harmful.")[47] Some people, Aristotle indicates in these lines, choose the bad but pleasant course of action in preference to that which they consider to be to their own advantage. It is natural to read in this passage a description of the classic case of incontinence. But it may also apply to the apolaustic, intemperate life in which long-term goals and distant consequences are disregarded or coolly overruled. Debauchees, ignominious deserters, joy riders, spongers, and blackmailers do not necessarily suffer from weakness of the will. Yet, they all choose the pleasant at the expense of the prudent. Considered on their own, therefore, these lines appear to be applicable to both the incontinent and the wicked. We shall come back to this issue.

C. The lines οἷς δὲ πολλὰ καὶ δεινὰ πέπρακται καὶ διὰ τὴν μοχθηρίαν μισοῦνται, καὶ φεύγουσι τὸ ζῆν καὶ ἀναιροῦσιν ἑαυτούς ("They who have done terrible actions hate and shun life because of their vice, and destroy themselves")[48] stress the fact that wickedness generates its own peculiar kind of misery, and for that reason they do not apply to the incontinent. Even Gauthier admits as much.[49] The meaning of the phrase ἀναιροῦσιν ἑαυτούς ('they destroy themselves'), as used in the present context, is peculiarly Aristotelian; in the *De Sophisticis Elenchis*[50] it refers to self-contradiction.

Vice appears here to be the moral equivalent of logical self-confutation: just as the illogical person's assertions conflict with and ultimately cancel each other, the vicious person is a *locus* of disorderly and uncoordinated pulls and tensions. Wicked actions and dispositions impede the development of one's selfhood, just as the utterance of contradictions empties one's discourse of declarative content.

D. ξητοῦσί τε οἱ μοχθηροὶ μεθ' ὧν συνημερεύσουσιν, ἑαυτοὺς δὲ φεύγουσιν· ἀναμιμνήσκονται γὰρ πολλῶν καὶ δυσχερῶν, καὶ τοιαῦθ' ἕτερα ἐλπίξουσι, καθ' ἑαυτοὺς ὄντες, μεθ' ἑτέρων δ' ὄντες ἐπιλανθάνονται (". . . vicious people seek others to pass their days with, and shun themselves. For when they are by themselves they remember many disagreeable actions, and expect to do others in the future; but they manage to forget these in other people's company.")[51] Baseness ultimately leads the wicked to shun themselves and to seek the anaesthetizing company of others. Further, Aristotle claims, just as their past affords them no joy, they cannot expect the future to be any less disagreeable. Although Aristotle explicitly makes the wicked the subject of the sentence, one criterion applies to the akratic, too. Weak-willed alcoholics, for instance, are prone to take comfort in the undemanding company of their boozing companions. As for the other criterion, however, it does not fit the akratic who is prone to deceive himself that he will mend his ways on the morrow. Only the wicked, or hardened sinners, expect their future actions to resemble their past ones. But why should such anticipation be vexatious (*duscherēs*) rather than complacent, as one might more readily expect? This, the main point of the passage, is further developed in Aristotle's claim that the wicked is alienated from both his past and his future.

E. οὐδε δὴ συγχαίρουσιν οὐδε συναλγοῦσιν οἱ τοιοῦτοι ἑαυτοῖς· στασιάξει γὰρ αὐτῶν ἡ ψυχή, καὶ τὸ μὲν διὰ μοχθηρίαν ἀλγεῖ ἀπεχόμενόν τινων, τὸ δ' ἥδεται, καὶ τὸ μὲν δεῦρο τὸ δ' ἐκεῖσε ἕλκει ὥσπερ διασπῶντα. εἰ δὲ μὴ οἷόν τε ἅμα λυπεῖσθαι καὶ ἥδεσθαι, ἀλλὰ μετὰ μικρόν γε λυπεῖται ὅτι ἥσθη, καὶ οὐκ ἂν ἐβούλετο ἡδέα ταῦτα γενέσθαι αὐτῷ· μεταμελείας γὰρ οἱ φαῦλοι γέμουσιν ("Hence such a person does not share his own enjoyments and distresses. For his soul is in conflict, and because he is vicious one part is distressed at being unable to perform certain actions while another part is pleased; and so each part pulls in a different direction, as though they were tearing him apart. Even if he cannot be distressed and pleased at the same time, still he is soon distressed because he was pleased, and wishes these things had not become pleasant to him; for base people are full of regret.")[52] There is no compelling reason to read this passage as Gauthier does,[53] viz., as an account of the akratic's state of mind at the exclusion of anything else, since Aristotle explicitly presents wickedness as a cause of distress. There is no indication in the text, however, that such distress as the wicked experiences is of a moral nature. There are other grounds, beside moral ones, on which to deplore one's own past misdeeds. Nor has it, in any case as yet, been established that, in Aristotle's usage, *metameleia* unfailingly designates a moral emotion.

Taken together, Aristotle's claims are somewhat perplexing and raise a number of issues. Firstly, as already stated, they contradict the view, expressed in book VII, that there are clear differences of quality between incontinence and wickedness. In book IX, as has just been seen, Aristotle does not appear any more to rely on the neat dividing line between incontinence and wickedness that he had drawn in the earlier book. Wickedness, he now appears to indicate, is a risk that all weak-willed persons run and a condition into which some of them will inevitably slide. No longer is regret presented as a differentiating criterion between incontinence and vice. No longer is incontinence clearly circumscribed as correct but inoperative desire, expressible in a major premise of a practical syllogism. Instead, Aristotle now presents it as much closer to wickedness than he had been doing earlier in the *Nicomachean Ethics*. As noted earlier, this view has become counter-intuitive. Modern readers on whom the Judaeo-Christian tradition has been influential value remorse either in itself or for its salutary effects and, hence, consider incontinence and wickedness to be very different states separated by the watershed of redeemability.

Secondly, we must wonder to what extent Aristotle's characterization of the vicious as utterly wretched is theory-driven. Indeed, Aristotle's objectivist ethics in general and his current discourse on *philautia* in particular both require that he paints a gloomy picture of the wicked character. Besides which, he may not have thought that the ghost of Thrasymachus had been laid for good and therefore seeks to reiterate in his own words the Socratic argument that injustice does not pay.[54] However, if wickedness brings distress and misery, we shall want to know how and why the wicked became wicked and why he perseveres in his wicked ways. Indeed if regret can act as a spur in the case of incontinence, why does it not do so in the case of wickedness? Some brief remarks on Aristotle's conception of wickedness need here to be made.

Surprisingly, the issue of wickedness as such does not arise in the *Eudemian Ethics*; it is merely presented as the genus of which incontinence is as a species.[55] In the *Nicomachean Ethics*, on the other hand, where no such classification is made, it tends to be considered only through the analysis of particular vices, such as pusillanimity, cowardice, or, most frequently, intemperance. Wickedness, *qua* such, is not discussed. The reason may have been that Aristotle considered that vice, like virtue, is unitary. Just as one cannot have one moral virtue to the exclusion of the others, the dispositional flaws which produce particular vices would affect the whole of the soul and eventually debilitate the decision-making processes altogether. On this assumption, wickedness, rather than being characterized as the cumulative effect on a person's character of several individual vices, would be the name of a class to which individual vices, with the possible addition of incontinence, belong. Wickedness would then properly be discussed in connection with whatever vice happens to be at issue in the current argument. And the claim, made in *N.E.* VII, 8, that the wicked, in the person of the intemperate, will remain unregenerated, would be of direct relevance to the later discussion of the problem as to whether genuine self-love can co-exist with the absence of virtue, itself due either to incon-

tinence or to vice. In *N.E.* VII Aristotle had unambiguously
stated that absence of remorse impedes self-improvement
and ultimately leads to the vicious state becoming endemic
in the soul. This view is consonant with the conclusion of his
discussion of voluntariness and responsibility in *N.E.* III to
the effect that ". . . it was originally open to the person who
is [now] unjust or intemperate not to acquire this character;
hence he has it willingly, *though once he has acquired it he
can no longer get rid of it.*"[56] This appears to indicate that in
book III Aristotle had already presented a 'thin end of the
wedge' conception of wickedness according to which every
weak-willed, as well as every self-indulgent, agent is potentially wicked. Indeed, paralyzing though vice eventually
turns out to be, it is not to be compared to a disease for
which the agent could not be held responsible: ". . . the
virtues, as we say, are voluntary, since in fact we are ourselves in a way jointly responsible for our states of character,
and by having the sort of character we have we lay down the
sort of end we do. Hence the vices will also be voluntary,
since the same is true of them."[57]

In this well-known passage Aristotle addresses the
Socratic paradox that no one does evil willingly, and claims
that such lack of knowledge as produces incontinence,
wickedness or vice can itself be culpable. Aristotle's way of
tackling the paradox reveals how he conceived the relationship between wickedness and regret and contributes to
explaining why, in his view, wickedness is incompatible with
self-love. Indeed, since "each type of activity produces the
corresponding character,"[58] adult agents are responsible for
their character even when they have reached a point at
which they no longer could act out of character. Although
wickedness inevitably disables the will of the wicked, it cannot ever, of itself, Aristotle contends, mitigate blamewor-
thiness. On this account, wickedness is ultimately to be
traced to earlier voluntary wrong choices and decisions. In
other words, the wicked himself had been the agent of his
enslavement. Before the cumulative effect of wrong-doing
had taken over his life, he could have resisted the promptings of his pleasure drive, made other choices, sought, and

steadfastly abided to, a correct conception of the end of human life. Every akratic lapse progressively enfeebles not only the will but also the capacity for making and keeping to coherent long-term plans. Ultimately, the decision-making agencies in the soul become harnessed to the pursuit of short-term, irresistible, and un-coordinated impulses. Thus *akrasia* may in the end deprive an agent of moral sagacity altogether. More concretely, we can easily envisage the case of an individual who, finding himself increasingly unable to resist certain impulses, comes to accommodate himself to the progressively irresistible motivation that they offer, and uses his capacity for rational calculation to secure the realization of unworthy goals.[59] The remorse he initially felt after each lapse will very likely transform itself into complacency and cynicism. Alternatively, self-deceit may conveniently exert upon him an anaesthetizing influence. In this manner *akrasia* may transform itself into vice. An obvious case in point is that of Shakespeare's Macbeth. From being "full of the milk of human kindness,"[60] as well as brave and loyal, Macbeth is driven by weakness and ambition to murder Duncan in order to secure the crown of Scotland for himself. Although acute, his initial remorse proves inoperative and further murders are plotted in an attempt to consolidate his position. Ultimately, Macbeth alienates himself from his closest associates, loses his capacity for love, and lays Scotland bare.

These considerations indicate that, in some cases at least, remorse is ineffective in preventing the slide from weakness of the will into vice, and hence that Aristotle may have been justified in subsuming the former under the latter in *E.E.* 1223a36-b31 and in not drawing a sharper distinction between them in *N.E.*, 1166b2-25. What still remains to be shown, however, is that the waning of remorse, which in my presentation signals the moral deterioration of the akratic, will, in turn, itself give way to a mental malaise and discontent which correspond to what Aristotle, in *N.E.* IX, 4, calls '*metameleia*'.

Let us first note that the vicious person's goals are, strictly speaking, not of his own choosing; their presence in his soul is a fact over which he has little or no control. Though vice may, in some cases, leave the decision process (*proairesis*)[61] unimpaired, it nevertheless signals a (culpable) failure to bring order into one's various commitments, needs and wants, and to harmonize short-term and long-term goals. Even when the vicious is successful in devising means to gratify his appetites, he is unable not only to abate them but also to subject them to rational control. In that sense he is quite literally alienated from "what is mostly him," *viz.*, the dianoetic part of his being. His reason is the slave of his passions. But it ought not to be. In Aristotle's brand of ethical objectivism the achievement of happiness (*eudaimonia*) is conditional upon desires and reason operating in harmony towards the realization of the human specific function (*ergon*). Failure in that respect cannot but lead to psychic strife (*stasis*), and, in so far as the wicked suffers from a divided self, he can properly be said to be his own worst enemy. No more according to Aristotle than according to Isaiah is there peace unto the wicked.[62]

To conceive of such psychic strife in terms of the conflict between reason and the passions would, however, be oversimplistic, and it must be kept in mind that the wicked person's passions themselves are likely to be at variance with each other. In the words of Bishop Butler, they surround him "like so many harpies, craving for their accustomed gratification."[63] Not only will the base find it difficult to satisfy their various passions concurrently, but it is also likely that the present satisfaction of one passion will impede satisfaction of a different passion, present or future. Not only does the apolaustic and appetitive life require the sacrifice of one current appetite in favour of another, but it also involves privileging the present self at the expense of the future self.[64] Thus, although most wicked and base persons are beyond the reach of the moral emotion of remorse, it is nevertheless highly probable that, at some point in their lives, they will come to bemoan the effects of their vice, if not the vice itself. As Aristotle indicates, regret will not only stand between them and happiness, but it will eventually poison the very pleasure they used to derive from the satisfaction of

their (excessive) wants. Macbeth's lament at the end of his
reign might have been written to illustrate Aristotle's point:

> I have liv'd long enough: my way of life
> Is fall'n into the sear, the yellow leaf;
> And that which should accompany old age,
> As honour, love, obedience, troops of friends,
> I must not look to have; but, in their stead,
> Curses, not loud but deep, mouth-honour, breath,
> Which the poor heart would fain deny, and dare not.[65]

These lines express not so much remorse as the belated
and bitter realization that wrongful deeds preclude self-fulfilment and make impossible the cultivation of fully-fledged
and durable personal relationships. Another fictional example is provided by Lorenzo da Ponte's Don Giovanni, who
refuses to the last to repent but cannot altogether prevent
his past from haunting and tormenting him.

Seen in this way, Aristotle's presentation of the wicked
as regretful loses its air of paradox, and the discrepancy
between *N.E.* VII and IX on the matter of intemperance
and remorse is correspondingly lessened. *N.E.* VII, 7 to 9 are
devoted to drawing fine conceptual distinctions between a
range of related concepts which include incontinence and
intemperance. There Aristotle uncontentiously asserts that
while the presence of remorse is a defining criterion of
incontinence, the intemperant, with his warped values and
single-mindedness, has neither reason nor opportunity to
experience compunction on moral grounds. In this context,
intemperance, i.e. the excessive indulgence in bodily pleasures, is presented as paradigmatically vicious, and
Aristotle makes no attempt at relating it to other kinds of
vice. In book IX, by contrast, he is concerned with wickedness in general and its effects on the wicked. Since it is
unlikely that vice be confined to one area of life, wicked persons generally find themselves at the mercy of a number of
discrepant passions, all vying for satisfaction. They soon
discover that they cannot satisfy them all: while some passions will needs remain frustrated, others will grow more

tyrannical. Past self-indulgences, injustices, and cruelties will altogether turn out to be incapacitating in one way or another. They will then be the object of *metameleia* in the non-moral sense.

In other words, Aristotle's mutually contradictory statements on the matter of *metameleia* occur in the discussion of two different problems, viz., (1) How do we distinguish between incontinence and intemperance? and (2) Can the wicked experience the inner peace that is characteristic of self-love properly so-called? While Aristotle can safely rely on remorse to settle the first question, the drift of his argument requires a negative answer to the second. In view of the reflexive and private nature of self-love, Aristotle faces the difficulty of identifying an internal feature that could serve to distinguish from inside the good form of self-love from the bad. What else, save regret and its attendant anxieties, could stand between wickedness and the serenity of true self-love? As for the use of *metameleia* in both a moral and a non-moral sense, we have seen that it does not run counter to Greek usage of the time.

If incontinence and vice each engender a form of remorse or regret, moral virtue, by contrast, in Aristotle's presentation generates a state of serene internal peace. While the wicked "murders" his own personality,[66] the virtuous person successfully effects the integration, within his *psychē*, of intellection, desires, and passions and, in so doing, eliminates not only the risk of tension between discrepant impulses and goals but also that of prejudicing his future for the sake of his present. Insuring the continuity between his past, his present, and his future, he makes himself "one and indivisible"[67] or, in the words of Plato's Socrates, "fair within."[68] Thus building his own 'self', he nurtures his inner freedom[69] and can confidently expect, in future, not only to be able to do what he pleases but also what he truly wants. Barring adverse contingent circumstances the virtuous person's self-determination is as complete as is humanly possible.

In this context Aristotle can convincingly pronounce the virtuous person to be a self-lover in the correct sense of that phrase.[70] Far from misguidedly indulging either his appetites or his emotions, the virtuous person correctly identifies himself with the specifically human element in his *psychē*, viz., reason. His virtue results from a long process of empowering reason to guide, inform, and integrate the other sides of his personality. Hence, in his case, the self which is loved, and for the sake of which goods are wished, is not the appetitive element in his soul but the well-balanced whole that his personality constitutes. Hence, too, the self which loves is not an avid, capricious, and blind emotion, but a desire made rational, an emotion enlightened by sagacity. Only the virtuous has a correct conception of his own interest, and only in his case is self-love truly reflexive. Since he is not inwardly torn or divided, all the parts of his soul share in the same joys and sorrows, and never need one part grieve because another has received satisfaction.

In chapter 2 above it was argued that the self, which the virtuous self-lover is enjoined to nurture and honour, is of an inter-personal nature. In cultivating his *nous*, the virtuous man renders himself more, rather than less, akin to other virtuous agents. Further and more importantly, primary friendship opens up the self of each partner to the other's loving knowledge and, in the process, grafts them together. The resulting relation is uniquely strengthening and actualizing. Thus does Aristotle proceed to justify his claim not only that self-love, in the proper sense of the word, is compatible with true friendship,[71] but also that it is a *sine qua non* of it.[72] We shall return to this justification in the next chapter. As for the claim itself, it is both plausible and generally uncontested; psychologized and popularized versions of it abound. "One must love oneself," goes a piece of sound and homely advice, "to stand a chance of forming durable and satisfying personal relationships."

> This above all: to thine own self be true,
> And it must follow, as the night the day,
> Thou canst not then be false to any man:[73]

Polonius' utterance of the precept shows how common-place it is. In more sober language, it will be said that self-love, itself the effect of psychic health, gives virtuous agents the inner resources without which primary friendship cannot be initiated and cultivated. Not only will they choose their friends wisely, but they will also cherish them for what is truly lovable in them.

In Aristotle's presentation, however, the priority of love of self over that of others is rooted in definitional considerations as well as in moral psychology. "The defining features of friendship," he writes, "would seem to be derived from features of friendship towards oneself."[74] As virtuous agents live in harmony with themselves[75] and delight in their own being,[76] in like manner are they in deep-rooted agreement with their primary friends and rejoice in their excellence. Such definitional primacy of self-love is later used to ground what appears to be a norm, i.e., that one *should* love oneself more than any other being.[77] As V. Politis has noted,[78] this is a questionable move, since the contention that the better the friendship the more it approximates the virtuous man's self-love, does not, of itself, legitimize the inference that the virtuous should love himself most of all. In that respect the biblical injunction to 'Love thy neighbour as thyself',[79] though vaguer, is less problematic. There, self-love, viewed as primary because inevitable, is merely used as a criterion against which to assess love of others.

Politis argues extensively and convincingly that the offending inference is not amenable to validation within the framework of Aristotle's analysis of self-love. This, however, need not worry us unduly since the inference occurs within the context of an unmistakably dialectic chapter. "There is also the puzzle about whether one ought to love oneself or someone else most of all,"[80] Aristotle opens the discussion, before canvassing diverse views in the matter. He then brings his own distinction between two kinds of self-love to bear on the issue and concludes, in his own name but *in the terminology of the aporia*, that the virtuous agent *must* love himself most of all. In other words, the problematic inference is generated by the juxtaposition, in *N.E.*, IX, 8, of two discourses, viz., Aristotle's own and that which is common to both parties to the discussion. Nowhere in *N.E.* IX, 4, an earlier chapter devoted to self-love but of a non-dialectical tenor, does Aristotle assert or imply that love of self should (*dei*) surpass love of others. In any case, this contention itself goes against the grain of Aristotle's identification of self with reason. Indeed, how could he have enjoined the virtuous to love his own reason, or virtuous self, more than that of his friend, since reason is not amenable to that kind of individuation, and virtue is not a contested, competitive good?

To conclude: in his analysis of virtuous *philautia*, Aristotle has achieved two things. To begin with, he has shown how sweet are the rewards of virtue. His portrait of the true self-lover is that of a serene person who has internalized the values and norms of the moral life and, as a consequence, is untroubled by the discomforts of remorse or regret. Secondly, by freeing true self-lovers from the sway of their appetites and false conceptions, he has shown their readiness for what he viewed as the most satisfying personal relationship of all, i.e., primary friendship. Not being prompted by what Plato called *'penia'*[81] (lack), their love can be freely given, disinterested, and attentive to the needs of others in themselves. Paradoxically, as we shall now see, love of others may even carry the true self-lover to the extreme of self-sacrifice.

5

SELF-LOVE
AND
EGOISM

From the examination of self-love, its nature, varieties, conscious (and not so conscious) manifestations, effects, and consequences, we now move to a consideration of its connection with friendship. At one end of the spectrum we find that those who, out of vulgar self-love, seek the lion's share of contested, competitive goods, can only form unsteady, crudely utilitarian or unashamedly hedonistic associations. Their self-partiality, in effect, precludes friendship. Leaving out of account the many compromises that the run of men make between crass self-love and benevolent friendship, Aristotle proceeds to an examination of the purest forms of self-love proper and altruism. In the process, he makes a number of highly puzzling claims.

Having remarked, uncontentiously, that the virtuous self-lover, who honours and gratifies his reason, is universally praised,[1] Aristotle proceeds: (a) to generalize the normative claim there implicit by stating that the common good is served by virtuous agents *competing* to achieve what is fine (*to kalon*);[2] and (b) to specify that the true self-lover will sacrifice not only contested goods for his friend(s) but also, if need be, his life. In so doing, he will secure "the fine" for himself.[3]

Either claim entails a paradox. To begin with, Aristotle appears to sanction a situation where the virtuous can only achieve his goal, i.e., the fine, by effectively elbowing out his competitors, some of whom will inevitably be his primary friends. Not only does this contention present the fine as a fit object of competition, but it also jeopardizes the above-stated second claim that primary friends are willing to sacrifice competitive goods to each other. As for this latter claim itself, it appears to legitimize the inference that truly to love one's self might require the sacrifice of that very self, even to the point of annihilation, for the sake either of one's friend(s) or that of the community. In so far as the ultimate self-sacrifice prevents the virtuous from living his allotted span of life, it is likely to stand between him and the fulfilment of one of *eudaimonia's* conditions, viz., completeness of life.[4] This second paradox (hereafter the *aporia*), which is not stated in, but implied by, the text, has much troubled modern commentators. In the hope of dissipating it, I shall attempt to identify and spell out the reasons which may have prompted Aristotle to recommend, in certain circumstances, what is, in effect, a form of altruistic suicide. If successful, my exegesis will contribute to showing how self-sacrifice and competition might co-exist with reference to the same objects. For this reason, the second paradox will be discussed first.

In an attempt to ease the *aporia*, Gauthier characterizes the difference between the two forms of self-love as that between "vulgar egoism" and "virtuous egoism":[5] while the vulgar egoist seeks self-gratification at the ready expense of others, the virtuous egoist is motivated exclusively by "an aspiration towards moral beauty" without regard for his own material advantage. Gauthier thereby lends the weight of his authority to the view that Aristotle is an exponent of both psychological egoism (i.e., the view that human beings always act from self-love) and ethical egoism (i.e., the view that they ought to act only from self-love and that the common good is the end product of enlightened self-interest).[6] Gauthier's interpretation is unhelpful; not only is his notion of virtuous egoism obscure, but, in so far as he treats the concepts of self-love and virtue as synonymous, he fails to ease the paradox of the self-sacrificial self-lover. Any serviceable interpretation of Aristotle's claim will have to take on board his view that a true self-lover will in certain circumstances deliberately choose self-destruction.

In his *Aristotle's Theory of Moral Insight* Troels Engberg-Pedersen endeavours, in the name of Aristotle, to resolve the *aporia* by construing the rational, objective considerations which might have prompted him to recommend, in certain circumstances, the ultimate self-sacrifice. Reading "acting for the sake of the *kalon*" as "acting for the sake of others," Engberg-Pedersen claims that ". . . noble acts consist in sharing out natural goods. According to the chapter on self-love, it is reason that states how they should be shared out."[7] Engberg-Pedersen's resulting argument appears to owe much to Thomas Nagel's well-known justification of the possibility of altruism.[8] Rationality, Nagel had claimed, can motivate agents to perform actions which are recognized to promote "an objectively valuable end,"[9] even when such actions are against their own self-interest. Thus, in Nagel's view "To apply a principle to oneself impersonally, one must be able to apply it to the person who one is, in abstraction from the fact that it is oneself."[10] This is the very line of thought that Engberg-Pedersen unhesitatingly ascribes to Aristotle: ". . . when a person 'pays no attention to himself', as opposed to doing everything for his own sake (. . .), what he does is to leave out of account 'his own' desires. But the point is not that he pays no attention whatever to himself or neglects all his desires. What he does is just to take account of himself *as one among others* (. . .) (S)ince the basic problem is that of how natural goods should be shared, reason can find no foothold for a criterion anywhere else than in properties that are impersonal; reason sees that initially all human beings have an equal claim."[11] According to Engberg-Pedersen, therefore, Aristotle is committed to the view that self-sacrifice is required when ". . . there is no legitimate ground for ascribing to oneself a claim to the goods that is any stronger than that of any other human being who will be affected by the goods being shared out in one way or another."[12] This, he concludes, constitutes "the basic insight that Aristotle wishes to express by his concept of τὸ καλόν[13] [the fine]."

Can this attractive interpretation be sustained? Though the resolution of the aporia of self-love and self-sacrifice can clearly benefit from a Nagelian analysis of the relationship between selfhood, motivation, and rationality, Engberg-Pedersen's analysis is open to a number of serious objections. Firstly, as has been noted,[14] it lacks the backing of positive textual evidence. Secondly, Engberg-Pedersen leaves out of acccount the surely crucial fact that Aristotle's treatment of self-love occurs within the general framework of an analysis of friendship. What the Danish scholar identifies as the expression of a universal moral requirement (i.e., a requirement grounded in the equal moral status of persons *qua* persons) is, in fact, the recognition that the friend's status *qua* friend constitutes for the virtuous a motivational, as well as justificatory, factor. It can only be insofar as an individual person is his friend—not insofar as he is a human being—that the Aristotelian virtuous agent will be moved to treat him as the bearer of entitlements similar to, or as weighty as, his own. Is the friend not his other self? I shall come back to this point.

Thirdly, Engberg-Pedersen's exegetical hypothesis, according to which the *kalon* principle enjoins universal altruism, is not entirely convincing. Although it tallies with passages in which Aristotle shows "fine" actions to involve self-sacrifice, it arguably miscontrues these texts by inferring from them that altruism must be the primary motivating force of "fine" actions. Although Aristotle sometimes describes fine actions as those that are meritworthy "when viewed from an impersonal standpoint,"[15] in Michael Woods' words, this does not mean that he ascribes their merit to the fact that they were motivated by the agent's desire to promote the good of others. In the *Eudemian Ethics*, only those ends are pronounced fine which are both praiseworthy and valuable in and for themselves.[16] To act for the sake of the fine, as I argued earlier,[17] is not the same as acting for the sake of some presumably altruistic end which is beyond the act itself. The fact that the fine does encompass altruistic action holds no definitional relevance since its extension is wider than that of altruism. To be motivated by the fine consists more generally in acting from the recognition of the appropriateness[18] of the act or the end itself. As N. Sherman has well said, "To act for the sake of the fine . . . is the end of virtue, but an immanent end—not some additional value posited over and above the value of virtuous action itself."[19]

In his commentary on *N.E.*, IX,8, Stewart relies on Spinozistic theses to account for the emergence of the *aporia* within Aristotle's analysis of self-love.[20] More particularly, he draws attention to the close resemblance between Aristotle's notion of genuine self-love and the rational self-love that Spinoza advocates in the *Ethics*.[21] Following Stewart's lead but pushing the comparison between the two philosophers further than he did, I shall invoke a number of Spinozistic theses to support my contention that Aristotle is justified in his claim that genuine love of self may require full sacrifice of self. Three passages from the *Ethics* directly relate to the problem at issue: (1) ". . . the power of passion cannot be defined by the power with which we endeavour to persist in our being; but (. . .) it must necessarily be defined by the power of some external cause compared with our own";[22] (2) (with Stewart) ". . . men who are governed by reason, that is, men who, under the guidance of reason, seek what is useful to them, desire nothing for themselves which they do not also desire for the rest of mankind, and therefore they are just, faithful, and honourable";[23] and (3) "A free man never acts by fraud but always with good faith."[24] As the note to this proposition specifies, this principle admits of no exception: "If it be asked, 'If a man can liberate himself from a present danger of death by deception, would not consideration for the preservation of his own being advise him to deceive?' it may be answered in the same manner, 'That if reason advise him that, it would advise it to all men, and therefore reason would advise men not to unite their forces and have laws in common save in deception one to the other, that is, not to have common laws, which is absurd.'"[25]

These extracts show plainly that Spinoza's definition of virtue as the striving to persist in one's own being (*conatus*)²⁶ does not prevent him explicitly to commend, in certain circumstances, the choice of death over life. As the first text quoted above indicates, Spinoza explicitly mentions cases in which clinging to life amounts to allowing oneself to be overwhelmed by causes from outside one's own being. When pushed to extremes, such visceral, non-rational love of life is alienating since it places those who cannot but act upon it not only at the beck and call of their own passions but also at the mercy of external circumstances. Those individuals are unfree, Spinoza indicates, and it would even be a misnomer to call them *agents* in the full sense of the term.²⁷

Both Aristotle and Spinoza thus argue that self-love properly so-called rules out the choice of life over everything. The agreement of the two philosophers in this respect would, in itself, not only be unsurprising but also devoid of any real philosophical interest if it were not for the fact that Spinoza's system provides a full justification for the view that endeavour to persist in one's being may require the sacrifice of one's life. The question may now be raised as to whether Spinoza's justification of self-sacrifice can throw light on Aristotle's terse and puzzling parallel text.

It is on purely rational grounds that Spinoza justifies his claim that it is not always appropriate to ensure one's own continued existence. As the third of the above extracts from the *Ethics* makes clear, to perjure oneself amounts not only to letting oneself, in one specific case, be overpowered by passive emotions, but also implicitly to condone the subjection of reason by the passions in all relevantly similar circumstances. In other words, those who rely on a narrowly conceived notion of self-interest to justify, e.g., perjury, undermine reason in general, since they would put it at the service of the instinctual and emotional drives. Whether they realize it or not, they force reason, which by its very nature is universal, effectively but absurdly to prescribe its own demise. Such subordination of reason cannot be rationally willed by the free Spinozistic agent, since in the process his own freedom would be correspondingly diminished and his *conatus* enfeebled. For Spinoza, as is well-known, rationality and morality coincide.

Could a variant of this view be ascribed to Aristotle? As we have seen, Aristotle locates selfhood in *nous* and argues that the achievement of *eudaimonia* is conditional upon the dominance in the soul of the rational element. Being the expression of such dominance, moral virtue involves the coordination of the passions, their harnessing to appropriately desired ends, and the correct assessment by practical reason of ever-changing particular circumstances. Further, as was shown in the preceding chapter, baseness and wickedness, as characterized by Aristotle, cannot but be accompanied by a state of general psychic disharmony and discomfort resulting from the enslavement of reason. Thus, as can be seen, the two philosophers use similar arguments to support an identical conclusion. Nevertheless, they differ in one important respect. Unlike Spinoza, Aristotle does not appear to rely on considerations of universalizability to establish the compatibility of self-love and self-sacrifice. This is especially intriguing in view of his insistence that it is on rational grounds that self-sacrifice may be required.[28]

Although Aristotle presents moral considerations as rational, he does not appear to consider impersonality to be entailed by moral rationality or, indeed, to view universality as a defining feature of moral concepts. As K. Dover pointed out, both impersonality and universality seem rather foreign to the spirit of Aristotelian, not to say Greek, ethics.[29] Although this is too large an issue to address here, it is nevertheless warranted to state, within the context of the present argument, that while Spinoza views the moral community as encompassing the whole of humanity, Aristotle restricts it to those who are capable of moral virtue. At its widest the moral community coincides with the *polis* (city-state), and at its narrowest it consists of the circles of primary friends. Yet, within such restricted confines, the argument from universalizability, central to Spinoza's solution of the *aporia*, can arguably be said to apply. Before attempting to make the Spinozistic argument fit the Aristotelian claim, however, we need to consider not only the background of this claim itself but also some examples of ultimate self-sacrifice.

"If he must,"[30] the friend of virtue will give his all, life included, for his partner. Occasions for self-sacrifice could conceivably arise either when circumstances are such that the partners cannot expect both to survive (in, e.g., wartime situations and dangerous expeditions) or when a greater good is likely to accrue through the survival of one partner than the other. In the first case the self-sacrifice is likely to be made out of love; in the second, presumably rarer, case, one friend's continued existence might be viewed as more justified or more desirable than the other's. In those cases the person who considers his own claim to life to be slenderer than his friend's might be moved to sacrifice himself either for the sake of the other (*ekeinou heneka*) or for the sake of a common and important cause that the friend would be better able to promote on his own. In other words, both situations might arguably justify the decision of an altruistic suicide. An example in point is that of Captain Oates, a member of Scott's second antarctic expedition, who deliberately walked out into the blizzard to increase the expedition's likelihood of success and his fellows' chances of survival. As Richard Kraut concludes his discussion of a similar example, ". . . there are situations that call upon one person and no others to act courageously."[31] It will here be usefully recalled that Aristotle's great-souled man (*ho megalopsychos*), who is said not to face dangers frequently, will nevertheless be willing on exalted occasions to take great risks.[32] Whenever the great-souled man does face danger, Aristotle states, he is "unsparing of his life, since he does not think life at all costs is worthwhile."[33] Unfortunately Aristotle does not, in this passage, specify the type of conditions which will prompt this paragon of virtue to lay down his life, and although it is natural to assume that he has military situations in mind, we must heed the clue provided later in the passage by the assertion that the great-souled man ". . . cannot let anyone else, *except a friend*, determine his life."[34]

Since documented instances of ultimate self-sacrifice from love are hard to come by, a fictional example will be invoked. In Euripides' eponymous play, Alcestis dies to save the life of her husband, Admetus, whose impending death can only be avoided if another agrees to die in his place. All refuse but she. Although Euripides' play is not concerned with what Aristotle was later to call primary friendship, it nevertheless is a study in the morality of accepting, and refusing, the ultimate self-sacrifice. Admetus' parents are implicitly castigated not only for refusing to die instead of their son but mainly for failing to appreciate the fact that, at their stage in life, their continued existence is of lesser value than his. Although Alcestis' matter-of-fact agreeing to die for Admetus and instead of him is presented as a reflection of her own (and her society's) estimation of a wife's value as inferior to her husband's, the heroic selflessness of her devotion arguably constitutes the main theme of the play. Further, it is only through her death that Alcestis acquires the heroic status that, as a woman, she could never have achieved otherwise. Indeed, after her death Admetus comes progressively to think that she may, after all, have had the better part and feel due shame: "I count my wife's lot happier than my own, though it seems not to be . . . How then, my friends, is it profitable for me to live, when I both fare so badly and then hear such evil of myself?"[35] A short but honourable life career, Admetus reflects, might have been preferable to the mournful, undistinguished, and regretful existence which followed the loss of Alcestis.

Alcestis' self-sacrifice could well be described as the choice of "a single fine and great action over many small actions,"[36] a choice which Aristotle sees as characteristic of the excellent person. By contrast, the part of Admetus should most probably be taken to show that the choice of life at all costs cannot be expected to bring self-fulfilment, honour, or, indeed, "the fine." This particular lesson signals a meeting point between Aristotle's sophisticated philosophy of friendship and the earlier heroic and Homeric conceptions of morality to which he was heir. This can be seen, e.g., in the reasons invoked in the *Iliad* by Achilles before rejecting his mother's counsel of restraint: "Straightaway may I die, . . . seeing I return not to my dear native land, neither proved anywise a light of deliverance to Patroclus nor to my other comrades, . . . but abide here by the ships a profitless burden upon the earth."[37] The principle that heroism at the cost of life is to be chosen over life at the cost of glory is also ascribed to Pericles by Thucydides in the famous Funeral Oration: "In the fighting they thought it more honourable to stand their ground and suffer death than to give in and save their lives. So they fled from the reproaches of man, abiding with life and limb the brunt of battle; and, in a small moment of time, the climax of their lives, a culmination of glory, not of fear, were swept away from us."[38] Later, as is well known, Socrates was, in turn, approvingly to quote the Homeric lines in the *Apology* and praise Achilles for "not taking death and danger into consideration."[39]

Let it be noted, however, that the right-doing that Plato's Socrates would place higher than life is conceived in terms of what would now be termed pure morality rather than seen in terms of honour. This shift of emphasis from socially to internally centred morality is significant and prepares the way for Aristotle's own use of the principle to resolve one of friendship's moral dilemmas. Although Aristotle still upholds the old Homeric principle that a short but glorious life is preferable to a long and dreary one, his justification of the principle owes little to the tradition. His own claim is that proper concern for the integrity of one's own self may, in extreme circumstances, require the forsaking of that very self. Cases where one's other self's continued existence is perceived to be of greater value, to oneself or to the community, than one's own can, I argued, be included under the heading of 'extreme circumstances'.

Occasions for ultimate self-sacrifice are bound to be rare, and we should not assume that the excellent person will be on the look out for them. As we noted, Aristotle specifies that the excellent person will sacrifice his life for his friend only "if he must."[40] Commentators who, like Madigan,[41] fail to register this point will find it well nigh

impossible to reconcile Aristotle's view that "every understanding chooses what is best for itself"[42] with the claim
that immediately follows it, i.e., that the excellent person
will be prepared to die for his friends and/or country.
Although Aristotle may not always be fully systematic, it is
unlikely that he would have remained oblivious to the conflicting nature of two claims made in the space of a few
lines. We must work on the assumption that they present a
single argument. Most of the time, Aristotle claims, *nous*
will choose what is best for itself and thus ensure its continued existence, but in certain cases it will prefer its own
demise to the loss of its due sovereignty. Such evils as serious perjury, desertion, and the preventable loss of a primary friend must be avoided at *all* costs. Whenever the
choice is between death and one of such evils, *nous* will act
on the understanding that its passing away is preferable to
its subjection to what may well be considered to be ignominious passions. In these circumstances and whatever the
choice turns out to be, *nous* ceases to operate *qua* such, and
the agent, as Aristotle tells us,[43] effectively chooses betweeen
two evils. Unsurprisingly, the virtuous person chooses
death, while the wicked and the weak cling to a debased
existence. Be it noted that those who make the supreme
sacrifice of their self do not do so for the sake of obtaining
the fine; if the fine comes into it, it is through the realization
that their choice is an appropriate one. The alternative possibility would, in any case, rule out the performance of
future virtuous acts, since *nous*, having once lost its
sovereignty by yielding to the passions, would no longer be
capable, if it ever was, of performing 'fine' actions.

In his appraisal of situations and circumstances likely
to make the continuation of friendship dependent upon his
performance of self-sacrificial actions, the virtuous will not
disproportionally weigh his own love of life or fear of death.
Being a self-lover in the proper sense of the expression, he
will not make a choice that would have the effect of harnessing reason to the passions and thus of alienating his
own self. Although his self-sacrifice, which may have to be
total, will not exactly be joyful, it will nevertheless be freely

chosen and unaccompanied by unseemly lamentations. As for the egoist, whose love of life has to be deemed excessive and, for that reason, deserves reproach,[44] he will sacrifice his friend's good, or even life, to his own misconceived advantage. Such a choice constitutes evidence that the friendship had not progressed beyond the hedonistic or utilitarian stage. Other selfhood is unattainable to those who are not selves in Aristotle's sense.

Thus is the *aporia* resolved: in certain situations proper regard for one's own integrity inevitably requires the sacrifice of one's life. The virtuous both understands this and acts on his understanding. Although Aristotle never explicitly faces up to the *aporia*, it may justifiably be claimed that the above resolution is faithful to the spirit of his analysis both of self-love and of primary friendship. Just as Spinoza's definition of virtue, as the endeavour to persist in one's own being, is consistent with his recommendation to die rather than commit perjury, Aristotle's view that understanding chooses what is best for itself can be made to cohere with his claim that virtuous agents will, in certain circumstances, choose to die for or instead of their friends. While for Spinoza immoral acts stem from inadequate ideas formed under the dominance of the passions and the imagination, for Aristotle failure to be motivated by the fine results from the prominence in the soul of the wrong kind of self-love.

A further similarity between Spinoza's argument and that of Aristotle should now be discernible. The Aristotelian virtuous agent who sacrifices his life for his friend thereby shows that he is capable of viewing his own life on a par with that of another. He has the morally commendable ability to step outside of his own concerns and circumstances and to survey them objectively and impersonally. In Nagel's striking terminology he takes "the view from nowhere."[45] In the process he discovers that his life is not intrinsically more worthwhile than that of his friend. On the assumption that the argument constructed above is recognisably Aristotelian, it can now be concluded that the crucial concept of universalizability, central to Spinoza's substantiation of a parallel claim, is operating here too, although on more modest a scale. As Spinoza claims that the choice of one's own survival at the cost of perjury would, in effect, sanction the death of reason in all similar situations, Aristotle indicates that the status of a friend as an other self entails moral obligations which require of the virtuous that he ceases to consider his own case as relevantly different from that of (some) others, i.e., his other self or selves. While some commentators will indulgently point out the deficiencies of Aristotle's under-developed concept of universalizability, others will praise him for recognizing what many later philosophers neglect, viz., the relevance to morality of particular ties, commitments, and close relationships. The difference between Engberg-Pedersen's interpretation and the one here presented is that, while the former ascribes "the community of humans as a whole" to Aristotelian universalizability, the latter restricts it to the community of primary friends. What I consider to be an anachronism on Engberg-Pedersen's part may be explained by the fact that, as Dover puts it, "It may often be the case that what appears to be a commendation of generalized beneficence and generosity in fact refers to the conduct towards *philoi*."[46]

If self-sacrifice for the sake of a friend can, on some rare occasions, be thus justifiably called for, what must we make of Aristotle's next contention, viz., that the virtuous will also be prepared to die for his native country? This looks like an amendment and is not supported by the argument that precedes it. Commentators have long wondered whether the addition, in 1169a19, of 'and for his native country' to 'for the sake of his friends' as a possible beneficiary for the virtuous' self-sacrifice, was genuine.[47] Some have even suggested excising the words or emending the text.[48] This seems a little hasty. Aristotle, who sets store by common opinions, could expect his audience to be well acquainted with a principle repeatedly invoked or quoted by Homer, the tragedians, Thucydides, and Plato. For that reason alone, the inclusion of a reference to the fatherland in a discussion of the moral obligations of primary friendship should not be surprising. Strictly speaking, it has nothing to do with the argument at hand, but the author of the *Politics*, for whom the various forms of association which can be described as friendships promote the good life, i.e., the end of the state,[49] was unlikely to consider that such an amendment required much additional argument.

In any case, the inclusion of a reference to the fatherland into the argument follows naturally from the contention, which almost immediately precedes it in the text, that the whole community stands to benefit from all its virtuous members' striving to perform virtuous or even heroic actions: ". . . when everyone *competes* to achieve what is fine and strains to do the finest actions, everything that is right will be done for the common good, and each person individually will receive the greatest of goods, since that is the character of virtue. Hence the good person must be a self-lover, since he will both help himself and benefit others by doing fine actions."[50] This passage contains a number of pitfalls for the unwary modern reader. Its first verb, *hamillaomai*, here used in the present participle, can, but need not, include an idea of rivalry. Translators who, in this context, render it by 'compete', as opposed to 'strive', can arguably be said to bias their Greekless readers towards an egoistic interpretation of Aristotle's text. Unless, of course, these readers are prepared to entertain the view that a competition can have all winners and no losers. Let us briefly review these possible interpretations.

If, in *N.E.*, IX, 8, Aristotle is taken to extol the advantages of virtuous rivalry, *and* his interpreters consider that competitions, by definition, involve losers as well as winners, then his contention that the self-lover is he who strives to outdo others in the pursuit of the fine is uncautious in the extreme. Firstly, it runs counter to other Aristotelian texts[51] in implying that "the fine," as such, is a fit object of competition. Secondly, it appears morally to sanction the possibility that one virtuous individual could successfully achieve his goal by effectively preventing others from reaching theirs. Even, we shall want to ask, when these others are his primary friends? This question will presently be addressed further.

Alternatively, the view might be taken that although *hamillaomai* involves competition, the challenge here envisaged by Aristotle need not be such that one participant's success spells another's loss. For instance, a running race[52] may be organized at the outcome of which all those participants are declared winners who have bettered their own individual score. It is not inconceivable that in one such race, all participants should be winners; although nobody comes first, all have won, i.e., progressed, helped along by the eagerness and enthusiasm of the others. They have broken their own record rather than some other person's. Not only are the individual participants in such a race fitter for having taken part in it but the standard of marathons in general has improved. Likewise, in the terms of Aristotle's contention, according to this interpretation, the community at large benefits from the endeavour by its individual members to eliminate all unworthiness from their own thoughts and actions.

The fact that this reading of *hamillaomai*, which retains the positive aspects of competition while eliminating its mean sides, would considerably ease our exegesis of the chapter, does not, of course, constitute a decisive reason for adopting it. Neither is one's general and vague feeling that it is implausible and anachronistic, a ground for rejecting it. What is directly relevant to the issue, however, is the fact that Aristotle appears to have felt no compunction in stating that the good person, in pursuing the fine, awards himself a part that is *better* than that which others, friends included, are likely to obtain. The dialectical tenor of the context[53] does not alter the fact that comparatives ('a *greater* good', '*finer*', 'a *bigger* part of the fine')[54] are used, indicating the possibility that one person's gain implies another's loss or lesser gain. A comparison with a scriptural passage might here prove helpful. While Mary Magdalen and Martha were not competing against each other in Jesus' service, the circumstances made it likely that one would succeed better than the other. In telling Martha that her sister had had "the better part," Jesus was not adjudicating a contest, but he was nonetheless administering a mild rebuff to her, pointing out that Mary Magdalen's choice has been the finer and wiser of the two.[55] Likewise, Aristotle may, in the passage in question, have been alluding to the possibility that, in their eagerness to benefit the state, some virtuous citizens would achieve their aim better or more speedily than some others. The mere fact that they might, in the process, incur heavy personal losses should, however, make us wary of describing such a competition as a rivalry. Whether this is the kind of situation that Aristotle had in mind is, alas, a matter of speculation.

According to the third exegetical possibility, Aristotle need not here have competitions, virtuous or otherwise, in mind. He might simply be counting the advantages of virtuous persons' *straining* to achieve the fine.[56] The fact that, in classical Greek, *hamillaomai* does not always connote rivalry and can simply mean 'to strive', allows one to entertain this possibility. This usage can be found in Plato,[57] as well as in Aristotle himself earlier in the *Nicomachean Ethics*.[58] Unfortunately, the reason which militates against the second reading makes this one implausible, too. Besides which, one may care to note that in the *Memorabilia* Xenophon lends Socrates the view that "a man's virtue consists in outdoing his friends in kindness."[59] The fact that Xenophon, who often expresses common opinions, uses the unambiguous *nikan* (outdoing, winning) should, in this instance, make us wary of removing any competitive connotation from Aristotle's use of a semantically related verb. Unfortunately, we have to conclude that there is no way of precisely ascertaining either the meaning of *hamillaomai* in this passage or, indeed, the nature of Aristotle's views on competition.

What is certain, on the other hand, is that Aristotle considered that the community, however small or large, stood to benefit from its individual members' moral virtue, and it is to the relationship between one's own and others' good that we must now turn. Is Aristotle saying in this passage that, appearances to the contrary notwithstanding, moral and, for that matter, altruistic behaviour is ultimately more advantageous to the individual than prudence? It will here be argued that in spite of the use, in 1169a9-10, of the contrasting adverbs *koinē* and *idiai* to designate the community's good and one's own personal advantage, respectively, this would not represent the thrust of Aristotle's argument. He was no precursor of Hobbes or of game-theory analysts. The difference in outlook clearly emerges from Aristotle's claim that the vicious person "will harm both himself and his neighbours by following his base feelings."[60] As we saw in chapter 4 above, Aristotle argues that the base, who fail to be guided by what is mostly themselves, i.e., reason, suffer from self-alienation. Hobbes, by contrast, describes the "fool," who says that justice is contrary to reason,[61] as simply misguided insofar as he fails to take into account external factors such as the likelihood of being found out by his peers, as well as divine retribution. Unlike Hobbes and his numerous successors, Aristotle does not view morality as a device to counteract the limitations of human sympathies. Indeed such a device would be redundant in an ethics of virtue which centres on the education of the emotions as well as on practical reasoning. Aristotle's allegiance to the centrality of virtue in the moral life leads him to assert that the virtuous man will benefit his partners because he wants to, *not* because he surmises that it will ultimately benefit himself. Although Aristotle states that fine actions are praiseworthy because they benefit the community, it is not primarily because they benefit the community that they are to be performed. The role he allots to praise and blame in the moral life is but a supporting one. Honouring one's reason, or self, and benefiting the community go hand in hand in Aristotelian ethics. As for the *Nicomachean* statement, quoted above, which may or may not, as we saw, sanction virtuous competition, I shall argue that it need not be interpreted as an attempt to convince naturally selfish agents that it pays to be good. In so far as Aristotle argues all along that self-love properly so called is a prerequisite not only of primary friendship but also of excellent citizenship,[62] he need not address what has become a key problem for many modern moral philosophers, viz., how to reconcile the natural self-partiality of agents with the altruistic demands of the moral life.

If moral motivation cannot here be at issue, we must nevertheless inquire into the possibility that the high-principled competition or rivalry that Aristotle envisages might actually reduce communal benefit. More precisely, what would be the outcome of a situation where several virtuous agents were vying with each other in the pursuit of the fine? A reference to game theory, which has evolved an altruist's dilemma, alongside the better known prisoner's dilemma, is here relevant. As described by E. Ullman-Margalit, the outcome of an altruist's dilemma, i.e., a situation where both partners strive to "increase the pay-off of the other," can be "worse for both than the outcome which would be brought about had they both acted selfishly."[63] The example of altruistic dilemma that she provides appears to be a case of Aristotelian virtuous rivalry: "an elderly man and a lady (. . .) both refrain from approaching the single unoccupied seat on the bus, which *can* seat them both although not too comfortably, with the altruistic intention of leaving it free for the other to occupy."[64] Just as the elderly man and the lady would (separately and possibly even jointly) be better off for not behaving altruistically, Aristotle's virtuous competitors or rivals, while individually aiming at performing a fine action, could conceivably fail to maximize the common good. *Pace* Aristotle, we must wonder, therefore, whether the vying for the *kalon* could turn out to have disadvantageous consequences for all concerned.

The very raising of this question, which must, in the end, be answered in the negative, highlights interesting differences between Aristotle, on the one hand, and Hobbesians and game theorists, on the other. Firstly, the Aristotelian virtuous agent does not essentially conceive of morality as the conciliation of his own interest with that of others. Neither is 'to live and act for others', *qua* such, and in the absence of further specifications, a moral ideal for an Aristotelian. Whenever the virtuous man strives to perform a fine action, it is not primarily in order to benefit others but because he correctly understands that the action is required by the circumstances and is consonant with the *telos* of human life. To that extent the situation envisaged by Ullman-Margalit would not constitute a failure for an Aristotelian. Secondly, Aristotle seems to have been conscious of the need to forestall the kind of difficulty highlighted in the altruist's dilemma: "It is also possible to sacrifice actions to one's friend, since it may be finer to be responsible for one's friend's doing the action than to do it oneself."[65] In such a situation, Aristotle replies, the virtuous will let his friend perform the decent action and, in so doing, ensure that no advantage is lost in vain. He will take the seat on the bus, allow his friend the honour of endowing a much needed chair of Greek at the local University, or let him stay with their sick elderly neighbour while he goes to the Opera. As we saw, benevolent actions which involve some renunciation on the part of the agent are not performed *in order to* increase the other's payoff but either for their intrinsic value or out of love for the other. In any case, the renunciation in question could not be of the fine since it would itself be finer than the forsaken action and, as such, be a better manifestation of due self-love. In this sense, the fine, which can only be secured through disinterested motives, can never be renounced, and the virtuous person, who, in Aristotle's words, endeavours to secure for himself "the greater part of the fine," must, in the process, paradoxically be willing to make great sacrifices. Since the fine, alongside love, can provide that kind of motivation, as well as justification, it is not unreasonable to conclude, as Aristotle appears to do, that a community will generally benefit from its members' eager and possibly competitive pursuit of the fine. The claim that self-interested action occasionally maximizes social utility more than altruistic behaviour need not seriously concern an Aristotelian.

This difference in outlook between Aristotle and Hobbesians of all descriptions should make one wary of scouting his texts for a handling of their key ethical problem, viz., Why be moral? It is only when the self is viewed as an entity made up of a unique cluster of raw emotions, passions, and drives that the problem arises of reconciling self-interest with the superior and other-regarding demands of morality.[66] In a system where the moral life is defined as a process of mutual adaptation between the emotions and rationally evolved goals, where the self is assimilated to reason, the possibility of conflicts between 'I' and 'you' loses its sting. That this is indeed the case is clear from Aristotle's handling of the concept of self-love, which he claimed justifiably, as I hope to have shown, to be compatible with very considerable self-sacrifice.

6

SELF-SUFFICIENCY

Most ancient philosophers, from Plato to the Stoics, praised self-sufficiency in one form or another. Whether they called the self-sufficient man *hikanos*, *autarkēs*, or *se contentus*, whether or not they considered that such a paragon had ever lived or was likely to exist, they viewed him as a high moral ideal. Compared with the modern notion of self-sufficiency or autarky, which mostly denotes economic independence, the ancient concept has a rich moral aura. Complete autarky, which involves both immunity to chance and independence from appetitive desire, pertains only to the divinity, unless, of course, it lies within the reach of the wise man, too. Ordinary human beings who seriously aspire to autarky need a rare degree of virtue to achieve a fair measure of it. So deep, as a result, is their happy self-possession likely to be that it may well appear to make normal affective ties redundant. Will the autarkic, wise, contented man have friends, since it is agreed that he does not *need* them? Plato, Aristotle, the Epicureans, and the Stoics asked the question.

The tension between the aspiration to self-sufficiency and the need for lovers and friends is vividly and differently handled in a number of Platonic dialogues. According to the *Symposium*, love born of penury is an attempt to recover lost wholeness. When it takes an individual for its object, love is misguided, pathetic, ridiculous even, as Aristophanes' grotesque tale of cart-wheeling Humpty-

Dumpties shows. When it seeks the unalloyed and unchanging beauty of impersonal forms, by contrast, love brings wisdom and true immortality. In the main, Diotima's panegyric of philosophic love and Alcibiades' description of Socrates as self-sufficient because detached from close human ties thus resolve the tension between autarky and affective ties by effectively downgrading affective ties. Such is also the conclusion of the *Lysis*, although it there appears to be more reluctantly drawn. Assuming that friendship is of one kind only and that it cannot but be based in need, which, in turn, generates desire, Socrates forces Lysis to conclude that the better a person is, the fewer friends he will have and the less he will value friendship. Since both regard this conclusion as unsatisfactory, the dialogue ends with an admission of failure. In his treatment of friendship, Aristotle, as will presently be seen, endeavours to resolve this *aporia* by showing that the best kind of friendship supersedes need and to that extent is compatible with individual autarky. In this he may paradoxically have been inspired by Plato's *Phaedrus*. In that dialogue, it will be recalled, Socrates argues that love of individuals actually prepares the best of human souls for the contemplation of truth. The beauty of the beloved, i.e., the object of their divinely manic love, actually inspires them to leave earthly concerns behind and gaze upwards to the abode of reality. In the terms of Plato's metaphor, they grow wings again and recover some of the "wholeness" which was theirs before incarnation. Plato's claim in the *Phaedrus* that the love of individuals can have cognitively beneficial effects was not lost on Aristotle, whose discourse on the effects of primary friendship on individual autarky could be seen as a sober re-interpretation of Plato's wings analogy. His long and intricate arguments must now be examined.

Aristotle approaches the problem of self-sufficiency or autarky (*autarkeia*) through his teleological conception of nature. A self-sufficient entity, he holds, is an entity whose essence is fully realized: ". . . what each thing is when fully developed, we call its nature, whether we are speaking of a man, a horse, or a family. Besides, the final cause and end of a thing is the best, and to be self-sufficing is the end and the best."[1] This emphatic declaration notwithstanding, no systematic and comprehensive analysis of the concept of autarky can be found in the Aristotelian corpus, and it is only from the collation and integration of a number of scattered remarks and comments that a rounded conception of his ideal of self-sufficiency will emerge.

Self-sufficiency, which in the first place characterizes the divinity,[2] can nevertheless also pertain to ends (*eudaimonia*, most notably[3]), types of life (the life of study[4]), as well as individuals (great-souled men,[5] kings,[6] as well as lesser mortals) and, of course, states, since, according to Aristotle's famous definition, "a state is not a mere aggregate of persons but . . . a union of them sufficing for the purposes of life."[7] Admitting of degrees, self-sufficiency accrues to individuals through the possession of goods both internal (i.e., goods of the soul and of the body) and external (e.g., good birth, friends, money, and honour).[8] The fact that neither kind of good, as defined, is immune to chance[9] in no way lessens the moral demands they can make, or the responsibilities they can place, on individuals.

The positive value ascribed to self-sufficiency carries serious implications for friendship. Friendship, Aristotle maintains, is something "most necessary for our life," and "no-one would choose to live without friends even if he had all the other goods."[10] Yet, he also teaches that the virtuous person aims at self-sufficiency. How are these two ideals to be combined? Clearly, the instrumental nature of the friendship of utility and that of pleasure precludes the achievement of even a modicum of individual *autarkeia*. In those relationships, even when they are mutual, friends are cultivated mainly for the sake of the goods they are expected to provide. As for morally excellent persons, on the other hand, Aristotle has to explain how they are to pursue the external but desirable good of primary friendship while simultaneously striving to be sufficient unto themselves. As so often, the problem was first set out by Plato. Here is Socrates closing in on the child Lysis:

> Will not the good man, in so far as he is good, be found to
> be sufficient for himself?
> Yes.
> And if sufficient, he will want nothing so far as his suffi-
> ciency goes.
> Of course not.
> And if he does not want anything he won't feel regard for
> anything either.
> To be sure not.
> And what he does not feel regard for, he cannot love.
> Not he.
> And if he does not love, he won't be a friend.
> Clearly not.
> How then, I wonder, will the good be ever friends at all
> with the good, when neither in absence do they feel regret
> for each other, being sufficient for themselves apart, nor
> when present together have they any need of one another?
> Is there any possible way by which such people can be
> brought to care for each other?
> None whatever.
> And if they do not care for each other, they cannot possibly
> be friends.
> True, they cannot.[11]

Socrates is here claiming that (1) the good, in so far
as they are good, are not in want of anything, and (2)
one cannot have regard for that which one does not need.
The unpalatable conclusion seems to follow that friendship's only function is to fill a gap in second-rate individuals. In his own analyses of *philia* Aristotle disposes
of the second, highly contentious, Socratic premiss by
distinguishing between kinds of friendship and showing
that the friendship of need is but an inferior variety of
friendship. Complete or virtuous friendship, as we saw in
chapter 3, requires that friends be loved in and for themselves. In such a relationship the friends will both care
and have regard for each other, *qua* selves, and will not
use each other. Experience of the best kind of friendship,
Aristotle in effect claims, shows some of Socrates'
assumptions in the *aporia* to have been either wrong or
merely ironical.

Judging by the amount of space devoted to it in both *Ethics*, Aristotle must have felt very keenly the challenge posed by Socrates' first premiss, and the arguments he deploys against it require careful exegesis. In *N.E.* I,7, Aristotle supports his claim that *eudaimonia* is the ultimate end of human action by outlining the characteristics that it uniquely possesses. Firstly, it is *teleia* (final, endlike) to a higher degree than other human ends, such as honour, pleasure, or virtue. While each of the latter can be taken as a means to some end other than itself, *eudaimonia* cannot, without conceptual confusion, be made subservient to some further goal. Secondly, *eudaimonia* is *autarkēs* (self-sufficient); Aristotle's intention in ascribing this characteristic to the supreme end of human action will be discussed below. Thirdly and lastly, *eudaimonia* is *hairetōtatē* (most choiceworthy): "If it were counted as one among many, then, clearly, we think that the addition of the smallest of goods would make it more choiceworthy; for the smallest good that is added becomes an extra quantity of goods [so creating a good larger than the original good], and the larger of the two goods is always more choiceworthy."[12] For the purposes of the present enquiry, this complex passage can minimally and safely be taken to mean that happiness should not be placed on a footing with clearly circumscribed and easily numbered goods, such as wealth, health, physical beauty, and the parenting of successful children.

The inclusion of self-sufficiency amongst the criteria of happiness is highly significant. In the *Nicomachean Ethics*, it will be remembered, the claim that happiness is the best good immediately follows the rejection of the Platonic conception of the good. It is wrong as well as useless, Aristotle there argues, to postulate a single form of goodness to account for all instances of good, since "good is spoken of in as many ways as being is spoken of."[13] More specifically, certain states of affairs are good as ends, while others derive their goodness from their appropriateness as means to bring about desirable ends. Even of intrinsic goods there is no single form, Aristotle continues, before concluding that good is, in effect, a relational property, i.e., one whose account requires a consideration of the object to which the property is ascribed.[14] In other words, what is good is so, not through participating in the Form of Goodness, but either through being an object of desire or through being the objective end of an activity. It is in this latter sense that the goodness of a thing, a being, or an activity depends on its nature: ". . . it [the good] is that for the sake of which the other things are done; and in medicine this is health, in generalship victory, in housebuilding a house, in another case something else. . . ."[15] As far as the human good is concerned, it, too, is defined by reference to function (*ergon*)[16] and consists in the human soul's activity that expresses reason.

The relational nature of *eudaimonia* is reflected in each of its three characteristics but most explicitly in the self-sufficiency that Aristotle ascribes to it: ". . . we regard something as self-sufficient when all by itself it makes a life choiceworthy and lacking nothing."[17] In this instance it is explicitly species-related, since Aristotle had taken care to note that ". . . what we count as self-sufficient is not what suffices for a solitary person by himself, living an isolated life, but what suffices also for parents, children, wife, and in general friends and fellow-citizens, since a human being is a naturally political [animal]."[18] In the *Politics*, too, Aristotle had explicitly warned against viewing the individual as potentially self-sufficient outside the political context: "The proof that the state is a creation of nature and prior to the individual is that the individual, when isolated, is not self-sufficing; and therefore he is like a part in relation to the whole."[19] According to Aristotle's striking and famous analogy, a stateless person is like "an isolated piece of draughts,"[20] i.e., unable to function *qua* such. Thus, it is because sociality is a part of human nature that the polity is logically prior to the individual, and any inquiry into the criteria of human self-sufficiency needs to take account of the fact that human flourishing requires the fulfillment of innate social tendencies. Such fulfillment will normally accrue to humans through participation in the affairs of the city-state but may also derive, we can assume, from the formation and cultivation of primary friendships or, for that matter, from a combination of both.

In the *Eudemian Ethics*, Aristotle exploits the dialectical format to drive home the point that human autarky cannot ever be complete. It has been suggested, he writes, that since God is not in need of friends, the happiest and best human beings, who most resemble the divine, will not need them either. This inference, Aristotle in effect replies, is hasty. While the divine nature constitutes its own, uniquely suitable, cognitive object, human beings need to apprehend objects external to themselves before they can, derivatively, gain reflexive awareness. While divine autarky is total, therefore, ours cannot be other than sporadic and incomplete, since it depends upon our relations with others. As Aristotle concludes, ". . . for us well-being [*to eu*] has reference to something other than ourselves, but in his [God's] case he is himself his own well-being."[21]

Taken together, these passages invite two general comments on the Aristotelian ideal of self-sufficiency and, for that reason, warrant a brief interruption of the present argument. Let it be noted, firstly, that Aristotle's commitment to the ideal of self-sufficiency does not lead him either to deplore or to seek in any way to minimize the mutual dependence of human beings. In his theory of knowledge, he provides a deep and comprehensive account of what must have struck him as an ineradicable aspect of human nature, viz., that human beings, *qua* such, cannot take the measure of their own being in the absence of things or beings other than and external to themselves. Holding that, few exceptions apart, the good life for humans is social, he therefore made the management of human interdependence into the prime concern of the prudent lawgiver.[22] Secondly, as far as the paltriness of man's autarky, as compared to God's, is concerned, it did not prompt Aristotle to bemoan the wretchedness of the human condition. On the contrary, he sought to demonstrate, through his philosophy of primary friendship, that human beings need not remain locked within the confines of their own private and imperfect world, but could reach out to the moral excellence of those they love and integrate such excellence into their own selves. His contention, which shall be considered presently, that primary friendship contributes to blessedness shows that his ideal of self-sufficiency is anything but constraining or mean-spirited.

Aristotle's argument that *autarkeia* is species-related has an important moral dimension in so far as it is part of his thesis that the virtuous life is more autarkic than would be an existence devoted to the pursuit of pleasure or of material gain.[23] Indeed, while the friendship of virtue fulfils a need rooted in the human essence, its lesser varieties meet merely individual, peripheral, and contingent needs. Only of essential human needs can it be claimed that their frustration precludes the achievement of *eudaimonia*. This argument, in turn, enables Aristotle to resolve Socrates' *aporia* in the *Lysis*. Primary friends, far from being necessary in order to make good psychological gaps in each other, he claims, bring about the fulfillment of the social instinct that nature has implanted in all human beings. Indeed, since sociality has been defined into human nature, friendly relationships in general are necessary for the actualization of what Aristotle presents as an essential human potentiality. On such a view, a friendless, stateless person should *prima facie* be an object of suspicion: he might be wrapped up in contemplation and to that extent be god-like, but, as Aristotle tells us in the *Politics*, he is more likely to be "a beast."[24] The psychological deterioration of Philoctetes in Sophocles' eponymous play is arguably an example in point. Having been left marooned on deserted Lemnos on account of a stenching wound, a neighbour to no-one but himself, Philoctetes reverts to inarticulate babble, allows himself to be overtaken by blind bitterness, and loses his (human) dignity. Only when reintegrated in human society will he become himself again. As Aristotle holds, friends are not a good with which the strong and psychologically mature could dispense; on the contrary, complete friends are a necessary component of the good life for man. To maintain that friendship precludes psychological self-sufficiency would be as absurd as claiming that the need of food and drink signals the absence of physical self-sufficiency and, hence, of health.

This argument, which sets limits to the ideal of human self-sufficiency, also accounts for the *prima facie* surprising classification of friendship amongst external goods.[25] Indeed, a number of commentators have claimed that this classification goes against the spirit of Aristotle's philosophy of primary friendship. Thus Stewart: "The value of the *heteros autos* (. . .) is scarcely that of an *external* good."[26] Thus Gauthier attempts to iron out what he deems to constitute a difficulty in Aristotle's argument by calling attention to the dialectical nature of the passages in which the classification appears.[27] These strictures notwithstanding, Aristotle's classification can be shown to be justifiable. Let it be noted, firstly, that the exercise of most moral virtues requires the presence of a number of factors and circumstances: justice cannot be practiced without people to be treated justly, and liberality requires recipients of largesse and patronage. In like manner, agents cannot display the virtues involved in friendship in the absence of specific individuals whom they love and whose good they aim at furthering. On the assumption that the virtuous will have friends, the mutual fulfillment brought about by primary friendship will therefore depend upon a number of contingent and, to some extent, external factors, amongst which figure luck, health, survival, geographical location, and a modicum of material goods. Forever a realist, Aristotle explains that since any benefactor, *qua* such, depends on the beneficiary for his actualization,[28] the excellent person "will *need* people for him to benefit."[29] For this reason, the theorizer, who cultivates the most divine element in himself and can contemplate on his own, surpasses the morally excellent person in self-sufficiency and, to that extent, comes closer to, though he never reaches, the ideal of full and divine *autarkeia*.[30] The background to the distinction between internal and external goods, as well as the distinction itself, therefore, appears fully to validate Aristotle's classification of friends amongst external goods. *Pace* Stewart and Gauthier, it can be claimed that not only does this classification take the

limitations of human life into account, but it also accommodates the distinction between virtuous friendship, which
contributes to the actualization of the human essence, and
its imperfect varieties, which mostly aim at compensating
the partners' individual deficiencies.

So far it has been argued that Aristotle's conception of
human nature as essentially social contributes to substantiate his contention that virtuous friendship fosters, rather
than jeopardizes, such self-sufficiency as virtuous human
agents are capable of achieving. A full justification of this
claim, however, requires an analyis of a number of noetic
arguments, and it is upon these that the remainder of this
chapter will concentrate.

The claim that the cultivation of virtuous friendship
actually fosters *autarkeia* is put forward in both *Ethics* with
minor but quite significant variations. Firstly, while in the
more dialectical *Eudemian Ethics* the comparison with the
divinity runs as a thread through the whole argument in
VII, 12, there is no mention of God in the corresponding
Nicomachean chapter, IX, 9. Secondly, in the *Eudemian
Ethics* Aristotle addresses at length the objection that
friendship of all kinds, including the primary form, under-
mines the very possibility of self-sufficiency. The fact that a
primary friend, it is here countered,[31] is a 'separate' (*diaire-
tos*) being as well as an other self, causes him to be, for his
friend, an (external) cognitive object and, hence, an occasion for self-awareness of the most choiceworthy kind. Far
from endangering any pre-existing self-sufficiency that the
friend might have enjoyed, such self-awareness actually
enhances and increases it. Although this Eudemian argument is circuitous in form and, at times, clumsy, Aristotle
appears to set great store by it. He may have considered
that the rebuttal of Socrates' conclusion in the *Lysis*
required heavy artillery rather than mere psychological considerations on the pervasiveness and depth of the human
need for companionship. Although his Eudemian observations on self-knowledge are tantalizingly brief, they nevertheless show that his reasons for insisting on the compatibility of friendship and self-sufficiency are similar[32] to those

presented in the *Nicomachean* version. Fortunately there the *aporia* is more discursively resolved by means of two different and ampler arguments, both relying on two fundamental theses of Aristotelian noetic, i.e., the claim that awareness of self occurs only through the apprehension of other objects and the view that, during the cognitive process, the knowing mind becomes the object known. The first argument (1169b22-1170a4), which is often and unduly neglected, centres on pleasure, while the second (1170a11-1170b19), which has not entirely benefited from the exposure it has received, rests entirely on noetic theses.

Argument No. 1:
The blessedly happy person needs friends.

In *N.E.* IX,9, let it first be noted, it is of the blessedly happy person (*makarios*) that Aristotle argues that he will need friends. While the concepts of happiness (*eudaimonia*) and blessedness (*makaria*) have the same denotation, their connotations can arguably be said to differ. As Aristotle had noted earlier,[33] blessed people are so called because of 'enjoyment' (*chairein*). While both *makarios* and *eudaimōn* apply only to virtuous agents, the former predicate lays the stress on the pleasure which is inherently theirs. Aristotle's first argument thus aims at showing that friends are a *sine qua non* of the unconditionally pleasurable life.

The argument relies on three premises. Firstly, *eudaimonia*, insofar as it is an activity, cannot be continuous: ". . . it comes into being, and does not belong, as a possession does."[34] Although Aristotle does not explicitly say so here, it is important to bear in mind that he consistently characterizes divine, as opposed to human, activity as continuous.[35]

Secondly, we are reminded that "what is our own is pleasant."[36] The assumption embodied in this second premise is a familiar one. In the early stages of *N.E.*, VIII, Aristotle had brought the issue of pleasure to bear on that of complete friendship: virtuous people, he had claimed, are pleasant for each other because ". . . each person finds his own actions and actions of that kind pleasant, and the actions of good people are the same or similar."[37] This had constituted an argument in favour of the superiority of virtue friendship over its inferior varieties. While the latter are incomplete because they are unconcerned with virtue, the former, which accommodates the demands of utility and of pleasure within the context of a virtuous association, is complete. It is worth pointing out that in both passages quoted above, *oikeios* refers exclusively to what is one's own. The actions of friends are not, as yet, said to be *oikeiai*.

In the third premise to the argument Aristotle states that "We are able to observe our neighbours more than ourselves, and to observe their actions more than our own."[38] This is an ambiguous statement. Does it allude to the genesis of self-awareness? That seems unlikely since this topic will constitute the hub of the second argument. Further, Aristotle here merely observes that it is *easier* to contemplate others than oneself, not that the latter is impossible without the former. Accordingly, we should work on the assumption that the premise means what it appears at first glance to say, i.e., that self-observation presents obstacles which are all but absent in the observation of others. This interpretation has the incidental advantage of being favoured by the author of the *Magna Moralia*: ". . . we are not able to see what we are from ourselves (and that we cannot do so is plain from the way in which we blame others without being aware that we do the same things ourselves; and this is the effect of favour or passion, and there are many of us who are blinded by these things so that we judge not aright); as then when we wish to see our own face, we do so by looking in the mirror, in the same way when we wish to know ourselves we can obtain that knowledge by looking at our friend."[39] The fact that this passage provides a simplified and psychologized version of what are complex noetic arguments in the *Eudemian* and the *Nicomachean Ethics* should not fundamentally affect the discussion of the point at issue. What matters here is that all three *Ethics* contain statements to the effect that, for whatever reason, self-knowledge cannot be direct and immediate. The recognition that an intermediary is required paves the way for the conclusion that virtuous people generally require the proximity of other, similarly virtuous, agents in order to secure the unconditional pleasure that arises from the contemplation of excellent actions.

At this stage of the argument Aristotle has yet to bring in friendship. The question arises as to why the virtuous agent should be *friends* with those whose performance of virtuous deeds gives him unconditional pleasure. In 1170a3, for the first time in this argument, Aristotle unequivocally intimates that the actions of one's friend are to be seen as 'one's own' (*oikeiai*). The excellent actions of a friend, we are told, exhibit two features which are "pleasant by nature,"[40] i.e., as spelled out in 1169b32-33, they are pleasant both in themselves and because they are *oikeiai*. Aristotle's use of this adjective in the present context is highly significant. Normally, *oikeios*, derived from *oikia* ('household'), means 'one's own, related by blood', and, as G.B. Kerferd has stated, "The normal way to become member of an *oikia* is to be born and brought up in the family, not to be brought in from outside."[41] Outlining the philosophical significance of this fact, Kerferd specifies: "In the important opposition between *oikeion agathon* [one's own good] and *allotrion agathon* [another's good] developed by Thrasymachus in the first book of the *Republic oikeion agathon* is not any good which is acquired, it is the good which belongs most intimately to oneself because it is rooted in one's very nature, and so is opposed to the good which is not so rooted."[42] In the passage under discussion, Aristotle starts off by using *oikeios* to refer to a person's own actions. His extension of the concept to cover the actions of one's primary friends can only mean that an additional, but not explicitly stated, premiss has been brought into the argument: a primary friend is another self. Only on such a condition can the virtuous man, as we shall see, be in a position to *domesticate* actions performed by another. Without this premise, whose meaning and implications were analyzed in chapter 2 above, the argument that the company of virtuous friends crucially contributes to the excellent person's virtuous enjoyment cannot get under way. In other words, the premiss allows Aristotle to incorporate within the virtuous person's own private sphere a good which *prima facie* appears external to it, i.e., a friend's excellent actions.

It can now plausibly be claimed on Aristotle's behalf that the virtuous agent will derive more pleasure from the observation of the excellent activities of his virtuous friends than from those of mere acquaintances. Indeed, the status of primary friends as other selves to each other causes a number of their actions to be, practically if not literally, *oikeiai* to both parties. The virtuous man who nobly lets his friend perform a morally right action in his stead acquires, in the process, some "co-ownership" of his friend's action. More frequently, however, it is through empathetic understanding that he will integrate his friend's actions into his own life. Their close, long-standing friendship, which has intimately acquainted him with the circumstances, motivation, and character of his partner, puts him in the rare position of being able to take the full measure of his moral excellence. As was argued in chapter 2 above, such knowledge, which proceeds by direct acquaintance, causes the knower to become the object known and, coincidentally, to gain awareness of himself in possession of what is, in Aristotle's presentation, a highly determinate good. Thus can morally excellent actions become *oikeiai* to both partners in primary friendship, i.e., to him who performs them and to him who draws from them a form of noetic sustenance not readily available otherwise. This process, which could be described as a further domestication of the good of moral excellence into their joint lives, is a source of unconditional pleasure for virtue, or primary, friends. Since such pleasure is unavailable in the absence of friends, Aristotle can conclude that "the blessedly happy person will *need* such friends since he chooses to observe excellent actions which are also his own and since such are the actions of his virtuous friend."[43] The occurrence of *deēsetai* ('will need') at the conclusion of this argument is significant. To the above-mentioned arguments, some of which had remained implicit in the text, Aristotle now adds an extra consideration; human beings, for whom continuous activity is difficult,[44] do require virtue friendship for blessedness and self-sufficiency. Unsurprisingly, this conclusion is soon to be followed in both *Ethics* by a discussion of the optimal number of friends. Aristotle commonsensically argues that the exacting demands of complete friendship could not be met within a large circle. Had he not done so, the paradoxical conclusion might have followed that blessedness is directly proportionate to the number of one's friends.

Argument No. 2:
Friendship leads to self-actualization.

The second argument which Aristotle offers in *N.E.* IX,9, to demonstrate that primary friendship fosters human self-sufficiency, is compressed, highly complex, and somewhat jagged. Burnet,[45] Ross,[46] and Gauthier[47] have attempted to articulate it by means of series of syllogisms. Although the number of syllogisms that these commentators claim to have uncovered in the text varies, all three broadly agree as to the substance of the arguments there deployed by Aristotle. Unimpeachable as these formalisations appear to be, they are dismissed by Hardie on the ground that "The weak link in the argument of the chapter lies in the claim that a friend is an *alter ego* in the sense that we can be aware of his thoughts as we can be aware of our own. No chain is stronger than its weakest link." For this reason, he pronounces himself unwilling "to say more about the details of the reasoning in the second part of *N.E.*, IX,9."[48]

In chapter 2 above, it has been argued that the *allos autos* premiss, which underpins Aristotle's philosophy of primary friendship, directly follows from his noetic. In chapter 3, the further claim was defended that far from being "the weakest link in the chain," this premise and its implications do shed light on aspects of friendship which most modern analyses neglect. *Pace* Hardie, Aristotle's second presentation of the claim, in *N.E.*, IX,9, viz., that primary friendship ensures human self-sufficiency, thus appears worthy of serious consideration, especially since, as argued earlier, it can be buttressed by the inclusion of *Eudemian* developments. While being indebted to Burnet, Ross, and Gauthier for their formalizations of Aristotle's reasoning, I shall here concentrate almost exclusively on its contents.

Aristotle begins by rehearsing some fundamental tenets of his philosophy. These are included amongst the premisses for the complex argument that follows:

(1) The virtuous person values and takes pleasure in what is objectively good, i.e., good by nature (*phusei*);[49]

(2) Since the life of any species is defined by reference to its specific activity (the *ergon* argument), human life is characterized by the activities of perceiving (*aisthēsis*) and of thinking (*noēsis*);[50]

(3) Every potentiality (*dunamis*) refers to its corresponding activity (*energeia*);[51]

Inference A (from 2 and 3): An actualized human life consists in perceiving or thinking;[52]

(4) What is good by nature (e.g., life) is determinate (*hōrismenon*);[53]

Inference B (from A and 4): Unlike the vicious life, the virtuous, i.e., actualized, human life is determinate;[54]

(5) Everyone desires life;[55]

Inference C (from 1, B, and 5): The virtuous life is both eminently choiceworthy and objectively pleasant;[56]

Inference D (from 1, 2, and C): Virtuous agents desire life more than others do.[57]

Thus starkly formulated and in spite of the fact that it falls neatly within the context of the overall argument, this statement, inference D, is counter-intuitive. Those inclined to feel annoyance at what they may perceive to be Aristotle's lack of psychological insight, would do well to bear in mind, in addition to (5) above, this sentence from the *Politics*:

". . . men cling to life even at the cost of enduring great misfortune, seeming to find in life a natural sweetness and happiness."[58] This latter passage does not contradict inference D. Although love of life is a deeply rooted feeling which takes no heed of value, Aristotle held, the virtuous life, which best fulfils the human function (premiss 2), is objectively more desirable than a morally indifferent existence. As such, it is more keenly—and rightly—desired by those whose emotions are in harmony with reason. Aristotle does not mean that akratic, vicious, and intellectually feeble persons do not love their lives, but he here implies that they are less justified in so doing than the virtuous.

(6) Perception and cognition are accompanied by awareness of themselves;[59]

Inference E (from A and 6): Perceptual and cognitive awareness amount to awareness of self;[60]

Intermediate Conclusion No. 1: Awareness of self, i.e., the perception that one is alive, is pleasant in itself, especially for virtuous agents whose lives are determinate and actualized.[61]

Only in the final stages of this top-heavy argument does Aristotle introduce the topic of friendship. This he does by integrating yet another highly compressed premiss into the argument:

(7) "The excellent person is related to his friend in the same way as he is related to himself, since the friend is another himself."[62]

Intermediate Conclusion No. 2: Just as his own being is choiceworthy for the excellent person, so is the being of his friend or other self.[63] Just as the excellent person rejoices in his own excellent and highly actualized being, he will rejoice in the excellent and similarly actualized being of his other self. The sharing of conversation and thought, which best allows for the joint perception (*sunaisthanesthai*) of one's own being and that of the friend, provides opportunities for such profound and justifiably valued satisfaction.[64]

Final Conclusion: "Whatever is choiceworthy for him [the virtuous] he must possess, since otherwise he will to this extent lack something [and hence not be self-sufficient]. Anyone who is to be happy, then, must have excellent friends."[65]

Considered on its own, this laborious and convoluted exposition is not altogether convincing; the argument is top-heavy, and its seventh premise appears very much to be invoked as a *deus ex machina*. No wonder that Stewart speculates: "Perhaps something has dropped out (. . .) which served to make the transition from the individual's simple *aisthanesthai* (perception) of himself to his *sunaisthanesthai* (joint perception) of his alter ego."[66]

In chapters 1 and 2 above, it was argued that this initially puzzling premise, on which the present argument stands or falls, is a direct inference from Aristotle's views on the nature and genesis of self-awareness. A brief summary of some of the main contentions of these chapters should, accordingly, shed much necessary light on Aristotle's second argument that primary friendship fosters self-sufficiency. Let it first be borne in mind that Aristotle locates selfhood in the noetic part of the soul and that, as a result, he holds that the underdevelopment of this part constitutes a failure of selfhood. Further, he characterizes cognition as the taking over, by the knowing mind, of the form(s) of the object(s) it apprehends. Lastly, he presents self-awareness as a by-product of cognition. As was argued in chapters 1 and 2, these views license the conclusion that primary friendship, which closely familiarizes virtuous individuals with each other's excellent lives and personalities, is a crucial factor in self-actualization. Indeed, not only does each partner in primary friendship apprehend the moral excellence of the other, but concomitantly he also becomes the excellence he discerns in his friend. Since it is a matter of definition that the partners in primary friendship have succeeded in becoming what they truly are, viz., their noetic element, it can be inferred that this relationship involves the noetic conflation of the friends' selves. Virtue or primary friends become each other's actualized self, and this very process furnishes them with an awareness of their own highly actualized being. As stated in the second intermediate conclusion of the present argument, such awareness is inherently pleasurable. The noetic processes involved in the intimacy of primary friendship thus constitute a source of self-fulfillment not to be found elsewhere, and primary friendship can justifiably be deemed to be one of the greatest goods which a human being is capable of enjoying.

Arduous and cumbersome though the second argument in *N.E.* IX,9 initially appears, it is thus entirely consonant with Aristotle's general noetic and ethical stances and *within that framework* does not lack plausibility. The noetic benefits of friendship, on which it focuses, ground the conclusion that the friendship of virtue is a necessary component of the good life for agents whose natural and essential sociality means that, in the absence of virtuous friends, they could not be sufficient unto themselves.

Aristotle's emphasis on self-knowledge as a benefit uniquely afforded by friendship should not be construed to mean that the virtuous person will choose and cultivate his friends *in order*, primarily, to gain noetic actualization and bathe in the good constituted by the awareness of his own actualized being. Since self-awareness cannot occur in the absence of an object of cognition, neither can the specific kind of self-realization brought about by friendship be aimed at from the friendless state. Aristotelian agents therefore simply could not seek virtue friends in order to secure a good they would be unable even to conceive in their absence.

In *N.E.* IX,9, it can now be concluded, the *aporia* presented by Socrates in the *Lysis* is resolved. Humans are so constituted that they require others actually to become what they essentially are, and virtuous agents are those who succeed in actualizing their nature to the fullest extent. In this process of self-actualization primary friendship plays a major role, since it uniquely provides the virtuous with goods, both cognitive (i.e., the awareness of themselves *qua* fully actualized) and moral (i.e., deepened moral understanding and a regard for others in and for themselves) which would otherwise be unavailable to them. To that extent primary friendship, which had earlier been argued to constitute a source of unconditional pleasure, is also a necessary component of the self-sufficient life. Though such friendship depends, to some extent, on external contingent factors, it could be said to constitute a bulwark against chance, and Nietzsche may well have been alluding to friendship when he wrote: "The Greeks, in a way of life in which great perils and upheavals were always present, sought in knowledge and reflection a kind of security and ultimate *refugium*."[67]

The focus of the present chapter, so far, has been the exegesis of Aristotle's two arguments in defence of the claim that primary friendship fosters individual self-sufficiency. Leaving this theoretical framework aside, I shall now very briefly address the broader substantive issue of the value of individual self-sufficiency within the context of affective relationships. Is Aristotle right to place a high value on it, and, if so, could the dedicated and earnest pursuit of autarky induce virtuous agents to exert undue caution in the choice of their friends? After all, a certain amount of risk-taking, in friendship and elsewhere, not only adds spice to life but can also be claimed to be morally enriching.

In his influential article *Persons, Character, and Morality*,[68] Bernard Williams castigates Aristotelian self-sufficiency as an "unappetizing ideal." In order to reconcile this ideal with friendship, claims Williams, Aristotle presents partners in virtuous friendship as mere reduplications of one another (or other selves). Williams objects to this move on the ground that it effectively promotes safety and complacency in interpersonal relationships at the expense of commendable risk-taking. As he writes: "Once one agrees that a three-dimensional mirror would not represent the ideal of friendship, one can begin to see both how some degree of difference can play an essential role, and, also, how a commitment or involvement with a particular other person might be one of the kinds of project which figured basically in a man's life."[69] Such commitment, Williams contends, ". . . would be mysterious or even sinister on an Aristotelian account."[70] These are somewhat bemusing claims. Williams appears to assume that a willingness to take risks constitutes one of the morally commendable aspects of friendship,[71] and he further argues that the more different the friends are from each other, the more risks the friendship holds for their individual self-sufficiency, and thus the nobler their relationship. On this interpretation, Aristotle's description of friends as other selves to each other cannot but be construed as a desperate and "unappetizing" attempt to secure the combination of friendship and self-sufficiency. The exegesis presented in chapter 2 above will, I hope, have shown that this latter contention is based on an unjustifiable reading of a number of key passages. Williams' other contention, however, is not so easily dismissed.

It should, firstly, be asked whether a willingness to take risks in friendship is, *in itself*, morally commendable. True, deliberately to restrict one's choice of friends to one's own religious, social, ethnic, political, or intellectual sphere would smack of narrow-mindedness and pusillanimity and positively hinder the cognitive function that Aristotle and Williams agree in ascribing to friendship. Those, however, who abstain from initiating friendships with manic-depressives, workaholics, or explorers addicted to wintering in the Antarctic are certainly mindful not to take risks; while we may hesitate to commend them as courageous, we should be equally reluctant to denounce them as pusillanimous. In these examples, the taking of risks is morally neutral insofar as the worst that can befall the partners is the atrophy of their friendship. There are situations, however, in which risk-taking in the choice of one's friends can be positively foolish. It is not so much because of risks to person and liberty that friendships across certain political and religious divides should be ruled out as because such loyalties are apt to run so deeply in the would-be friends' personalities as to make openness to an antagonistic cause well nigh impossible. In the absence of a common commitment, born-again Christians, for instance, are unlikely to derive much benefit, cognitive or affective, from friendships with committed humanists, although each party may well admire the dedication and earnestness of the other. When such individuals share at least one serious commitment (e.g., ecological concern) or interest (e.g., authentic music) they are, to that extent, similar, and a friendship, albeit a limited one, is possible between them. Indeed, the intimate and complete friendship of which Aristotle writes does require overall mutual sympathy with and interest in the concerns of the other.

It should, secondly, be pointed out that Williams' criticism rings a somewhat anachronistic note. His intimation that friendships across deep-seated political or religious divergences are somehow nobler because riskier than safe friendships between like-minded individuals, presupposes some form of ideological pluralism, the identification of tolerance as a virtue, and a commitment to the ideal of personal growth. None of these would have been live issues to a Greek writer of Aristotle's time and temperament. Aristotle's commitment to the *polis*,[72] together with his view that friendship between citizens best preserves states from revolutions,[73] would have prevented him from seriously considering the possibility of friendships across certain boundaries. It is presumably for these reasons, that he pronounced similarity, albeit restricted to virtue, to be a condition of primary friendship[74] and relegated relationships arising "from contraries" to the inferior varieties of friendship.[75] True, he recognized that it is possible to take a disinterested delight in persons unlike oneself,[76] but he explained this on the ground that ". . . accidentally love of the good is love of the opposite, but essentially it is love of the middle, for opposites do not strive to reach one another but the middle."[77] Aristotle's reference to the middle ground, as well as his examples of attraction of opposites (viz., the stiff and the witty, the active and the lazy)[78] show clearly that it is temperamental differences rather than ideological divergences that he has in mind. Neither *Ethics*, we can conclude, contains any evidence that Williams' strictures would have been even intelligible to Aristotle.

Finally, it is worth recalling here the counter-claims that Martha Nussbaum directed at Williams: "When we consider the full requirements of Aristotelian living-together and the requirements it imposes, the vulnerabilities it creates, we cannot think that Aristotle has courted self-sufficiency to the neglect of richness of value. Indeed we are more likely to be awed and alarmed at the risk such a person runs in valuing so difficult and unlikely a goal."[79] Since, as we saw in chapter 5 above, the pursuit of this goal might even require the sacrifice of one's life, the presiding motive of primary friendship cannot be the cozy and undemanding companionship that Williams depicts. In the same manner as genuine love of self does not, in Aristotle's ethics, entail ethical egoism, the ideal of autarky does not signal moral complacency.

To conclude: Aristotle's arguments to support his claim that primary friendship fosters rather than, as might at first appear, impedes the virtuous person's *autarkeia* have been shown to have considerable force. Not only are they entailed by his general noetic, but they also illuminate his concept of self-sufficiency itself. They show that it presupposes both the ability to sustain exacting personal relations and the moral discernment required for valuing and choosing what is truly good. Regrettably but perhaps unsurprisingly, Aristotle does not appear to have questioned the ideal itself. To do so he would have had not only totally to transcend the spirit of his age but also, as we shall presently see, question the very foundations of his political philosophy.

7

FRIENDSHIP,
JUSTICE,
AND
THE STATE

Primary, or virtue, friendship, it has so far been established, constitutes a source of high self-realization for virtuous persons. Firstly, it affords them a semi-theoretical insight into the nature of the moral life. Through the process of making another self they gain not only an awareness of themselves *qua* morally actualized, but also a deeper insight into the nature and variety of moral experience. Secondly, to the extent that it meets their inherently social need to give and to receive from others, virtue friendship contributes to render excellent persons as self-sufficient as humanly possible.

This latter good, unlike the former, is not exclusively within the gift of primary friendship. As we saw, Aristotle generally presents the state as the end of the moral life and, as such, the ultimate fulfilment of human social nature: ". . . if the earlier forms of society are natural, so is the state, for it is the end of them, and the nature of a thing is its end. For what each thing is when fully developed, we call its nature, whether we are speaking of a man, a horse, or a family. Besides, the final cause and end of a thing is the best."[1] In any case, friendship is, to some extent, an external good which chance may deny the virtuous. Although he viewed friendlessness as "a very terrible thing,"[2] there is no

147

evidence that Aristotle thought that it constitutes some kind of moral failure on the part of the friendless. Furthermore, he often intimates that the sublimity of primary friendship is due, at least in part, to its rarity, and that it cannot but be the preserve of a few rather exceptional men. While this reveals the profoundly aristocratic character of the Aristotelian morally ideal life, it fails to provide much guidance for the many, who are as inherently social as the wise, on the best way to conduct their lives. Although primary friendship is a moral good of the highest order, we thus conclude, it is not a goal at which most people can realistically aim. Not only do the many stand little chance of achieving it, even when they can conceive of it, but even the virtuous may be prevented from achieving it by contingent factors. Participation in the affairs of the state, on the other hand, should be available to all (decent) citizens who seriously seek it, Aristotle held, and the concept of political or civic friendship (*politikē philia*) was generally in use to describe the bond which can and should link all those who take part in the affairs of a state or are united in their allegiance to a party. Bearing in mind Aristotle's distinction between utility, pleasure, and virtue friendship, I shall now investigate the nature of civic friendship and of its relation to the friendship which has been described in the preceding chapters. More specifically, I shall address the issue as to whether primary friendship is a rare and precious bloom which can only grow in the fertile soil of civic friendship or, on the contrary, as some commentators have argued, it is the rich and abundant crop of civic friendship which, in appropriate conditions, grows from the seed of primary friendship among a few rarely high-minded individuals.

Unfortunately, Aristotle never directly confronted this issue, which, as later philosophical developments were to show, is both complex and amenable to different, though equally plausible, solutions. One may well ask, for instance, how civic friendship in the relatively provincial framework of a *polis* actively contributes to the fulfilment of those who have virtuous friends. Indeed, participation in the affairs of the state might arguably appear irksome to those who have achieved virtue friendship, and we can readily imagine that it would be a sacrifice for them to descend from the height of other selfhood into the fray of the committee room, the assembly, and the law courts. After all, consorting with their few virtuous friends, in addition to bringing them noetic actualization, might sufficiently fulfil the social side of their nature. As is well known, Epicurus was soon to present private friendship not only as necessary but also as sufficient for the actualization of the human social tendency. Moreover, why did Aristotle argue not only that civic but also primary friendship could not flourish outside the framework of the *polis*? Inter-state friendships were far from unknown in antiquity.[3] Would Aristotle have denied the accolade of primary friendship to the association enjoyed, e.g., by Plato and Dion of Syracuse? As we know, the Stoics were soon plausibly to argue that wise men, *qua* such, are citizens of the cosmos (*kosmopolitai*). Concord (*homonoia*) or friendship, they claimed, inevitably prevails between those who obey reason and recognize the irrelevance of such contingent factors as custom, ethnicity, and geography.[4] Why, lastly, did Aristotle claim that individual friendships act as a safeguard to the state[5] when they could so easily come to threaten it? After all, Cicero's discussion, in the *De Amicitia*, of the conflicts of loyalties generated by political obligation and private friendship[6] did and has continued to address a live issue. All these questions are complex, and Aristotle's implicit or putative answers to them must now be considered.

Let it first be noted that, compared with his present day commentators, Aristotle is fairly economical with the phrase 'civic friendship'. Although he uses it repeatedly in one *Eudemian* passage (VII,9 and 10), he resorts to it but rarely in the corresponding *Nicomachean* chapters and appears never to have needed it in the *Politics*.[7] *Politikē philia*, clearly, was not for him the semi-technical expression it has since become, and the large claims that some of his recent commentators have made for civic friendship need to be squared with the reality of infrequent Aristotelian usage. What Aristotle does discuss at some length, however, is friendship in communities (*koinoniai*), both small- and large-scale. Restricted communities, such as families, travelling parties, religious societies, etc., as well as the political community at large, Aristotle notes,[8] generate some kind of friendship between their members. While all friendship presupposes a form of community, the general well-being of a community, in turn, depends on the extent of the friendly feelings that prevail between its members.[9]

Aristotle identifies advantage as the presiding motive of friendship in communities, and, accordingly, in both versions of the *Ethics* he presents civic or political friendship as a variety of the friendship of utility. "Civic friendship," we read in the *Eudemian Ethics*, "is constituted in the fullest degree on the principle of utility (*kata to chrēsimon*), for it seems to be the individual's lack of self-sufficiency that makes (. . .) unions permanent."[10] To that extent it differs from primary friendship.[11] Aristotle is similarly explicit in the *Nicomachean* version: "political friendship (. . .) is concerned with advantage (*ta sumpheronta*) and with what affects life,"[12] although no explicit contrast is drawn in this passage between civic and primary friendship. I here assume that, in the above two contexts, the expressions *to chrēsimon* and *ta sumpheronta* are broadly synonymous and refer to the expedient as contrasted with the fine.

Although the friendship of utility, in Aristotle's presentation, can be manipulative and exploitative, it need not be. As John Cooper[13] has forcibly argued, a modicum of mutual and even disinterested well-wishing can soften what is fundamentally a self-regarding and self-benefiting relationship. Aristotle's own distinction in both *Ethics* between two sub-classes of the friendship of utility bears out Cooper's claim. While one kind of utility friendship depends on rules (*nomikē philia*) and expects returns proportional to outlay, the other proceeds from character (*ēthikē philia*), involves a certain amount of trust, and takes a broad-minded view of what counts as repayment.[14] Under which of these two categories does civic friendship fall? In the *Eudemian Ethics*, contrary to what one might expect, it gets relegated to the morally inferior *nomikē philia*: "When . . . it is based on a definite agreement (*kath' homologian*), this is civic and legal friendship."[15] Being a kind of "ready-money transaction,"[16] this friendship often gives rise to recriminations. Aware of the fact that hypocrisy is the last homage that vice renders to virtue, Aristotle wrily notes that civic friends occasionally like to pass their association for something higher than it is, i.e., for "a moral friendship."[17] Earlier in this *Ethics* Aristotle had claimed that the political life is generally chosen "for the sake of money and gain."[18]

The jaundiced tone of Aristotle's account of political friendship in the *Eudemian Ethics* is worth stressing, especially in view of the fact that most commentators appear to have missed it. Not only is civic friendship claimed to be a *do ut des* arrangement, but it is also presented as a particularly mean-spirited, petty, opportunist, and hypocritical type of exchange. It is a temporary and unsteady compact on the part of self-seeking individuals to refrain from harming one another. Aristotle does not, in the *Eudemian Ethics*, appear to envisage that a measure of public spirit, concern for the common good, or interest in the well-being of one's associates could enter into the motivation or the dispositions of those who are civic friends. Which type of constitution, one wonders, had Aristotle in mind when he wrote this account of civic friendship? We shall come back to this question.

On the whole, as we shall have further opportunity to note, Aristotle's analyses of civic friendship in the *Nicomachean Ethics* are far less cynical and disparaging. Although there, too, he stresses the self-regarding nature of civic friendship, he does not specify whether it comes under the rule-governed or the character variety of the friendship of utility. This enables him in this treatise to outline the moral and political benefits of civic friendship, to moot the claims that "if people are friends, they have no need of justice,"[19] and, therefore, later, in the *Politics*, to present friendship as "the greatest good of states."[20]

Having located civic friendship within Aristotle's general classification of friendship in the ethical treatises, we must investigate its nature further. In both *Ethics* it is defined as a species of concord (*homonoia*).[21] Although Aristotle's remarks on concord are brief, one can extrapolate from them without too much difficulty. Concord is a state of harmony prevailing between those whose "purpose and desire are for the same objects."[22] Its scope, depth and duration vary considerably. Pertaining to practical matters as opposed to theoretical concerns,[23] concord effectively enables joint members of associations to work together smoothly and effectively. In the case of civic friendship such unison mostly concerns large questions,[24] the paradigm of concord being a generally agreed political decision like the election of a ruler or the conclusion of a treaty. As such, civic friendship need not, although, of course, it may, involve the affectivity of the partners.

Can concord or civic friendship promote shabby, as well as worthy, goals, or does its very existence tell of the political health of a state? Aristotle's answers to this question need to be studied in their variety. While the *Eudemian* version allows for the existence of some sort of inferior and, therefore, limited concord between the base (*hoi phauloi*),[25] the *Nicomachean Ethics* contains the explicit claim that, in civic matters at least, concord is the preserve of those who are decent (*hoi epieikeis*).[26] Indeed, the definition of civic friendship as concord in *N.E.*, IX,6 is followed by a comparison between the harmony that prevails between all decent citizens in a sound constitution and the inner stability enjoyed by good men who "are in concord with themselves."[27] Far from allowing that there can be honour amongst thieves, Aristotle, in *N.E.*, IX,6, appears to claim that civic concord cannot obtain unless the citizens themselves are morally sound. The base, whose motivation is generally unsteady, can neither feel due concern for the common good nor cooperate with others in its pursuit. Their general psychic disharmony causes them to be unjust, prone to undue acquisitiveness (*pleonexia*),[28] and to steer clear of genuinely public service. In *N.E.*, IX,6, therefore, the gap between civic and primary friendship is relatively narrow, and Cooper's remark that "Civic friendship makes fellow-citizens' well-being matter to one another, simply as such"[29] is faithful to the spirit of that chapter.

Unfortunately, as the evidence of book VIII, chapters 9 to 13, indicates, Aristotle does not appear consistently to have held civic friendship in such high regard, even in the *Nicomachean* version. In an earlier lengthy passage (1159b25-1162a33) he presents a mainly descriptive, classificatory, even sociological account of various forms of friendship in communities.[30] Rather than mounting an argument or making specific points, Aristotle in that passage appears to be rehearsing material presumed to be already familiar to his audience and rounding off his account of the varieties of friendship before turning to his next topic, i.e., the disputes arising in friendship. As we shall have further opportunity to note, civic friendship is not singled out here for special treatment; it is merely listed as one of the several forms of friendship in communities. Julia Annas may well have had this passage in mind when she wrote that, *pace* Cooper, "Aristotle is not especially interested in civic friendships."[31] The fact that the phrase *politikē philia*, as we saw, most probably does not occur in the *Politics*, i.e., where one would most expect to find it, would appear to support Annas' remark.

As can be seen, therefore, the divergent opinions of commentators reflect Aristotle's own fluctuations on the matter of civic friendship from disparagement to eulogy *via* indifference. These fluctuations are disconcerting because Aristotle's views on human nature and on the role of the state in the economy of the good life lead one to expect from him a fuller, more consistent, and generally more sympathetic analysis of the bond between fellow citizens. More particularly, in view of the use-value that Aristotle ascribes to friendship in the safeguard of the state, why do the practical treatises not include advice to legislators as to how friendship amongst the citizenry can best be promoted?[32]

The answer to these perplexities lies, I submit, not in Aristotle's unconcern with civic friendship but in his assumption that civic friendship is but the reflection, in the lives of individuals, of the constitution of the state.

Considered in itself, civic friendship is neither noble nor pettily contractual, neither disinterested nor manipulative, neither stable nor unsteady. It is the constitution of the state which, to a large extent, determines not only the nature and the extent of the civic bond but also its moral worth. Like the criteria of good citizenship, those of civic friendship, according to this interpretation, will vary with the constitutions. While sound constitutions encourage all citizens to have regard for each other, defective and deviant ones prompt rulers to be solely concerned with securing a balance of power, however skin-deep and precarious, between antagonistic parties, or with establishing a truce among them. There is little in common between the kinds of civic friendship that these constitutions generate. To support this interpretation I shall now offer some reflections on the inter-relations between constitution, justice (universal and particular), and friendship (civic and primary), as sketched out in the practical treatises. These reflections will unfortunately have to remain both speculative and tentative since full textual support in these matters is unavailable.

In *N.E.*, VIII the classification of civic friendship amongst utility friendships is followed by an investigation into the specific obligations of justice incurred by members of restricted communities. Aristotle there emphasizes that the concepts of community, friendship and justice are co-extensive.[33] In communities or associations formed for the sake of a common purpose or *koinōniai*, ties of friendship evolve which, in turn, generate specific obligations of particular justice: "It is more shocking, e.g., to rob a companion of money than to rob a fellow citizen, to fail to help a brother than a stranger."[34] In the framework of *koinōniai*, Aristotle avers, the requirements of particular justice increase with friendship; the closer the tie the greater the demands of justice and, correspondingly, the deeper the injustice. Accordingly the (particularly) just person always includes his membership of communities, big or small, as a relevant consideration in his moral deliberations.

In accordance with his view that limited associations are subsidiary and "subordinate to the political community,"[35] Aristotle proceeds to extend his analysis of friendship in restricted communities to cover joint membership of a state. Contrary to what we might expect, however, Aristotle does not, at least in *N.E.*, VIII, appear to consider that the political community (*politikē koinōnia*) is of a different, nobler nature, nor that the friendship of fellow citizens is different in kind from the friendship of associates, nor, lastly, that it generates its own specific obligations of justice. In that book the main difference between the political community, on the one hand, and limited communities, on the other, would seem to be their respective areas of concern; while the former aims at "advantage for the whole of life,"[36] the latter aim at partial advantage only.[37] What is true of smaller associations is also said to be true of political systems, viz., the friendship they generate is co-extensive with the amount of justice they display.[38] The amount and presumably the quality of civic friendship in a state are therefore directly proportional to the worth of its political system. Before further developing this point, however, the Aristotelian distinction between universal and particular justice must be brought into the argument to clarify the difficult matter of the relationship between civic and primary friendship.

As defined in the *Nicomachean Ethics*, universal justice is complete virtue in relation to another;[39] in a perfect state it will be co-extensive with law-abidingness. Its opposite, universal injustice, constitutes the whole of vice, and "The worst person (. . .) is the one who exercises his vice towards himself and his friends as well."[40] As for particular justice, it closely corresponds to what we call fairness and pertains to the apportioning of competitive or contested goods (e.g., honour, wealth, and safety) between the members of a society or group; its opposite, particular injustice, is ascribed to undue acquisitiveness or greed.[41] In the *Politics*, where the distinction between universal and particular justice is not explicitly drawn, Aristotle describes justice as "the bond of men in states; for the administration of justice, which is the determination of what is just, is the principle of order in political society."[42] In so far as it essentially incorporates a

concern for the common interest, justice is the good of political science,[43] and a state cannot exist[44] nor a government
stand[45] without it.

Following on from this formal definition, Aristotle notes
that conceptions of justice vary in kind with the constitutions, and rehearses some of the main *Nicomachean* themes
in order to fill in his current notion of common interest. It is
the life of moral excellence, which consists in acting well, he
reiterates, that best secures the happiness of cities as well
as that of most human beings, and law-givers should accordingly let themselves be guided by this principle. As always a
political realist, Aristotle draws a distinction between the
perfect constitution, which is aristocratic, and the best constitution, all things considered, which is the polity. Locating
my interpretation within the framework of this Aristotelian
distinction, I shall now endeavour to argue that, while *universal justice* constitutes the ideal of the *aristocratic constitution*, it is *particular* or *distributive justice* that the *polity*
is expected to foster in the citizen body. As universal justice
differs from particular justice, so, I shall contend further,
does primary friendship differ from civic friendship. As far
as oligarchies and democracies are concerned, Aristotle
appears to claim,[46] they cannot ever generate a true sense of
community among the citizenry since they are based on
deficient or incomplete notions of justice. Civic friendship, in
these constitutions, is unlikely to be anything but base-
minded.

The ideal or perfect constitution, mentioned in book III
of the *Politics* and described at length in book VII, is aristocratic. It aims at the happiness of the city and proceeds
from a correct understanding of the end of human life.[47] In
such a constitution power is invested in men of absolute
goodness who enjoy the excellences of leisure, and citizens'
rights and prerogatives are, accordingly, restricted to only
and all such men.[48] This is consonant with Aristotle's definition of a citizen as one "who has the power to take part in
the deliberative or judicial administration"[49] of the state,
and his view that those equal in status and worth should
take it in turn to rule and be ruled.[50] Young citizens will

carry arms and protect the city before increasing wisdom equips them to serve as legislators and councillors. Since moral excellence is the aim of the aristocratic community as a whole, the criteria for being a good man and those for being a good citizen do, in its case, coincide completely.[51] What its laws prescribe as just is just absolutely, and not, as in lesser constitutions, just "relatively to the principle of the constitution."[52] Lastly, in contrast with deviant constitutions, the best form of political organization ensures that the advantage of the ruling party is congruous with the interest of the state as a whole, since only those who have the ruling element in themselves are eligible to rule over others.

Although Aristotle's remarks on justice in the *Politics* are not only sketchy but also generally focused on the justice which he describes as "particular"[53] in the *Nicomachean Ethics*, references and allusions to comprehensive or universal justice do creep into his account of the perfect constitution. For instance, his characterization of the virtue of the citizens of the aristocratic constitution includes the remark that "justice has been acknowledged by us to be a social excellence, and *it implies all others*."[54] His earlier identification of human excellence with justice[55] must likewise be taken to point to universal rather than particular justice. Constitutions such as the aristocratic one, in which citizenly and individual virtue are co-extensive, draw their excellence from the fact that they promote universal justice amongst the citizen elite. As he had stated in the *Nicomachean Ethics*, compliance with good laws fosters universal justice, since such laws encourage the decent to co-operate in the (correctly conceived) public interest and coerce the many who fall short of full virtue. Aristotle's ultimate preference for the aristocratic constitution over other forms of political organization, however, raises the problem as to how many fully virtuous citizens a state can realistically be expected to contain. Aristotle's answer to this question is not unambiguous. In book VII of the *Politics* he seems to indicate that there will be a fair number of such individuals,[56] while in book III he describes the aristocratic state as a state where "more than one, but not many, rule."[57] The latter, more likely view, as we shall see, must be taken to explain why Aristotle came to view the polity as the constitution best adapted to most men in most circumstances.

The presence of both a utopian and a realistic strand in Aristotle's political thought directly pertains to the issue of civic friendship. When, as we saw, he claims in the *Nicomachean Ethics*[58] that general civic harmony results from the inner psychic concord which characterizes morally virtuous citizens, i.e., those who value the just in and for itself, we must assume that he has in mind the constitution later to be described as aristocratic in the *Politics*. Being few in number, the fully-fledged citizens of this state will not only, in the words of the *Politics*, be individually excellent,[59] but they will also be in a position intimately to know one another's characters and abilities.[60] In other words, conditions in the aristocratic state will be propitious for the formation of bonds of primary friendship, and there will be a significant overlap between civic and primary friendship.

Mindful of the gap between the best life and the life in which the majority are able to share,[61] Aristotle outlines a constitution situated in a mean between democracy and oligarchy,[62] i.e., the polity (*politeia*). His advocacy of the polity appears to be based on the realization that most states cannot be composed entirely of morally excellent citizens and that circumstances may make it advisable to select statesmen, not only on the grounds of intellectual and moral excellence, but also on those of wealth and freedom. In line with his earlier claim that the principle of fairness should be applied when apportioning power in the state,[63] Aristotle claims that fairness is best secured when councillors and magistrates have neither much to gain nor stand to lose through holding office.[64] Thus the city which has the benefit of a constitutional government is mostly governed by middle class citizens (*hoi mesoi*) who, in Aristotle's optimistic estimation, are most likely to follow reason.[65] Indeed, being equal or similar, these "do not, like the poor, covet other men's goods; nor do others covet theirs, as the poor covet the goods of the rich."[66] This, in turn, guarantees that the citizens will "pass through life safely,"[67] since they will neither plot against those better placed than themselves nor have to fear the revolt of their inferiors in wealth or status. The mean condition of the polity, Aristotle tersely comments, fosters friendship[68] and political stability.[69] Although he does not here specify which kind of friendship he has in mind, we can assume that it is the civic friendship that he had described in book VIII of the *Nicomachean Ethics*. That this is indeed most likely to be the case follows from his assertion, in the *Politics*, that friendship in the polity generates "good fellowship" which, in turn, enables men "to share the same path" and, in so doing, safeguards the community from factions and dissensions.[70] Clearly, what is here described is less a personal relation between individuals than a state of internal peace and concord in which a community can function effectively and as a whole. As the polity is inferior to the perfect constitution, so does civic friendship fall short of primary friendship. While the latter brings self-fulfillment to morally excellent persons, the former involves them *qua* citizens only, and its value is mainly instrumental.[71] We shall come back to this point.

Considerations of particular justice thus appear to be uppermost in Aristotle's mind in his discussions of the polity. Although "the best life" of full virtue or universal justice retains its function as an ideal, such ideal is explicitly assumed to be beyond the reach of the many. What the latter deserve, however, is a political organization that allows them to coexist peacefully and to go about their daily business without fear of being molested. This will be best achieved when the many, who have a vested interest in the common good, are given an opportunity, however modest, to participate in the care of the state. Such sharing of power, which initially presupposes at least a modicum of harmony amongst the citizens, is, in turn, expected to bond them further in their regard for the laws and general care for the state.

Aristotle's view that the quality of justice in a state varies according to the constitution leads him to present oligarchical and democratic justice as imperfect.[72] Indeed, once legally in power, the rich and the poor alike generally pursue their own narrowly conceived interest at the expense of the good of the whole community. When this is the case, civic friendship cannot bond the citizen body in the pursuit of common, genuinely civic goals, but fragments it into alliances, compacts, factions, and parties, each of which is dedicated to the pursuit of its own advantage. There is little trust, not only between members of different sub-groups but even between co-members of restricted associations. Indeed, as Aristotle envisages it in the *Eudemian Ethics*,[73] trust is likely to be replaced by contracts. Lacking any sense of common enterprise, oligarchies and democracies are more unstable than aristocracies and polities, and therefore more prone to revolutions.[74] They make the formation and cultivation of civic friendship well-nigh impossible.

It can now be concluded that in Aristotle's presentation both the moral worth and the political efficacy of civic friendship are functions of the state's constitution. Whether his account of the bond between citizens is commendatory (*N.E.*, IX,6) or pejorative (*E.E.*, VII,10) depends, as we saw, on the political system that he has in mind at the time, and there is little to gain from attempting an exegesis of civic friendship outside of the context of particular constitutions.[75] This unexceptionable conclusion would appear to apply as much to modern societies as it did to those of Aristotle's time. Although this is not the place for generalities on society and moral value, one may care to note that modern communal ties, too, in their extent and depth have tended to reflect the prevalent concept (collectivist, individualistic, etc.) of society. Compare, e.g., a liberal individualist's assertion, that "The community is a fictitious *body*, composed of the individual persons who are considered as constituting as it were its *members*. The interest of the community then is (. . .) the sum of the interests of the several members who compose it,"[76] with a normative communitarian's definition of a community as "a collection of humans associated by some tie or ties that are thought to have some value, and the members of which partake of cooperative activities in order to realize something that is thought to have value, and for which such association is necessary."[77] While, in the former view civic friendship can be little more than a disposition to perform felicific calculus before acting, the normative communitarian sees civic friendship as the expression of the goals and values shared by fellow citizens who respect and care for each other. At the level of everyday political rhetoric this opposition often degenerates into an exchange of slogans between, on the one hand, those who value self-reliance, the unimpeded operation of market forces, and the moral neutrality of the state and, on the other hand, those who promote free education, care, and social welfare in general and recommend or at least condone some degree of state intervention.

If civic friendship imposes varying obligations of justice in line with the principles of the constitution of the state, and if its best form, therefore, is a great good, the question arises as to whether in the perfect state it becomes co-extensive with primary or virtue friendship. While a positive answer to this question would generate the difficulty of explaining how primary friendship with more than very few individuals is possible, a negative answer would require an account of the manner in which these two kinds of friendship relate to each other. These issues will be addressed in the remainder of this chapter. Having first proceeded to a comparison between civic and primary friendship and investigated the possibility of conflicts between them, I shall then try and assess the contribution that each makes to the realization of the human good.

To prepare the ground, it will be useful, first, to flesh out Aristotle's sketchy account of the friendship of association, of which civic frienship is but one species. Invoking a modern example of such a friendship, let us investigate the nature of the communal ties that prevail between the various members of, say, a sports team, a teaching department, a professional association, or a parish. Clearly, such ties may, but need not, be of an affective nature or involve esteem for the moral and intellectual qualities of one's fellow members. Equally clearly, the members need not always choose to spend much time together and may wish to restrict their association to the common pursuit of their community or group. The community, however, gives rise to certain definite, though limited, ties and obligations, and its maintenance requires the co-operation of all its members. Upon such co-operation depends the well-being of the association; the greater the concord and harmony between its parts and the more genuine their mutual goodwill, the more successful the association will generally be in fulfilling the purposes for which it was set up or which it embodies. Internecine conflicts, bickering, and individual greed for power, fame, status, or material advantages undermine the strength and effectiveness of the association. As to the good of the association itself, it should usually take precedence over the private loyalties that may have developed between fellow members.

The viability of communities thus depends generally upon the social virtues of their members; as Aristotle said, community friendship is a variety of the friendship of utility. Of these virtues, justice is the foremost. Unlike Aristotle, we should probably not choose to call the ties of association described above as "friendships."[78] This is mainly because, as we have noted before, the modern concept of friendship has a more restricted extension than that of Greek *philia*. We should, however, generally agree that the health of associations such as the above is directly proportional to the amount of fairness and honesty that characterize the interpersonal relations which prevail between the members. In this case the grounds of such interpersonal relations cannot but be the recognition of both the benefits that individuals will derive from their membership of the association and of the demands that the common good of the association makes upon them. Those who care to use Aristotle's terminology will say that the extent of the community between the members will also be the extent of their friendship, as well as that of the fairness required of them *qua* members. The existence of specific moral obligations generated from inside associations does not, of course, *usually* invalidate the members' obligations to other associations or loyalties to personal friends.

Before discussing the possibility of conflicts between primary and community friendship, as described above in modern but broadly Aristotelian terms, the contrast between them needs to be brought out. Firstly and obviously, primary friends are chosen,[79] while civic friends and other associates come, as it were, ready-made; their status as members of specific groups or as fellow citizens suffices to entitle them to their peers' friendship of association. This is because community friendship unites a group, *qua* such, rather than, like primary friendship, individuals. Indeed, as Aristotle frequently intimates, the degree of cohesiveness of the citizen body reflects the soundness of the constitution rather than the worthiness, affective warmth, or intellectual eagerness of individual citizens. Secondly, as was argued in chapter 3 above, primary friends love their (chosen) friends for what they are in themselves rather than for their accidental properties, amongst which figure membership of restricted associations and fellow citizenship. While primary friends ascribe intrinsic worth to their association, civic friends value theirs for its benefits and the fact that these benefits can be as substantial as political stability and general prosperity does not alter their basically instrumental nature. This feature of civic friendship, in turn, causes it to be confined to one area of existence, while primary friendship permeates the whole life of those it touches. To that extent, as we saw, the latter is more fulfilling, both affectively and noetically, than the former. Thirdly, and in this context most importantly, primary friendship is described to be over and above considerations of particular justice. While all other *koinōniai* are regulated by the standards and values embodied in particular justice, the friendship of virtue is generally said to make particular justice redundant: ". . . if people are friends, they have no need of justice, but if they are just they need friendship in addition."[80] Virtuous friends need not have recourse to considerations of particular justice in dealing with each other, as they do when interacting with their fellow citizens, colleagues, associates, team-mates, fellow-parishioners, etc. The reason is twofold: not only are those capable of primary friendship fully virtuous by definition, but, more relevantly, their mutual affection is such that it precludes the need to keep their individual egoistic drives under control. In primary friendship, as was argued in chapter 5 above, the tension between egoism and altruism does not even arise, and the virtuous who sacrifices his life for his friend is said to be choosing "what is fine at the cost of everything."[81] The extreme or even supererogatory character of such a sacrifice shows that primary friendship is situated on a moral plane where ordinary considerations of particular justice have ceased to be relevant.

The existence of clear distinctions between primary and civic friendship lends some urgency to the question as to whether they can generate conflicting obligations. If primary friends can be relied upon to be perfectly honest in their mutual dealings, one will nevertheless wonder whether they might not on occasion be tempted to further each other's good at the expense of those outside the charmed circle of their perfect friendship. Is it conceivable, in other words, that the personal bond of primary friendship could come into conflict with the impartiality requirements of particular justice? Had this question, which expresses a real difficulty for most modern conceptions of friendship,[82] been put to him, Aristotle would almost certainly have answered in the negative. Firstly, as we noted before, the *main* spring of Aristotelian friendship is moral goodness rather than non-rational attraction. Secondly, Aristotle's ethics of virtue encompasses the moral personality as a whole and conceives of the moral virtues as inseparable.[83] Partners in such friendship, therefore, will ". . . neither request nor provide assistance that requires base actions."[84] In the unlikely event that otherwise virtuous agents be tempted to act basely, their (primary) friends would restrain them, since ". . . it is proper to good people to avoid error themselves and not to permit it in their friends."[85] The possibility of conflicts between the demands of primary friendship and obligations of justice is therefore ruled out in

Aristotle's ethics. Indeed, he who asks his (primary) friend to act unjustly thereby manifests his own lack of virtue, and he who is minded to act unjustly for his (primary) friend's sake thereby allows his rational element, i.e., his own self, to be subjugated by non-rational affection. To the extent that he makes his friend's mistakenly conceived good his own good, he fails to grasp the true end of human action. We may surmise that such considerations formed the background of Aristotle's famous epigrammatic allusion to Plato: "though we love both the truth and our friends, piety requires us to honour the truth first."[86]

From the extreme unlikelihood of conflicts between primary friendship and the requirements of justice it can more specifically be inferred that, exceptional cases apart, the demands of primary and civic friendship will not clash either. Sound constitutions in the persons of their legitimate rulers will neither demand nor condone betrayals and other base actions. The dilemma later envisaged by Cicero[87] and popularized in our time by E.M. Forster ("If I had to choose between betraying my country and betraying my friend I hope I would have the guts to betray my country"[88]) could therefore not arise in a true aristocracy or in a polity. As for perverted constitutions, where the ruling party pursues its own advantage at the ready expense of the public good, they only generate rival factions and alliances (*summachiai*)[89] whose claims on the virtuous person's loyalty cannot compare with those of primary friendship. The fact that despotic rulers often encourage the mass of citizens to view them as the embodiment of the fatherland and try to exact the loyalty which by right is owed to the political community at large is not really germane to the present discussion. Although a tyrant (e.g., Creon in Sophocles' *Antigone*) may well rely on the argument that "he who puts a friend above his country is his country's enemy"[90] to prevent a subject (viz., Antigone) from giving due burial rites to her dead friend/brother who had plotted the tyrant's overthrow, his edict does not generate a conflict between primary and civic friendship. All that is at issue in this case is a clash between political obedience, which is not to be confused with civic friendship, and loyalty to a friend.

Having argued that the extent of the overlap between primary and civic friendship reflects both the nature and the worth of the political constitution, and that they are unlikely to generate conflicts of duties, we now address the question of their mutual relationship. Is either an extension or a development of the other, and, if so, which is the more end-like of the two? These questions, which must now briefly be addressed, are difficult since textual support is thin or even non-existent, and any answer to them will therefore have to be correspondingly speculative. Further, they presuppose a stand on the notoriously complex issue of the nature, practical or theoretical, of the good life.

Predictably, there are a number of exegeses to choose from. Both Aubenque and Fraisse have argued that primary friendship is a more elevated form of association than civic friendship. In any case, they point out, it elicited Aristotle's most profound thoughts on the matter.[91] In Barker's wake,[92] on the other hand, Price has recently argued that civic friendship constitutes a moral and political development from primary friendship: "civic friendship is indeed an extended variety of the friendship of the good."[93] His complex and detailed argument rests on the assumption, claimed to be "Aristotelian,"[94] that "It is (. . .) necessary if a city is to flourish that its members should value the general well-being for its own sake, in short that they should have good-will towards one another; and goodwill presupposes a belief that the other has (or can develop) the virtues required for *eudaimonia*. Thus the foundation for a flourishing city must be a kind of friendship on account of virtue."[95] Irwin, who adopts a median position, argues that in the best city civic friendship will present some of the defining features of primary friendship, viz., cooperative deliberation about the good, worthy common aims, and other selfhood. It is for this reason, he intimates, that Aristotle can claim that "political activity, and especially the distinctively political form of rule that consists in ruling and being ruled, is an intrinsic good, part of the happiness of each citizen. It is one example of cooperative deliberation involving people who regard each other as other selves; and it is a distinctive example of such deliberation, in so far as it seeks the complete good in the complete association."[96]

All agree, of course, that happiness, as *eudaimonia*, cannot really be achieved outside a community. The vast majority of commentators, including all those mentioned above, further understand the community in question to be political. In this they are surely right. Indeed, supposing that an ordered and harmonious civic life could obtain without his active participation, the virtuous person would nevertheless not desire to restrict his social life to the small circle of his like-minded primary friends. He would understand that the excellence of the city requires the dedication of all its capable citizens, and he would act accordingly. It is the city, as Aristotle repeatedly states, which embodies the perfect good for humans: ". . . though admittedly the good is the same for a city as for an individual, still the good of the city is apparently a greater and more complete good to acquire and preserve. For while it is satisfactory to acquire and preserve the good even for an individual, it is finer and more divine to acquire and preserve it for a people and for cities."[97] In this respect Aristotle's viewpoint could not be further from Epicurus'. Yet, as I shall now try and argue, *pace* Price, Aristotle's views on the political nature of the good life need not entail that civic friendship be an extension of, and a development from, primary friendship.

Firstly, if Aristotle himself had viewed civic friendship as virtue friendship writ large, he would most probably have said so in his extensive treatment of the grounds and forms of civic association. In fact, as was noted before, the topic of friendship is only perfunctorily broached in the *Politics*; more likely than not, Aristotle saw no reason to improve on his recently completed analysis of the subject in the *Nicomachean Ethics*. Secondly, he states explicitly that primary friendship is likely to be rare (*spania*) precisely because those capable of it are few and far between.[98] If virtue friendship is rare, it cannot function as a base for the more common phenomenon of civic friendship, which Aristotle likens to a bonding agent for the state.[99] As he wrote in a decisive statement: "it is possible to be a friend of many in a fellow citizen's way (. . .) but it is impossible to be many people's friend for their virtue and for themselves."[100] Although virtue friendship might just conceivably obtain between the few outstandingly virtuous rulers of the perfect state, we cannot assume that it would be very common, even amongst the polity's citizens, however sincere and earnest they be in their pursuit of the common good.

The superiority of virtue friendship over civic friendship, however, rests ultimately on the former's noetic character. If successful, the arguments of the previous chapters have established that friends of virtue love one another for what they are in themselves, viz., their practical reason or understanding. Virtue friendship involves each partner in the cultivation of his own essential self and consists in the joint making of other selves. Other selfhood, in turn, ensures that the partners not only realize in themselves the conditions of the moral life, but also know that they so realize them. Primary friendship thus has a cognitive character which one might well describe as semi-contemplative. *Qua* citizen—and there is no doubt that Aristotle held that active citizenship in a sound *polis* is essential to human flourishing—the virtuous person is engaged in the practical activity of contributing to the public good. *Qua* other self to one or a few others, the virtuous person not only practices a range of moral excellences, but also gains self-awareness as well as a deeper understanding of the moral life lived at its best. In that respect primary friendship could be said to constitute a resting place for the virtuous and prepare him for the life of contemplation (*theōria*).[101]

While primary friendship brings higher actualization to the few, civic friendship is likely to further the good of the greater number. While it is conceivable although not likely that primary and civic friendship be co-extensive in a perfect state, i.e., a state where the citizens, few in numbers, are wise and fully virtuous, these two kinds of friendship will at best overlap in less than perfect constitutions.[102] More specifically, in the polity the goods of shared deliberation and common undertaking are made available to all sound citizens, although they fall short of full excellence. As far as deviant constitutions are concerned, where only debased forms of civic friendship prevail, the extent of primary friendship in them is determined by the moral integrity and the dedication of private, politically disengaged individuals. Aristotle's commitment to the *polis* prevented him from even envisaging how primary friendship could survive political instability and corruption, and it was left to Hellenistic philosophers to do it in his stead.

Civic friendship, it can now be concluded, is an altogether different bond from the friendship of virtue. It fulfills a primarily political function and is subject to the obligations of particular justice. As such it constitutes the fertile soil in which the friendship of virtue can grow freely between select individuals whose comprehensive virtue, or universal justice, is sustained by their full understanding of the end of human life. To claim that civic friendship constitutes the end point of the friendship of virtue is, in one sense, over-optimistic in so far as it ultimately negates the Aristotelian distinction between the many and the wise. In politically favourable circumstances the many can and should achieve civic friendship. Yet only the wise can ever hope to reach the height of primary friendship.

CONCLUSION

Those who study ethical matters, Aristotle professed, should not disregard common opinions or the experience of the ages. Since the study of Greek literature of the time gives us no reason to doubt that he practiced what he preached, we can assume that his substantive account of the different forms of *philia* in both *Ethics* does not significantly depart from contemporary views on the matter. Rather than attempting to innovate, convert, or reform, Aristotle tidied, refined, systematized, and attempted to provide comprehensive justification for such beliefs on the matter as had been expressed in his culture by the many and the wise. Yet, as the influence he continues to exert testifies, his was no mere parochial outlook. While discoursing on what then held good usually and for the most part, he elaborated theories that have withstood the test of time. While systematizing the spirit of his time and place, he often transcended it. His analyses of the various forms of friendship have remained the *terminus a quo* for later writers on the subject, from Cicero to the present day via Aquinas and Montaigne.

This notwithstanding, Aristotle's account of primary or virtue friendship does not fully match corresponding modern notions, and parts of it are prone to strike present-day readers as rebarbative or even repellent. Many students who first encounter Aristotle's philosophy of friendship brand it unrealistic, unfeeling, unacceptably elitist, and, therefore as holding no more than an antiquarian interest.

In this study, I have not sought to gloss over what must be recognized as significant discrepancies between ancient and modern intuitions on friendship. At the same time, I have tried to avoid approaching anthropologically a philosopher who formed the tradition from which we continue to feed. Accordingly, while reflecting on Aristotle's text—which was my primary concern—I have also tried to identify, describe, and explain those aspects of his thoughts on friendship which differ, or appear *prima facie* to differ, from ours. In the process, I hope to have helped elucidating some of our own, often unexamined and unchallenged, modern intuitions and presuppositions.

Aristotle's concept of primary friendship, I have here argued, lies at the very core of his ethics. From his considerations on the best human good and moral virtue, a normative view of selfhood emerges. According to it, only those individuals can be said to be selves who have succeeded in harmonizing, within their own lives, the claims of reason, emotion, and appetite. Although becoming a self is not, of course, the same as becoming virtuous, the two processes are co-extensive, and the wicked, as well as the akratic, remain mere *loci* of incongruous, dissonant, and divergent forces.

Making primary friendship, by reference to which all other forms of friendship are described, dependent on moral virtue, Aristotle further characterizes this personal relationship as a joint becoming, by the partners, of one another's selves. In so far as it can be transpersonal and represents a moral ideal, Aristotelian selfhood thus doubly departs from corresponding modern notions. While later philosophers are concerned with the continuing sameness of individuals through change, Aristotle sets out to identify the conditions which individuals must meet in order actually to become what they have it in them to become. While Aristotle's modern successors focus on the unicity of individuals, he is concerned with specific essences. Unsurprisingly, therefore, their theories of the identity of persons are descriptive in intent while his notion of self, following from prior claims on the human function (*ergon*), is primarily normative.

These differences bear directly on the issue of inter-personal affective relations and the moral issues that they raise. Modern theories of personal identity, which rule out other selfhood by definition and, in effect, promote a con-ception of human beings as locked within the confines of their own singularity, cannot easily account for the experi-ence of deep friendship. Indeed, a note of puzzlement creeps into even the most literary and famous accounts of elective affinities, as, e.g., Goethe's "they [Ottilie and Eduard] exerted upon each other an indescribable, almost magical, attraction"[1] bears witness. In Aristotle's ethics, on the other hand, we find a full and, at times, moving account of the reciprocal awareness, intimate communion, and benevo-lence that human relationships can provide.

Further, the ethical issue of egoism *versus* altruism, which directly pertains to friendship, is considerably less thorny for Aristotle than for a number of modern theorists. Viewing the self as a cluster of singular mental states, and human nature as inherently selfish and, thus, largely beyond moral education, the latter cannot easily account for the esteem in which disinterested friendship is generally held nor justify the moral requirements that it embodies. Aristotle, by contrast, for whom selfhood is a moral goal, can claim *both* that friendship benefits the agent *and* that it disinterestedly seeks the good of another. Reason, around which he centres the self, is for him no mere instrument at the service of the passions, but the agency which enables humans to identify the goal(s) of human life and to tutor their various wants and drives accordingly. Even though virtuous persons derive self-actualization from their mutual communing, he persuasively argues, the interpersonal nature of their goals and values ensures that they could never reduce each other to the status of mere instruments.

Although the moral precept that friends should be loved in and for themselves has been upheld from Greek antiquity to this day, its justification has reflected doctrinal shifts in conceptions of the self. When Aristotle writes that a primary friend loves his friend for his, i.e., the friend's, sake, he does not mean that he cherishes him, warts and all, in his uniqueness. Rather, he intimates, it is the "self" of the other that he loves, i.e., his virtuous rationality or, what amounts to the same, his rationally defined virtue. Only virtuous agents are lovable, he contends, and only of them does it make sense to say that they should be loved for themselves. Correspondingly, we infer, only virtuous agents are capable of loving disinterestedly.

If Aristotle's assimilation of the self to reason thus spares him and his followers some awkward problems, it arguably lands him in difficulties of another kind which modern theories succeed in side-stepping. Firstly, in making primary friendship the preserve of virtuous persons, Aristotle appears to exclude compassionateness, mercy, and lenity from the emotional landscape of friendship. Yet, as, e.g., Paul Gilbert has claimed, "We have a particular admiration for those people who are able to love others whose good qualities are far from obvious, and we think of the love they bear them as particularly precious."[2] This disparity between ancient and modern perceptions, which in this instance must be attributed to the influence of Christianity, cannot easily be overcome or settled. Having included equality of worth and reciprocity in the quality of affection among the necessary conditions of fully-fledged friendship, Aristotle could not but conclude that, whatever other personal relations virtuous men might have with their inferiors in moral excellence, it could not be friendship in the full sense of the term. Although, like Aristotle, we view friendship as reciprocal and the partners as equals *within the relationship*, we do not regard it as a source of unique moral or, indeed, noetic actualization. Unlike him, therefore, we can subsume under the name of friendship various associations in which reciprocal affection of a kind overrides differences in the partners' moral integrity or intellectual standing. How wide can such differences be before we want to call the relationship something else than friendship? Although the issue cannot be resolved in the abstract, it is worth noting that in the above quoted text Gilbert uses 'love' rather than 'friendship', thereby showing that he may have been influenced by current perceptions[3] of what constitutes Christian *agapē*.

In his seminal article "Plato: The Individual as an Object of Love,"[4] Gregory Vlastos has given authoritative formulation to a second criticism often levelled at Aristotelian friendship. Indeed, although Vlastos mostly directs his arguments at Platonic doctrines, he maintains that Aristotle's own views on the subject constitute no real improvement on Plato's.[5] According to Vlastos, Plato held that

> We are to love the persons so far, and only in so far, as they are good and beautiful. Now since all too few human beings are masterworks of excellence, and not even the best of those we have the chance to love are wholly free of streaks of the ugly, the mean, the commonplace, the ridiculous, if our love for them is to be only for their virtue and beauty, the individual, in the uniqueness and integrity of his or her individuality, will never be the object of our love. This seems to me the cardinal flaw in Plato's theory. It does not provide for love of whole persons, but only for love of that abstract version of persons which consists of the complex of their best qualities.[6]

As the sucess of his article indicates, Vlastos articulated a common modern intuition about love and friendship. Disregarding the extensive and protracted arguments generated amongst Platonic scholars by Vlastos' criticism, we must now ask whether it was justifiably extended to Aristotle.

Scholarly responses to Vlastos' criticisms have generally borne the stamp of their authors' (modern) intuitions. They have largely been attempts to vindicate Plato's and Aristotle's views on love against criticisms which, interestingly enough, are assumed to be unimpeachable. Although it may well be impossible to divest oneself of the intuitions of one's time and culture, the realization that others have, or have had, different intuitions should make us wary of leaving our own unscrutinized. In fact, the examination of our own presuppositions about love and friendship might well reveal that we are less than wholly committed to the view that true affection is directed at the unique individuality of its object.

Let it first be conceded that Aristotle's reliance on a noetic conception of selfhood effectively directs his attention away from what Vlastos calls "the uniqueness and integrity" of individuals. Ascribing such uniqueness mostly to contingency, Aristotle does not regard it as a fit object of wonder and respect to be cared for and judiciously nurtured. On the contrary, as we saw, he considers that any love that is motivated by the coincidental, accidental, and, to that extent, individual characteristics of another cannot but fall short of the best kind of friendship.

It may well be because most modern ethical theories provide a rule-governed and universalist account of moral obligation that, until recently, many writers on love and friendship needed to compensate by stressing, perhaps overly so, the uniqueness of the object of love. It should further be noted that the current renewal of interest in virtue, i.e., agent-centred, ethics has led philosophers to address once again the issue of friendship. The fact that these philosophers appear to draw much inspiration from Aristotle's writings on the topic indicates that his views cannot be as counterintuitive to modern minds as is sometimes professed.

Where, in any case, do we anchor the uniqueness we are alleged so to prize? Is it in our mental states? But these are mostly private and, to that extent, opaque to others. Is it more likely in the sum total of our innate, as well as acquired, characteristics, qualities, and dispositions? But we feel demeaned or insecure when we are loved for innate, possibly trivial characteristics (e.g., a classically shaped nose or a beautiful singing voice) whose presence in us is purely fortuitous. Further, we generally take care to hide from our prospective lovers and friends what we consider to be shortcomings on our part; although they may well contribute to making us different from all others, they do not, in our own view, constitute an adequate basis for love. Lastly, we tend to suspect the motivation of those whose love thrives on the less desirable characteristics of the beloved (e.g., "his singular inability to fill in forms," "her surely unequalled indecisiveness"); their unduly fragile egos, we surmise, need to be constantly reassured by the incompetence of the objects of their love. In so far as we generally want to be loved for qualities which are both commendable and central to our personality, our intuitions may not be so much at variance with Aristotle's contention that the best love is the meeting point of worth and feeling as Vlastos *et al.* appear to assume.

It must to be pointed out, lastly, that although Aristotle leaves out of philosophical account the singularity of the object of love, he does emphasize the uniqueness of each and every relationship that merits the accolade of primary friendship. The formation of friendship is a protracted affair, he repeatedly indicates, and "people need time to grow accustomed to each other."[7] Friendship itself involves living together, sharing pleasures and sorrows, successes and disappointments, and accumulating a rich stock of shared experiences. Although each partner could very well have had other friends and different friendships, the bond between them is made unique by the circumstances of its development as well as by the common past that sustains it. Montaigne's claim that his own friendship with Etienne de la Boétie "has not other model than itself, and can be compared only with itself"[8] can be extended to each and every primary Aristotelian friendship.

It can therefore be seen that although Aristotle accounted for the best of all interpersonal relationships in terms of rationality and noetic actualization, he did not for all that forget that it engages the affects of those it bonds. Further, in individuating moral virtue and in showing how the virtuous person's life is enriched by the excellence of his friend's particular commitments, goals, and actions, he succeeded in striking a balance between what is now seen as the rival claims of ethical impartialism and particularism.

NOTES

Introduction

1. L. von Ranke, *Geschichte der romanischen und germanischen Völker von 1492 bis 1535*, Berlin, 1824, preface.

2. R.-A. Gauthier and J.Y. Jolif, *L'Ethique à Nicomaque. Introduction, Traduction et Commentaire*, second edition, Louvain et Paris, Beatrice-Nauwelaerts, 1970, II, 2, p. 655-658.

3. A.W.H. Adkins, *Merit and Responsibility*, Oxford, 1960, p. 31 and chapter xvi, *passim* and "'Friendship' and 'Self-Sufficiency' in Homer and Aristotle," *The Classical Quarterly*, 1963.

4. E. Benveniste, *Le Vocabulaire des Institutions Indo-Européennes*, Paris, Editions de Minuit, 1969, p. 347 sqq.

5. A comprehensive state of the question is to be found in J. Hooker, 'Homeric φίλος', *GLOTTA*, Band LXV, 1987, to which I am indebted.

6. On this usage, and the misinterpretations to which it gave rise, cf., most notably E. Benveniste, *op. cit.*, p. 337-353.

7. *Iliad*, VI.

8. Cf. most notably A.W.H. Adkins, 1963.

9. See, e.g., M. Whitlock Blundell, *Helping Friends and Harming Enemies*, Cambridge University Press, Cambridge, 1989.

10. Herodotus, I, 53,56,69,70; II, 152; III, 21,74,138; V, 70; VII, 135; VIII, 90,140,143; IX, 33. I am here endebted to J. Enoch Powell, *A Lexicon to Herodotus*, Georg Olms Verlag, Hildesheim, 2nd ed., 1960 (1st ed. Cambridge, 1938).

179

11. Xenophon, *Memorabilia*, II, V.

12. *N.E.*, 1177a32-34.

Chapter 1

1. This phrase is borrowed from P. Huby, *Greek Ethics*, Macmillan, London, 1967, p. 62. A similar view is held by Robert Flacelière, *L'Amour en Grèce*, Paris, Hachette, 1960, p. 167, whose tone is clearly laudatory when he states that "Aristote garde toujours les pieds sur la terre et ne se perd pas dans les nuages."

2. Two commentators who have recently felt very 'provoked' are E. Millgram, "Aristotle on Making Other Selves," *Canadian Journal of Philosophy*, Volume 17, Number 2, June 1987, and J. Benson, "Making Friends. Aristotle's Doctrine of the Friend as Another Self," in A. Loizou and H. Lesser (eds.), *Polis and Politics. Essays in Greek Moral and Political Philosophy*, Avebury, Aldershot, 1990.

3. *M.M.*, 1213a23-24.

4. *E.E.*, 1245a29-30.

5. Aristotle, *The Eudemian Ethics*, translated by H. Rackham, footnote to 1245a31-32. This view is endorsed by F. Dirlmeier, *Aristoteles, Magna Moralia*, Akademie Verlag, Berlin, 1958, pp. 470-71. Dirlmeier further stresses that in this context *allos* means *alter* rather than *alius* before concluding that "Gefordert ist also der Gedanke: In eben dem Sinne, in dem man von eimem *zweiten Herakles* spricht, ist der Freund ein zweites Ich."

6. *E.E.*, 1245a34-35.

7. *N.E.*, 1161b28-29, 1166a32, 1169b6-7, 1170b6-7.

8. Cicero, *De Amicitia*, XXI, 80; transl. by W.A. Falconer, Heinemann, London, 1923.

9. Thomas Aquinatis, *In Decem Libros Ethicorum Aristotelis Ad Nicomachum Expositio*, Marietti, Romae, 1909, my translation and italics.

10. H. Bonitz, *Index Aristotelicus*, Berlin, 1870, p. 125, my translation.

11. A detailed analysis of these complex arguments is offered in Chapter VI below.

12. Cf., e.g., S.R.L. Clark, *Aristotle's Man*, Clarendon Press, Oxford, 1975, p. 101, B. Williams, *Shame and Necessity*, University of California Press, Berkeley, CA, 1993, pp. 21-26, and B. Knox, *The Oldest Dead White European Males*, W.W. Norton and Co., New York and London, 1993, pp. 37-47.

13. M. Foucault, *The Care of the Self. The History of Sexuality*, vol. 3, transl. by R. Hurley, Penguin Books, Harmondsworth, 1984, pp. 42-43.

14. J.-P. Vernant, *L'Individu, la Mort, l'Amour: Soi-même et Autre en Grèce Ancienne*, Paris, Gallimard, 1989, p. 214ff.

15. Ibid., p. 224, my translation.

16. Ibid., p. 225, my translation. Benveniste expresses a similar view: ". . . Homer's whole moral terminology is everywhere shot through with values that are, not individual, but relational," *op. cit.*, p. 340, my translation.

17. For *'hena thumon echontes,'* cf. *Iliad*, XIII, 487; XV, 710, XVI, 219, and XVIII, 267. For *'ison thumon echontes,'* cf. *Iliad*, XIII, 704 and XVII, 720. Both sets of references were culled from the *Iliad* by B. Snell in an attempt to show that these expressions do not constitute a serious counter-example to his well-known and controversial thesis that Homer conceived of the mental as a cluster of discrete parts, identifiable only by their external effects or objects. For more ample detail, see his review of J. Boehme, *Die Seele und das Ich im homerischen Epos* (Leipzig: Teubner, 1928), *Gnomon, Band 7*, 1931, p. 84, as well, of course, as his more famous *The Discovery of the Mind*, transl. by T.G. Rosenmeyer, Dover Publications Inc, New York, N.Y., 1953, chapters 1 and 3.

18. *Iliad* XVIII, 82.

19. As H. Monsacré has remarked in *Les Larmes d'Achille. Le héros, la femme et la souffrance dans la poésie d'Homère*, Paris, Albin Michel, 1984, pp. 59-60. Cf., too, C.H. Whitman, *Homer and the Heroic Tradition*, Harvard University Press, Cambridge MA, 1958, p. 201.

20. A.W.H. Adkins, "Friendship and 'Self-Sufficiency' in Homer and Aristotle," *The Classical Quarterly*, 1963, p. 30.

21. On the metonymical use of *kara*, (head) cf., e.g. J.-P. Vernant, 1989, pp. 11-12.

22. For an interesting discussion of these lines, and of the problems they generate for the translator, cf. G. Steiner, *Antigones*, Clarendon Press, Oxford, 1986, pp. 201-15.

23. Euripides, *Orestes*, 1042.

24. Ibid., 1192.

25. *E.E.*, 1240b3.

26. *N.E.*, 1168b7.

27. In addition to those mentioned above, see I. Meyerson, *Problèmes de la Personne*, Mouton and Co., Paris and The Hague, 1973, J.-P. Vernant, *Essai sur l'Individualisme*, Paris, 1983, and Charles Taylor, *Sources of the Self: The Making of the Modern Identity*, Cambridge University Press, Cambridge, 1989, chap. 6 and 7.

28. J.-P. Vernant, 1989, p. 224.

29. D.A., II, 5, *passim*.

30. Ibid., 418a14-15.

31. Ibid., 425b15-16.

32. Ibid., 425b20 and 426a7-8.

33. Ibid., 426b8-12.

34. Ibid., 426b17-23, my italics. Cf., too, 431a21-22 and *De Sensu*, VII.

35. *D.A.*, 426b29.

36. I here follow the interpretations of R.D. Hicks, *Aristotle, De Anima*, Cambridge University Press, 1907, of J. Tricot, *Aristote. De l'âme*, Paris, Vrin, 1977, p. 152 sqq, and of D.K.W. Modrak, *Aristotle. The Power of Perception*, The University of Chicago Press, Chicago and London, 1987, pp. 62-71. In his *Aristotle's De Anima Books II and III*, translated with commentary and notes, Clarendon Press, Oxford, 1968, pp. 128-29 and 146-47, D. Hamlyn argues against the identification of the unified faculty of sense with the common sense.

37. *D.A.*, 418a17-18.

38. Ibid., 427a9.

39. Ibid., 426b29.

40. Ibid., 426b18-20.

41. *De Somno et Vigilia*, 455a15-17, transl. by J.I. Beare.

42. *N.E.*, 1170a31-1170b1.

43. Ibid., 1170a33.

44. D.W. Hamlyn, *op. cit.*, p. XIII. Cf, too, D. Ross, *Aristotle*, Methuen, London, 1964 (first edition 1923), pp. 141-42, and D.K.W. Modrack, *op. cit.*, chapters 3 and 6, *passim*.

45. R. Descartes, *Philosophical Writings*, transl. by J. Cottingham, R. Stoothoff, and D. Murdoch, Vol. II, Cambridge University Press, Cambridge, 1984, p. 18.

46. As Charles H. Kahn notes, "The Greek of Aristotle's day has no term which really corresponds to the modern usage of 'consciousness' (. . .) It is the term for sense perception—*aisthesis*—which comes closest to providing a parallel to the modern notion of consciousness in Aristotle's language," "Sensation and Consciousness in Aristotle's Psychology," in J. Barnes, M. Schofield, R. Sorabji (eds.), *Articles on Aristotle*, Vol. IV, Duckworth, London, 1979, pp. 22-23.

47. R. Descartes, Ibid., p. 22.

48. I do not here mean to suggest that Aristotle's and Descartes' theories of perception are totally at variance with each other. Rather, I hold, with A. Plomer, to whose *Phenomenology, Geometry and Vision* (Avebury, Aldershot, 1991) I am here indebted, that such similarities between Aristotle and Descartes as their handling of 'common-sensibles', are more than offset by crucial differences in metaphysical outlook.

49. D. Hume, *A Treatise of Human Nature*, Bk. I, Pt. IV, Section VI., ed. by L.A. Selby-Bigge, Clarendon Press, Oxford, 1888, p. 252.

50. Ibid., p. 253.

51. G. Ryle, *The Concept of Mind*, Hutchinson, London, 1949, *passim*, but, more particularly, p. 167 ff.

52. *N.E.*, 1098a12-17.

53. Ibid., 1168b34-35.

54. Ibid., 1166a13-17.

55. Ibid., 1151a1, my italics.

56. Ibid., 1148a29, my italics.

57. Ibid., 1147a17, my italics.

58. Ibid., 1166b7, my italics.

59. *E.E.*, 1239b11-14.

60. *N.E.*, 1161b27-29.

61. Ibid., 1166a29-32.

62. Ibid., 1169b5-7.

63. Ibid., 1170b5-7.

64. Although the fact that in this case the implied subject to which αὐτάρκεις is attached is in the plural and the pronouns in the singular makes the sentence syntactically clumsy, it does not, I think, make it obscure.

65. This point has not been lost on modern commentators. Cf., e.g., W. Jaeger, *Paideia: the Ideals of Greek Culture*, trans. by G. Highet, Blackwell, Oxford, 1957, Vol. II, pp. 343-44 and S.R.L. Clark, *Aristotle's Man*, Clarendon Press, Oxford, 1975, III, 3, *passim*, who reach the same conclusion through different routes.

66. *N.E.*, 1107a1.

67. Ibid., 1177a12-18.

68. Ibid., 1177b26-30.

69. Ibid., 1177b31-1178a2.

70. Ibid., 1178a2-4.

71. Ibid., 1178a22.

72. As defended, e.g., by J. Cooper in "Contemplation and Happiness: A Reconsideration," *Synthese*, Vol. 72, no. 2, 1987, and R. Kraut, *Aristotle on the Human Good*, Princeton University Press, Princeton N.J., 1989.

73. F. Nuyens, *L'Evolution de la Psychologie d'Aristote*, Editions de l'Institut Supérieur de Philosophie, Louvain, 1948, pp 192-93.

74. R.A. Gauthier et J.Y. Jolif, *op. cit.*, II, 2, pp. 728-29 and 893-96.

75. Cf., notably W.F.R. Hardie, *Aristotle's Ethics*, Clarendon Press, Oxford, 2nd ed., 1980, p. 71 ff., and J.M. Cooper, *Reason and Human Good in Aristotle*, Harvard University Press, Cambridge, MA, 1975, p. 157n.

76. Be it noted here that Aristotle does not explicitly describe the active intellect as ποιητικός. What he does say is that this intellect has the ability το ποιεῖν πάντα ("to produce all things"), D.A. 430a12. In common with most commentators, ancient and modern, I nevertheless characterize the higher intellect as ποιητικός for brevity's and clarity's sake.

77. *D.A.*, 429b14-18.

78. Ibid., 430a10-19.

79. Ibid., 430a22-23.

80. As, e.g., S.R.L. Clark, following Alexander and Zabarella, claims in *op. cit.*, V.3, *passim*.

81. D. Ross, *op. cit.*, p. 151.

82. Ibid., ibid.

83. *D.A.*, 430a23.

84. *N.E.*, 1177b30-31. Cf., too, *Met.*, 1075a7-9.

85. This interpretation makes Nuyens' hypothesis superfluous. Additional evidence against it could conceivably be adduced from the use of a Platonic metaphor in *De Anima*, 430a15, where Aristotle compares the active intellect to light: ὁ δὲ τῷ πάντα ποιεῖν, ὡς ἕξις τις, οἷον τὸ φῶς ("there is an intellect which is so by producing all things, so a kind of disposition, like light"). This allusion to the famous analogy of the sun in *Republic*, 508a, would seem to indicate that Aristotle still found it useful to refer to the master's metaphors even when, as in this case, he had radically departed from the master's substantial doctrines.

Chapter 2

1. *E.E.*, VII,2; *N.E.*, VIII,3-7. Cf., too, *Rhet.*, II, 28.

2. *N.E.*, 1157a30-32; cf., too, 1158b5-8.

3. Ibid., 1156b7-8, 1157a10-11, 1164a9-10.

4. *E.E.*, 1236b22-4.

5. J.M. Cooper, "Aristotle on the Forms of Friendship," in *The Review of Metaphysics*, 30, 1976-7.

6. K.D. Alpern, "Aristotle and the Friendships of Utility and Pleasure," in *The Journal for the History of Philosophy*, 21, 1983.

7. J.M. Cooper, 1976-7, pp. 633-34.

8. *N.E.*, 1156a17-19.

9. Ibid., 1156b10 and 1166a4.

10. *E.E.*, 1237b4.

11. *N.E.*, 1158b23-28.

12. I. Kant, *Groundwork of the Metaphysic of Morals*, (1st ed., Berlin, 1785), transl. by H.J. Paton, Hutchinson, London, 1948, p. 65.

13. O. Hanfling, "Loving My Neighbour, Loving Myself," *Philosophy*, Vol. 68, no. 264, 1993.

14. R.W. Emerson, "Friendship." Thanks are due to Janet Seacombe for drawing this passage to my attention.

15. Luke, XV.3-31.

16. *E.E.*, 1241a40.

17. Ibid., 1237a36sqq.; *N.E.*, 1168a19-20.

18. *N.E.*, 1159a34-35.

19. Ibid., e.g., 1102b14-18, 1111b13-16, 1136b6-9.

20. *Met.*, 1048b18sqq. I am here indebted to J. Tricot's commentary, Paris, Vrin, 1966.

21. *Met.*, 1050a34-1050b2.

22. Ibid., XI, 7, *passim*.

23. *E.E.*, 1236a39-b1; *N.E.*, 1156a34-5.

24. *N.E.*, 1170b28-9.

25. Matthew, V.13.

26. J. Benson, *op. cit.*, pp. 50-69. A similar interpretation is

defended in N. Sherman, *The Fabric of Character. Aristotle's Theory of Virtue*, Clarendon Press, Oxford, 1989, pp. 148-49.

27. *N.E.*, 1161a16-17.

28. Ibid., 1168a3-5.

29. J. Benson, *op. cit.*, p. 58.

30. *N.E.*, 1161a18-20.

31. *Pol.*, 1253a2-3.

32. Ibid., 1262b7.

33. *N.E.*, 1155a23-24.

34. *Pol.*, 1252b30-2.

35. *N.E.*, 1155a26-28.

36. Ibid., 1169a18sqq. This passage is discussed at length in chapter 5 below.

37. Ibid., 1169b12.

38. Ibid., 1104b3-5.

39. Ibid., 1155a3-4.

40. Ibid., 1170b11-12.

41. Ibid., 1106b36-1108a1.

42. *E.E.*, 1216b21-23; likewise *N.E.*, 1179b2-3.

43. *N.E.*, 1139a21-26.

44. *D.A.*, 431a14-16.

45. Ibid., 432a7-9. Cf., too, *Posterior Analytics*, 81a38.

46. *D.A.*, 431a12-17.

47. *N.E.*, 1179b23-26.

48. *M.M.*, 1213a15-24. The fact that the authenticity of the *M.M.* is still open to question does not affect the issue, since the passage quoted conveys a well-known Aristotelian claim.

49. *N.E.*, 1169b33-35.

50. Ibid., 1169b33-1170a1.

51. *D.A.*, 429a13-24.

52. Ibid., ibid.

53. *D.A.*, 429b5-9.

54. Cf., e.g., *Met.*, 1015a3-5.

55. *E.E.*, 1245a35-37.

56. *E.E.*, 1245a5-9, my italics.

57. p. 21.

58. *N.E.*, 1170a29-1170b1.

59. Ibid., 1170b5-7.

60. Ibid., 1170b7-8.

61. I am here indebted to Jonathan Lear's account of νοῦς in *Aristotle: the Desire to Understand*, Cambridge University Press, 1988, chapter IV, sections 3 and 4.

62. *D.A.*, 424a17-19.

63. Ibid., 432a2.

64. Ibid., 429b3-4.

65. Ibid., 417b23-4.

66. Ibid., 417b24.

67. *Met.*, 1072b18-24.

68. *N.E.*, 1139b4-5.

69. *D.A.*, 433a22-25.

70. *N.E.*, 1141b12-14.

71. Ibid., 1144a29-30.

72. Ibid., 1106b36-1107a2.

73. C.H. Kahn, "Aristotle and Altruism," *Mind*, 1981, vol. XC, p. 38. My interpretation of the significance and implications of the *allos autos* premise is, in certain respects, close to Kahn's. His exegesis is, however, more daring than mine. Ascribing to Aristotle a fundamentally impersonal view of the self, he can provide an elegantly simple account of 'other selfhood'. As for my more convoluted argument, it could perhaps be said to have the advantage of bypassing the need for highly speculative exegesis on the thorny issue of the active intellect.

74. The interpretation here propounded is close to that intimated by Sidgwick in his statement that true Aristotelian friendship "gives them [the good], in fuller measure than their own virtue, the delight of contemplating excellent achievements as something belonging to them," *Outlines of the History of Ethics*, Macmillan and Co., London, 1946 (1st ed. 1886), p. 66.

75. *E.E.*, 1245a2-4.

76. *N.E.*, 1176a15-19.

77. Unless this specific condition is realized, the interpretation here defended of the 'other self' premise cannot get off the ground, since there is no reason to deny that an akratic could derive noetic actualization from contemplating his (virtuous) friend's moral activities. What he could not do, however, is provide his friend with the same benefit.

78. *E.E.*, 1244b23-26.

79. Ibid., 1244b26-27, here quoted with Bonitz's emendations.

80. Ibid., 1244b33-34.

81. Ibid., 1245a4-5.

82. Ibid., 1244b29-33.

83. Ibid., 1244b23-25.

84. Ibid., 1245a2-3.

85. Ibid., 1245a6-7.

86. Ibid., 1245a8-9.

87. Ibid., 1245a35-37.

88. Ibid., 1245b4.

89. Ibid., 1245b1.

90. Ibid., 1245b11.

91. Ibid., 1245b4.

92. Ibid., 1245b7-9.

Chapter 3

1. *N.E.*, 1156b10-11, 1157b3.

2. Ibid., 1156a15, 1156b7, and 1166a4.

3. *E.E.*, 1236b29-33, 1237a35-37, b1-5 and 30-35.

4. *Rhet.*, 1380b36-1381a3.

5. As L. Ollé-Laprune suggests in his *Essai sur la Morale d'Aristote*, Paris, 1881, p. 40ff.

6. B. Pascal, *Pensées*, 688, transl. by A.J. Krailsheimer, Penguin Books, Hammondsworth, 1966.

7. H. Sidgwick, *The Methods of Ethics*, Macmillan and Co, London, 1874, p. 437. Cf., too, E. Telfer, "Friendship," *Proceedings of the Aristotelian Society*, 1971, pp. 235-37.

8. See, for instance, M. Stocker, "Friendship and Duty: Some Difficult Relations," in O. Flanagan and A.O. Rorty, *Identity, Character, and Morality. Essays in Moral Psychology*, MIT Press, Cambridge, Mass., 1990.

9. Cf. Lawrence A. Blum, *Friendship, Altruism and Morality*, Routledge and Kegan Paul, London, 1980.

10. Cf. S. Stern-Gillet, "Epicurus and Friendship," *Dialogue*, XXVIII (1989).

11. E. Wharton, *Sanctuary*, Charles Scribners's Sons, New York, 1914 (1st ed. 1903), p. 260.

12. İ. Dilman, *Love and Human Separateness*, Basil Blackwell, Oxford, 1987, p. 126. Cf., too, P. Gilbert, *Human Relations*, Basil Blackwell, 1991, pp. 77-78.

13. M. de Montaigne, *Complete Works*, Essay 28, transl. by D.M. Frame, Hamish Hamilton, London, s.d., p. 139. The two short quotations from Montaigne later in the paragraph are from the same page of the same essay.

14. E. Telfer, *op. cit.*, p. 224.

15. Ibid., p. 225. J. Annas takes a similar view in her "Plato and Aristotle on Friendship and Altruism," *Mind*, Vol. LXXXVI, No 344, Oct. 1977, pp. 549-50.

16. I. Dilman, *op. cit.*, p. 133.

17. *N.E.*, 1156a9-10.

18. Ibid., 1156a10-16.

19. *E.E.*, 1237b32-34.

20. *N.E.*, 1162b16-21 and 1163a9-16; *E.E.*, 1243a2-b38.

21. *N.E.*, 1168b2-3, my italics.

22. Ibid., 1155a29.

23. *E.E.*, 1241a7-8.

24. Martha C. Nussbaum, *The Fragility of Goodness. Luck and Ethics in Greek Tragedy and Philosophy*, Cambridge University Press, Cambridge, 1986, p. 355. Cf., too, S.R.L. Clark, *Aristotle's Man*, Clarendon Press, Oxford, 1975, pp. 109-10.

25. *N.E.*, 1171b22-25.

26. Ibid., 1169a20sqq.

27. Ibid., 1156b9-11, my italics.

28. *E.E.*, 1237a40-1237b3.

29. *N.E.*, 1156a15-19 and 1156b11.

30. *E.E.*, 1237b10; N.E., 1156b11-12.

31. As it is set out, e.g., in *Met.*, E,2.

32. A.W. Price, *Love and Friendship in Plato and Aristotle*, Clarendon Press, Oxford, 1989, pp. 108-10.

33. A.W.H. Adkins, " 'Friendship' and 'Self-Sufficiency' in Homer and Aristotle," *The Classical Quarterly*, 1963, p. 39. I have translated, and placed between square brackets, the words and phrases that had been left in Greek.

34. Ibid., ibid.

35. Ibid., ibid.

36. Ibid., ibid.

37. Ibid., p. 41.

38. Ibid., p. 45.

39. e.g., *E.E.*, 1235b30sqq.

40. This distinction is akin to J. Rawls' distinction between exclusive goods (such as commodities and items of property) and excellences (e.g., wit, beauty, grace, and abilities) ". . . which are a condition of human flourishing; they are goods from everyone's point of view," in *A Theory of Justice*, Harvard University Press,

Cambridge, MA, 1971, p. 443. A. MacIntyre similarly distinguishes goods internal from goods external to a practice in *After Virtue*, Duckworth, London, 2nd edition, 1985, pp. 190-91.

41. *N.E.*, 1169a20-22.

42. Ibid., 1169a32-1169b1.

43. Aristotle, *Nicomachean Ethics*, translation with commentary by T. Irwin, p. 371. The issue is discussed further in chapter 5 below.

44. *E.E.*, 1248b20-21.

45. D.J. Allan, in P. Moraux (ed.), *Untersuchungen zur Eudemishen Ethik. Akten des 5. Symposium Aristotelicum*, Walter de Gruyter und Co., Berlin, 1971, p. 69.

46. See Aristophanes' speech in *Symposium*, 191a-d.

47. *E.E.*, 1236b5-6.

48. *N.E.*, 1156b12-13.

49. Cf. the 'peck of salt' analogy in *E.E.*, 1237b10-19, and *N.E.*, 1156b26-29, and 1158a15-16.

50. *N.E.*, 1165b15.

51. Quoted p. 63.

52. M.C. Nussbaum, *op. cit.*, p. 306.

53. Pierre Aubenque makes a claim that would prove very difficult to substantiate when he writes that primary friendship ". . . substituant à la contingence de la rencontre l'intelligibilité du choix réfléchi, . . . introduit dans le monde sublunaire un peu de cette unité que Dieu n'a pu faire descendre jusqu'à lui', in *La Prudence chez Aristote*, Presses Universitaires de France, Paris, p. 183.

54. *E.E.*, 1237b40. The fact that there is no comparable remark in the *N.E.* might provide *some* justification for A. Kenny's claim that "the treatment of friendship in the *E.E.* appears more altruistic, less self-absorbed than that in the *N.E.*," in *Aristotle and The Perfect Life*, Clarendon Press, Oxford, 1992, p. 52.

55. Quoted in full in W. Jaeger, *Aristotle: Fundamentals of the History of his Development*, transl. by R. Robinson, Oxford University Press, Oxford, 2nd ed., 1948, pp. 322-23.

56. *E.E.*, 1238a3-4, my italics.

57. Ibid., 1238a4-7. Cf, too, *Magna Moralia*, II, XI, 9, although the distinction there made between to *philēton* (worthy to be loved) and to *philēteon* (what one must love) needs further exegesis to be usefully brought to bear on the present argument.

58. This point is well brought out in J.-C. Fraisse, *La Notion d'Amitié dans la Philosophie Antique*, Vrin, Paris, 1974, pp. 253-54.

59. *Poetics*, 1451b5-7.

Chapter 4

1. J. Butler, *The Analogy of Religion, Natural and Revealed, to the Constitution and Course of Nature*, Sermon XI, *passim*.

2. I. Kant, *op. cit.*, p.17.

3. Most notably R. Kraut, in *Aristotle and the Human Good*, 1989.

4. *N.E.*, 1168b9-10.

5. Ibid., 1169a11-12.

6. H. Bonitz, *op. cit.*

7. *N.E.*, IX, 8, *passim*.

8. Ibid., 1169a11-12.

9. Ibid., 1166a10-31.

10. Ibid., 1169b1.

11. *Pol.*, 1263b1.

12. *N.E.*, 1168b15-19.

13. *E.E.*, 1240a19-21; the italics in the translation are mine.

14. *N.E.*, 1166a33-35.

15. Cf., e.g., Ibid., 1102a26-32.

16. *D.A.*, 432a22-b7.

17. *N.E.*, 1138a18-20.

18. Ibid., 1138b5-6.

19. Ibid., 1138b8-11, my italics.

20. Ibid., 1168b29-35.

21. Ibid., 1166b25-26.

22. Ibid., 1166b27-28.

23. Cf, e.g., *Republic* IV and IX, *passim*.

24. Ibid., 588c7-8, translated by G.M.A. Grube, Hackett Publishing Company, Indianapolis, 1974.

25. Ibid., 589a2-4; my italics.

26. Ibid., 589b5-6; my italics.

27. *Phaedrus*, 247b2-3, transl. by W. Hamilton, Penguin Books, Harmondsworth, 1973.

28. Ibid., 247c7-8.

29. Ibid., 250c5-6.

30. Ibid., 279b9.

31. *Leges*, 726a3, transl. by T.J. Saunders, Penguin Books, Harmondsworth, 1975.

32. W. Jaeger, *op. cit.*, p. 49, R.A. Gauthier and J.Y. Jolif, *op. cit.*, II, 2, p. 725. More cautiously than they Dirlmeier writes that "Schlichte Tatsache, die wir auch im Vorhergegangenen immer wieder aus den Texten beobachtet haben, ist dass sich Ar. auch in der NE, in ihr nicht selten mehr als in der EE, eng mit Platon verbunden zeigt," *Aristoteles. Nikomachische Ethik*, p. 551.

33. See pp. 32-33 above.

34. *N.E.*, 1166b2-25.

35. R.A. Gauthier and J.Y. Jolif, *op. cit.*, II, 2, p. 733ff.

36. *N.E.*, 1150a22 sqq.

37. Ibid., 1166b24-25.

38. Xenophon, for instance, uses μεταμέλεια in all three senses; cf. 42 below.

39. Luke, XV, 7.

40. R.A. Gauthier and J.Y. Jolif, *op. cit.*, II, 2, p. 732.

41. *N.E.*, 1128b19-21.

42. K.J. Dover, *Greek Popular Morality in the Time of Plato and Aristotle*, Basil Blackwell, Oxford, 1974, p. 222, my italics. It is worth noting that in Xenophon's writings the context of occurrence generally shows clearly in which sense *metameleia* is used. For 'remorse', see, e.g., *Cyropaedia* IV, VI, 5 and V, III, 7, while for 'regret', see, e.g., *Cyropaedia* V, III, 6 and VIII, III, 32.

43. Cf., Liddell, Scott and Jones, 9th ed., Clarendon Press, Oxford, 1940, and W.W. Goodwin, *A Greek Grammar*, Macmillan and Co., 1983, 1105 and 1161.

44. *N.E.*, VII, 8, *passim*.

45. The *Eudemian Ethics* is less clear in that respect. In 1240b23, its only occurrence in that treatise, *metameletikos* appears to refer to non-moral regret rather than to remorse. The base person, Aristotle writes, often regrets earlier actions just as the liar regrets his lies. This appears closer to Plato's usage in, e.g., *Phaedrus*, 231a2-4, where lovers are said to regret the favours that their own infatuation had led them to bestow onto the object of their desire. In translating *ho metameletikos* by 'the penitent', Rackham forces a moral interpretation onto the text.

46. *N.E.*, 1166b7-8.

47. Ibid., 1166b8-10.

48. Ibid., 1166b11-13.

49. R.A. Gauthier et J.Y. Jolif, *op. cit.*, II, 2, p. 734.

50. *De Sophisticis Elenchis*, 176b36.

51. *N.E.*, 1166b13-17.

52. Ibid., 1166b18-25; cf., too, *E.E.*, 1240b23-4. I have altered Irwin's translation of ἀπεχόμενόν as 'being restrained' to 'being unable to'. My rendering has the double advantage of relying on a sense of ἀπέχω used elsewhere in the *N.E.* (1109a10) and of not begging the question in favour of incontinence. Indeed, which part in the wicked soul would do the restraining?

53. R.A. Gauthier et J.Y. Jolif, *op. cit.*, II, 2, p. 735.

54. Cf. Plato, *Rep.*, book I.

55. *E.E.*, 1223a36-37 and b30-31.

56. *N.E.*, 1114a20-21, my italics.

57. Ibid., 1114b22-5.

58. Ibid., 1114a7.

59. Ibid., 1142b18-20.

60. Shakespeare, *Macbeth*, Act I, Scene V.

61. *N.E.*, 1151a6.

62. *Isaiah*, XLIII, 22.

63. J. Butler, *Analogy of Religion*, Pt. I, Chapter III, George Bell and Sons, London, 1897, p. 112.

64. *E.E.*, 1240b22-24.

65. Shakespeare, *Macbeth*, Act V, Scene III.

66. *E.E.*, 1240b27-28.

67. Ibid., 1240b14-15.

68.Plato, *Phaedrus*, 279b9.

69. *N.E.*, 1168a33.

70. Ibid., IX,4, *passim*.

71. Ibid., 1166a29-33.

72. Ibid., 1166b28-29.

73. Shakespeare, *Hamlet*, Act I, Scene III.

74. *N.E.*, 1166a1-2.

75. Ibid., 1166a13.

76. Ibid., 1166a17-25.

77. Ibid., 1168b9-10.

78. V. Politis, "The Primacy of Self-Love in the *Nicomachean Ethics*," *Oxford Studies in Ancient Philosophy*, Vol. XI, 1993.

79. *Leviticus*, XIX, 18, and Matthew, XIX, 19.

80. *N.E.*, 1168b28-9.

81. Plato, *Symposium*, 203b.

Chapter 5

1. *N.E.*, 1169a7-8.

2. Ibid., 1169a8-10.

3. Ibid., 1169a17-22.

4. *N.E.*, 1101a14-6.

5. R.A. Gauthier et J.Y. Jolif, *op. cit.*, II, 2, pp. 747-48.

6. I am using the expressions of 'psychological' and 'ethical egoism' as defined by W.K. Frankena in *Ethics*, Prentice-Hall, Inc., Englewood Cliffs, N.J., 1963, pp. 16-23.

7. T. Engberg-Pedersen, *Aristotle's Theory of Moral Insight*, Clarendon Press, Oxford, 1983, p. 44.

8. T. Nagel, *The Possibility of Altruism*, Princeton University Press, Princeton, N.J., 1970.

9. Ibid., p. 97.

10. Ibid., p. 109.

11. T. Engberg-Pedersen, *op. cit.*, pp. 44-45.

12. Ibid., p. 47.

13. Ibid, ibid.

14. A. Madigan, *"Eth. Nic. 9.8: Beyond Egoism and Altruism?,"* in J.P. Anton and A. Preus (eds.), *Essays in Ancient Greek Philosophy IV: Aristotle's Ethics*, S.U.N.Y. Press, New York, N.Y., 1991, p. 87.

15. M. Woods, *Aristotle's Eudemian Ethics, Books I, II, and VIII*, translated with a commentary, Oxford, Clarendon Press, 1982, p. 186.

16. *E.E.*, 1248b18-23.

17. Pp. 70-71.

18. *Topics*, 145a22 and *E.E.*, 1249a9.

19. N. Sherman, *op. cit.*, pp. 113-14.

20. J.A. Stewart, *Notes on the Nicomachean Ethics of Aristotle*, Clarendon Press, Oxford, 1892, pp. 375sqq.

21. *Ethics* IV, proposition 18, note. All subsequent quoted translations of Spinoza's *Ethics* are by A. Boyle, revised by G.H.R. Parkinson, Dent, London, 1989.

22. Ibid., IV, prop. V, proof.

23. Ibid., IV, prop. XVIII, note.

24. Ibid., IV, prop. LXXII.

25. Ibid., IV, prop. LXXII, note.

26. Ibid., IV, prop. XX.

27. Ibid., IV, appendix III.

28. *N.E.*, 1169a17-18.

29. Cf., K.J. Dover, *op. cit.*, pp. 277-78.

30. *N.E.*, 1169a19.

31. R. Kraut, *op. cit.*, p. 122.

32. *N.E.*, 1124b8.

33. Ibid., 1124b8-9.

34. Ibid., 1124b31-1125a1; my italics.

35. Euripides, *Alcestis*, 935-936 and 960-91, translated by D.J. Conacher, Aris and Phillips Ltd., Warminster, 1988.

36. *N.E.*, 1169a24-25.

37. *Iliad*, XVIII, 98-104, transl. by A.T. Murray, W. Heinemann Ltd., London, 1934. The fact that Achilles had earlier, in IX, 400-415, expressed his preference for a long and uneventful life might indicate that the principle was viewed as a positive ideal.

38. Thucydides, *History of the Peloponnesian War*, II, 42, translated by R. Warner, Penguin, Harmondsworth, 1954.

39. Plato, *Apology*, 28d4-5.

40. *N.E.*, 1169a19.

41. A. Madigan, *op. cit.*, pp. 78-80.

42. *N.E.*, 1169a17.

43. Ibid., 1169a20sqq.

44. Ibid., 1168b22-23.

45. T. Nagel, *The View From Nowhere*, Oxford University Press, Oxford, 1986.

46. K.J. Dover, *op. cit.*, p. 277.

47. See, e.g., R.-A. Gauthier et Y. Jolif, *op. cit.*, II. 2, pp. 748-50.

48. Ibid., ibid.

49. *Politics*, 1280b36-40.

50. *N.E.*, 1169a8-13, my italics.

51. The issue is discussed in chapter 3 above, pp. 70-71.

52. This example was suggested to me, in correspondance, by Anthony Preus. Richard Kraut offers a related, though more contrived, example to support a similar argument in *op. cit.*, pp. 116-19.

53. Discussed pp. 100-101 above.

54. *N.E.*, 1169a28, 33, and 35.

55. Luke 10:42.

56. As T. Irwin remarks in a note appended to his translation of *N.E.*, 1169a8-9.

57. Cf., e.g., *Rep*, 490a9.

58. *N.E.*, 1162b8.

59. Xenophon, *Memorabilia*, II, VI, 35.

60. *N.E.*, 1169a14-15.

61. T. Hobbes, *Leviathan*, Part I, chapter 15.

62. This contention will be further analyzed in chapter 7 below.

63. E. Ullman-Margalit, *The Emergence of Norms*, Clarendon Press, Oxford, 1977, p. 48.

64. Ibid., ibid.

65. *N.E.*, 1169a32-34.

66. Among the abundant literature on this problem, Kurt Baier, *The Moral Point of View*, Cornell University Press, 1958,

chapter 7, is noteworthy for his lucidity. The doctrinal gap that yawns between Aristotle and modern Hobbesians *cum* Classical Liberals is apparent in Baier's definition: "Moralities are systems of principles whose acceptance by everyone as overruling the dictates of self-interest is in the interest of everyone alike, though following the rules of a morality is not of course identical with following self-interest."

Chapter 6

1. *Pol.*, 1252b32-1253a1.

2. *E.E.*, 1244b7-10.

3. Ibid., 1238a12, *N.E.*, 1097b7-8.

4. *N.E.*, 1177a27-28.

5. Ibid., 1125a12.

6. Ibid., 1160b3-5.

7. *Pol.*, 1328b16-17.

8. *Rhet.*, 1360b26-28, and *N.E.*, 1099a31-b6 and 1169b9-10.

9. *Rhet.*, 1360b29. Cf., too, 1386a9-10.

10. *N.E.*, 1155a2-6.

11. *Lysis*, 215a6-c1, transl. J. Wright, in E. Hamilton and H. Cairns (eds.), *op. cit.*

12. *N.E.*, 1097b16-20.

13. Ibid., 1096a23-24.

14. Ibid., 1096b27-29.

15. Ibid., 1097a18-20.

16. Ibid., 1097b24 ff.

17. Ibid., 1097b14-15.

18. Ibid., 1097b8-11. Cf, too, 1169b16-19.

19. *Pol.*, 1253a25-27. Whether Aristotle's is an organic conception of the State, as S.R.L. Clarke, *Aristotle's Man*, III, 3, *passim*, and J. Lear, *op. cit.*, pp 200-01, maintain, is a question that

cannot here be discussed. Let it just be noted that in the above passage Aristotle is not saying that the citizen *is* a part but merely *compares* him to a part. Further, while in a true organism the part cannot function when isolated from the whole, it is arguable that in the *Nicomachean Ethics*, 1177a32-1177b1, Aristotle claims that in the contemplative life humans could function on their own.

20. *Pol.*, 1253a6.

21. *E.E.*, 1245b18-19.

22. Such a thesis, in its extreme and extended implications, is defended by Richard Bodéüs in his *The Political Dimensions of Aristotle's Ethics*, forthcoming, S.U.N.Y. Press.

23. As Plato had already argued in *Philebus*, 67a-b.

24. *Pol.*, 1253a27-33.

25. *N.E.*, 1169b9-10, and *Rhet.*, 1360b26-28. Cf., too, ibid., 1386a9-10 where Aristotle ascribes the evil of friendlessness to chance (*tuchē*).

26. J.A. Stewart, *op. cit.*, p. 384.

27. R.A. Gauthier et J.Y. Jolif, *op. cit.*, II, 2, pp. 751-52.

28. *N.E.*, 1168a5-9.

29. Ibid., 1169b13; my italics.

30. This point is made by J. Passmore, *The Perfectibility of Man*, Duckworth, London, 1970, pp. 49-50.

31. E.E., 1244b21-1245b19.

32. J-C. Fraisse, in "*Autarkeia* et *Philia* en E.E. VII, 12, 1244b1-1245b19," in P. Moraux und D. Harlfinger, *Untersuchungen zur Eudemischen Ethik*, Walter De Gruyter & Co., Berlin, 1971, and *Philia: La Notion d'Amitié dans la Philosophie Ancienne*, Paris, Vrin, 1974, has proceeded to a detailed comparison between the two versions. While insightful, his exegesis does not, I think, sufficiently take into account the dialectical nature of some of the arguments that Aristotle wields in the *Eudemian* version.

33. *N.E.*, 1152b7-8. Admittedly, the passage in which the line occurs is dialectical.

34. Ibid., 1169b29-30.

35. Cf., e.g., *Met.*, 1072a21.

36. *N.E.*, 1169b33.

37. Ibid., 1156b15-17.

38. Ibid., 1169b33-35.

39. *M.M.*, 1213a16-24.

40. *N.E.*, 1170a1.

41. G.B. Kerferd, "The Search for Personal Identity in Stoic Thought," *Bulletin of the John Rylands University Library of Manchester*, Vol. 55, no. 1, Autumn 1972, p. 180.

42. Ibid., pp. 180-81.

43. *N.E.*, 1170a2-4, my italics. I here depart from Irwin's translation.

44. Ibid., 1170a5-6.

45. J. Burnet, *The Ethics of Aristotle. Edited with an Introduction and Notes*, Methuen, London, 1900, note on 1170a18.

46. D. Ross, *Ethica Nicomachea*, in *The Works of Aristotle Translated into English*, vol. IX, 1, Oxford University Press, Oxford, 1925, commentary on 1170b19.

47. R.A. Gauthier et J.Y. Jolif, *op. cit.*, II, 2, pp. 755-62.

48. W.F.R. Hardie, *op. cit.*, p. 332.

49. *N.E.*, 1170a14-16.

50. Ibid., 1170a17.

51. Ibid., 1170a17-18.

52. Ibid., 1170a18-19.

53. Ibid., 1170a19-21.

54. Ibid., 1170a20-24.

55. Ibid., 1170a26-27.

56. Ibid., 1170a27-29.

57. Ibid., 1170a27.

58. *Pol.*, 1278b27-30, as noted by R.A. Gauthier and J.Y. Jolif, *op. cit.*, p. 758.

59. *N.E.*, 1170a29-32.

60. Ibid., 1170a31-1170b1.

61. Ibid., 1170b1-1170b4.

62. Ibid., 1170b5-7. The exegesis of this premise forms the object of Chapter 2 above.

63. Ibid., 1170b7-8.

64. Ibid., 1170b8-14.

65. Ibid., 1170b17-20.

66. J.A. Stewart, *op. cit.*, p. 393.

67. F. Nietzsche, *Daybreak*, translated by M. Hollingdale, Cambridge University Press, Cambridge, 1982, 154, p. 98.

68. B. Williams, *Moral Luck*, Cambridge University Press, Cambridge, 1981. This article first appeared in A.O. Rorty (ed.), *The Identities of Persons*, University of California Press, Berkeley, 1976. Cf., too, J. Lear, *op. cit.*, p. 201.

69. Ibid., pp. 15-16.

70. Ibid., p. 16.

71. In this Williams is in agreement with Epicurus who claimed that ". . . one must be willing to run some risks for the sake of friendship," *Sententiae Vaticanae*, XXVIII, translated by B. Inwood and L.P. Gerson, *Hellenistic Philosophy: Introductory Readings*, Hackett Publishing Company, Indianapolis, 1988. The problem of reconciling friendship with self-sufficiency, however, is much more acute for Epicurus than for Aristotle, since the former's hedonism requires him to explain how as chancy a relationship as friendship can lead to the achievement of *ataraxia*. For a detailed discussion of this problem, cf., S. Stern-Gillet, *op. cit.*

72. To be discussed in chapter 7 below.

73. *Pol.*, 1262b7-9.

74. *N.E.*, 1159b2-4.

75. Ibid., 1159b12-13.

76. *E.E.*, 1240a1; cf., too, *N.E.*, 1159b19-20.

77. *E.E.*, 1239b32-34. Cf, too, *N.E.* 1159b20-21.

78. *E.E.*, 1240a2.

79. M.C. Nussbaum, *The Fragility of Goodness. Luck and Ethics in Greek Tragedy and Philosophy*, Cambridge University Press, Cambridge, 1986, p. 369.

Chapter 7

1. *Pol.*, 1252b30-1253a1, first quoted on pp. 124-25.

2. *E.E.*, 1234b33.

3. On the problems posed by such friendships, see G. Herman, *Ritualised Friendship and the Greek City*, Cambridge University Press, Cambridge, 1987, pp. 116-28.

4. Cf., e.g., S.R.L. Clark, "The City of the Wise," *Apeiron*, 20:63-80.

5. *Pol.*, 1262b7-9.

6. Cicero, *De Amicitia*, XII, 40.

7. The expression arguably occurs in *Pol.* 1295b21-25: γίνεται οὖν δούλων καὶ δεσποτῶν πόλις, ἀλλ᾽ οὐκ ἐλευθέρων, καὶ τῶν μὲν φθονούντων τῶν δὲ καταφρονούντων · ἃ πλεῖστον ἀπέχει φιλίας καὶ κοινωνίας πολιτικῆς · ἡ γὰρ κοινωνία φιλικόν · οὐδὲ γὰρ ὁδοῦ βούλονται κοινωνεῖν τοῖς ἐχθροῖς · ("Thus arises a city, not of freemen, but of masters and slaves, the one despising, the other envying; and nothing can be more fatal to friendship and good fellowship in states than this: for good fellowship springs from friendship; when men are at enmity with one another, they would rather not even share the same path"). Cooper and Hunts (in G. Patzig, *Aristotle's Politik: Akten des XI Symposium Aristotelicus*, Vandenhoeck und Ruprecht, Göttingen, 1990), have invoked convincing arguments, respectively for and against, taking πολιτικῆς with φιλίας as well as with κοινωνίας. Although the issue cannot be settled with any certainty, I am inclined to think that, in this passage, πολιτικῆς goes only with κοινωνίας. Firstly, if this chapter contained any allusion to civic friendship, the whole sentence would be pleonastic. Indeed, as we shall see, Aristotle considers that whatever damages the political community *ipso facto* damages *civic* friendship. Further, there would be no point in adding that "good fellowship

pertains to the nature of friendship" unless non-civic friendship were meant. Lastly and crucially, even if the phrase 'civic friendship' occurred here, commentators would still have to contend with the fact that in his major political treatise Aristotle referred to it only this once.

8. *E.E.*, 1242a25-40 and *N.E.*, VIII,9, *passim.*

9. *N.E.*, 1161a30-b12.

10. *E.E.*, 1242a6-8.

11. Ibid., 1243a31-b14.

12. *N.E.*, 1167b2-4.

13. J.M. Cooper, 1976-77.

14. *E.E.*, 1242b35-7; *N.E.*, 1162b21-31.

15. *E.E.*, 1242b35-36.

16. Ibid., 1242b26-7.

17. *E.E.*, 1242b39-1243a1

18. Ibid., 1216a26-7.

19. *N.E.*, 1155a26-27.

20. *Pol.*, 1262b7-8.

21. *E.E.*, 1241a32-3; *N.E.*, 1155a24-26 and 1167a22. In common with most translators I render *homonoia* by 'concord' in spite of a revealing etymological difference between the Greek concept and its English equivalent. Indeed, while the English/Latin word relies on an affective concept (*cors*), the Greek notion involves a reference to *nous* which, as we shall see, is fully exploited in the Nicomachean analysis of civic friendship.

22. *E.E.*, 1241a26-27.

23. Ibid., 1241a16-17 and *N.E.*, 1167a22-29.

24. *N.E.*, 1167a29-32; *E.E.*, 1241a30-31.

25. *E.E.*, 1241a22-28.

26. *N.E.*, 1167b4-5.

27. Ibid., 1167b5.

28. Ibid., 1167b9-16.

29. G. Patzig, *op. cit.*, p. 235.

30. In their commentary Gauthier and Jolif explain: "La pensée qui s'exprime dans cette section (1159b24-1162a33) est de type nettement archaïque. Aristote y perd presque entièrement de vue l'amitié véritable, celle des vertueux, dont il vient de dégager la notion, pour y examiner sous le nom d'amitié les diverses formes de l'instinct de groupe, de la solidarité. De là la place prépondérante que va occuper dans cette section la notion *de koinonia*. Aristote n'avait pas eu besoin de cette notion pour définir l'amitié vraie. Elle apparait ici pour la première fois, comme le succédané sociologique de la similitude qui fonde l'amitié vertueuse et de la vie d'intimité où elle s'exprime. De même en effet que l'amitié vraie repose sur la similitude des amis en vertu et se traduit dans leur intimité, de même les diverses formes de la solidarité reposent sur la *koinonia*," *op. cit.*, II, 2, p. 696.

31. J. Annas, "Comments on J. Cooper," in G. Patzig, *op. cit.*, p. 248.

32. The fact that this question arises at all could well constitute a difficulty for Richard Bodéüs' bold claim, in *The Political Dimensions of Aristotle's Ethics*, SUNY Press, forthcoming, that the *Nicomachean Ethics* and the *Politics* are discourses addressed to law-givers rather than, as commonly supposed, to virtuous individuals. Indeed, if such were the case, one would expect Aristotle in the *Politics* to discuss lengthily the relationship which he viewed as most likely to protect the state against internecine conflict. One would further expect the *Nicomachean* account of friendship to be weighted in favour of civic friendship rather than, as is actually the case, in favour of primary friendship.

33. *N.E.*, 1159b29-31.

34. Ibid., 1160a4-6. It seems far from obvious that the existence of a bond of friendship makes a difference to obligations of particular justice. While friendship is a commitment to particular individuals, the obligations of justice are impersonal. It is thus not strictly speaking more *unjust* to cheat one's brother than a perfect stranger, although it is conceivably more unpalatable since it compounds injustice with a breach of trust. From the examples that he uses in this passage, I infer that Aristotle must have in mind particular justice rather than universal justice, which he identifies with morality.

35. Ibid., 1160a21; *E.E.*, 1241b24-5.

36. *N.E.*, 1160a22-3.

37. Ibid., 1160a14-5.

38. Ibid., 1161a10-11.

39. *N.E.*, 1129b25-7.

40. Ibid., 1130a5-8.

41. Ibid., V,2.

42. *Pol.*, 1253a37-39. Cf., too, *N.E.*, 1129b17-19.

43. *Pol.*, 1282b17.

44. Ibid., 1283a20-1.

45. Ibid., 1332b27-29.

46. This is an inference from *Pol.*, III, 9; as stated earlier, the issue of civic friendship, as such, is not discussed in the *Politics*.

47. Ibid., VII,13.

48. Ibid., 1332a32-6.

49. Ibid., 1275b17-20.

50. Ibid., 1332b25-7.

51. Ibid., 1288a37-39 and 1293b5-6.

52. Ibid., 1328b37-9.

53. Cf., e.g., Ibid., III, 9.

54. Ibid., 1283a38-40, my italics.

55. Ibid., 1277b18-9.

56. Ibid., VII,3,9, and 13.

57. Ibid., 1279a34-5; cf., too, III, 18. For a detailed discussion of this problem see R.G. Mulgan, *Aristotle's Political Theory*, Clarendon Press, Oxford, 1977, chapter 5.

58. As discussed on p. 152 above.

59. *Pol.*, 1332a32-4.

60. Ibid., 1326b14-16.

61. Ibid., IV, 1.

62. Ibid., IV, 8 and 9.

63. Ibid., III, 10.

64. Ibid., IV, 11.

65. Ibid., 1295b3-5.

66. Ibid., 1295b29-32.

67. Ibid., 1295b33.

68. Ibid., 1295b21-25.

69. Ibid., 1297a6-7.

70. *Pol.*, 1295b21-25.

71. The connection between particular justice and the friendship of utility in all its forms also emerges in the less weighty context of the casuistry of friendship. Recriminations, we are told, are most frequent in the friendship of utility (*N.E.*, 1162b5-6) since such friends ". . . deal with each other in the expectation of gaining benefits" (ibid., 1162b16-7). Far from considering such quarrels beneath his philosophical concern, Aristotle addresses them and recommends that the fairest way to resolve them is to measure the return against the benefit to the recipient rather than against the cost to the benefactor. Considerations of particular justice are thus brought in to check the egoistic drives of friends of utility.

72. *Pol.*, 1280a20-25.

73. *E.E.*, 1242b35-1243a2.

74. *Pol.*, V, 2, *passim*.

75. As Newman noted: "Aristotle does seem to imply (. . .) that not merely the justice of a good citizen, but also his virtue generally, will vary with the constitution," *The Politics of Aristotle*, vol. IV, p. 403.

76. J. Bentham, *An Introduction to the Principles of Morals and Legislation*, 1789, I,4.

77. J. Moravscik, "Communal Ties," in *Proceedings and Addresses of the American Philosophical Association*, suppl. to vol. 62, no. 1, Sept. 1988, p. 213.

78. Unless, of course, one adopts the Quaker terminology.

79. *E.E.*, 1243a32-3.

80. *N.E.*, 1155a26-7.

81. Ibid., 1169a32.

82. For an interesting discussion of this issue see L.A. Blum, *op. cit.*, chapter III.

83. *N.E.*, 1144b30-1145a2 and, probably, *E.E.*, 1246b32-3.

84. *N.E.*, 1159b5.

85. Ibid., 1159b6-7.

86. Ibid., 1096a16-7.

87. Quoted in note 6 above. Be it noted that Cicero and E.M. Forster hold opposite views on the issue.

88. E.M. Forster, *Two Cheers for Democracy*, Edward Arnold, London, 1952, p. 66. In the discussion that follows I benefited from Stephen Clark's observations, and from Judith N. Shklar's discussion of Forster's epigram in *Ordinary Vices*, The Belknap Press of Harvard University Press, Cambridge, MA, 1984, pp. 155-58.

89. *Pol.*, 1280a34-6.

90. Sophocles, *Antigone*, 182-83, trans. by J.V. O'Brien, Southern Illinois University Press, London and Amsterdam, 1977.

91. P. Aubenque, *op. cit.*, p. 6; J.-C. Fraisse, *PHILIA: La Notion d'Amitié dans la Philosophie Antique*, Paris, Vrin, 1974.

92. E. Barker, *The Political Thought of Plato and Aristotle*, London, 1906, pp. 235-37.

93. A.W. Price, *Love and Friendship in Plato and Aristotle*, Clarendon Press, Oxford, 1989, p. 204.

94. Ibid., p. 198.

95. Ibid., p. 197.

96. T.H. Irwin, "The Good of Political Activity," in G. Patzig, *op. cit.*, p. 95. Cf., too, his *Aristotle's First Principles*, Clarendon Press, Oxford, 1988, p. 410.

97. *N.E.*, 1094b7-10.

98. Ibid., 1156b24-25.

99. Ibid., 1155a22-3 and *Pol.*, 1262b7-9.

100. *N.E.*, 1171a17-20.

101. As C.H. Kahn has noted in *op. cit.*, 1981, p. 27.

102. As can be seen, my views on this issue are close to Irwin's, although they rely on a different argumentation. While his strategy involves him in adjusting the intension of the notion of civic friendship in Aristotle's political philosophy, mine consists in assessing its possible extension in a range of constitutions.

Conclusion

1. J.W. Goethe, *Die Wahlverwandtschaften*, II, XVII. Earlier, Montaigne had invoked "an inexplicable and fateful force" to explain the genesis of his friendship with Etienne de la Boétie, as discussed p. 63 above.

2. P. Gilbert, *op. cit.*, pp. 77-78.

3. Cf., on this issue, G. and S.R.L. Clark, "Friendship in the Christian Tradition," in R. Porter and S. Tomaselli, *The Dialectics of Friendship*, Routledge, London, 1989.

4. G. Vlastos, *Platonic Studies*, Princeton University Press, Princeton N.J., 1973.

5. Ibid., footnote no. 100.

6. Ibid., p. 31.

7. *N.E.*, 1156b25-6.

8. M. de Montaigne, *op. cit.*, p. 139.

SELECT
BIBLIOGRAPHY

A. Commentaries

J. Barnes, *Aristotle's Posterior Analytics*, Clarendon Press, Oxford, 1975.

H. Bonitz, *Index Aristotelicus*, Berlin, 1870.

J. Burnet, *The Ethics of Aristotle. Edited with an Introduction and Notes*, Methuen, London, 1900.

C. Dalimier and P. Pellegrin, *Aristote: Les Grands Livres d'Ethique*, Arléa, Paris, 1992.

V. Decarie, *Ethique à Eudème*, Paris, Vrin, 1978.

F. Dirlmeier, *Aristoteles. Nikomachische Ethik*, übersetzt und kommentiert, 3rd edition, Akademie-Verlag, Berlin, 1964.

R.A. Gauthier et J.Y. Jolif, *L'Ethique à Nicomaque. Introduction, Traduction et Commentaire*, second edition, Louvain et Paris, Publications Universitaires et Béatrice-Nauwelaerts, 1970.

D.W. Hamlyn, *Aristotle's De Anima, Books II, III*. Translation and Commentary, Clarendon Press, Oxford, 1968.

R.D. Hicks, *Aristotle, De Anima*, Cambridge University Press, Cambridge, 1907.

E. Hussey, *Aristotle's Physics*, Clarendon Press, Oxford, 1983.

H.H. Joachim, *Aristotle. The Nicomachean Ethics*, Oxford, Clarendon Press, 1951.

G.A. Kennedy, *Aristotle On Rhetoric*, newly translated, with introduction, notes and appendices, Oxford University Press,
New York and Oxford, 1991.

W.L. Newman, *The Politics of Aristotle*, Clarendon Press, Oxford,
1887.

D. Ross, *Aristotle. De Anima*, Clarendon Press, Oxford, 1961.

J.A. Stewart, *Notes on the Nicomachean Ethics of Aristotle*,
Oxford, Clarendon Press, 1892.

Thomas Aquinatis, *In Decem Libros Ethicorum Aristotelis ad
Nicomachum Expositio*, Marietti, Romae, 1949.

J. Tricot, *Aristote. Ethique à Nicomaque*, Nouvelle traduction avec
introduction, notes et index, Paris, Vrin, 1959.

J. Tricot, *Aristote. La Métaphysique*, Traduction, introduction,
notes et index, Paris, Vrin, 1974.

J. Tricot, *Aristote. De l'âme*, Traduction et notes, Paris, Vrin, 1977.

M. Woods, *Aristotle's Eudemian Ethics, Books I, II, and VIII*,
translation and commentary, Clarendon Press, Oxford,
1982.

B. Articles

A.W.H. Adkins, "Friendship and Self-Sufficiency in Homer and
Aristotle," *The Classical Quarterly*, 1963.

K.D. Alpern, "Aristotle on the Friendships of Utility and
Pleasure," *The Journal for the History of Philosophy*, 1983,
Vol. 21.

J. Annas, "Plato and Aristotle on Friendship and Altruism," *Mind*,
1977.

D. Bostock, "Pleasure and Activity in Aristotle's Ethics,"
Phronesis, Vol. XXXIII, No. 3, 1988.

P.A. Brunt, "'Amicitia' in the Late Roman Republic," *Proceedings
of the Cambridge Philological Society*, No. 191 (New
Series, No II), 1965.

S.R.L. Clark, "The City of the Wise," *Apeiron* 20, 1987.

J.M. Cooper, "Aristotle on the Goods of Fortune," *The Philosophical Review*, XCIV, April 1985.

J.M. Cooper, "Contemplation and Happiness: A Reconsideration," *Synthese*, Vol. 72, no. 2, 1987.

R. Develin, "The Good Man and the Good Citizen in Aristotle's *Politics*," *Phronesis*, 18, 1973.

P. Geach, "Good and Evil," *Analysis*, Vol. 17, 1956.

O. Gigon, "Die Selbstliebe in der Nikomachischen Ethik des Aristoteles," in *Dorema* Hans Diller zum 70. Geburtstag, *Dauer and Uberleben des antiken Geistes*, Griechische humanistische Gesellshaft, Internationales Zentrum für klassisch-humanistische Forschung, Zweite Reihe: Studien und Untersuchungen 27, Athen, 1975, 77-113.

C.H. Kahn, "Sensation and Consciousness in Aristotle's Psychology," in *Archiv für Geschichte der Philosophie*, Band 48, 1966.

C.H. Kahn, "Aristotle on Altruism," *Mind*, 1981.

G.B. Kerferd, "The Search for Personal Identity in Stoic Thought," *Bulletin of the John Rylands University Library of Manchester*, Vol. 55, no. 1, Autumn, 1972.

R. Heinaman, "Eudaimonia and Self-Sufficiency in the *Nicomachean Ethics*," *Phronesis*, Vol. XXXIII, no. 1, 1988.

E. Hoffman, "Aristoteles Philosophie des Freundschaft," in *Ethik und Politik des Aristoteles*, ed. F.-P. Hager, Wege der Forschung 208, Darmstadt, 1972.

J. Hooker, "Homeric φίλος," in *Glotta*, LXV Band, 1987.

A. Madigan, "E.N. IX,8: Beyond Egoism and Altruism?," in J.P. Anton and A. Preus, *Essays in Ancient Greek Philosophy IV*, SUNY Press, Albany, N.Y., 1991.

E. Millgram, "Aristotle on Making Other Selves," *Canadian Journal of Philosophy*, vol. 17, 1987.

J. Moravcsik, "Communal Ties," Presidential Address, 62nd Meeting of the Annual Pacific Division Meeting of the A.P.A., *Proceedings and Addresses of A.P.A.*, Suppl. to vol. 62, no. 1, Sept. 1988.

C. Osborne, "Aristotle, *De Anima* A 3.2: How Do We Perceive That We See and Hear?," *Classical Quarterly*, 33(ii), 1983.

V. Politis, "The Primacy of Self-Love in the *Nicomachean Ethics*," *Oxford Studies in Ancient Philosophy*, Vol. XI, Clarendon Press, Oxford, 1993.

J. Roberts, "Political Animals in the Nichomachean Ethics," *Phronesis*, 1989, Vol. XXXIV.

B. Snell, Review of Joachim Böhme, *Die Seele und das Ich im homerischen Epos*, (Leipzig, 1929), *Gnomon*, Band 7, 1931.

S. Stern-Gillet, "Epicurus and Friendship," *Dialogue*, XXVIII, 1989.

E. Telfer, "Friendship," *Proceedings of the Aristotelian Society*, 1971.

L. Thomas, "Friendship," *Synthese*, Vol. 72, no. 2, 1987.

A. Voelke, "Le problème d'autrui dans la pensée aristotélicienne," in *Revue de théologie et de philosophie*, 4, 1954, 262-82.

C. Books

A.W.H. Adkins, *Merit and Responsibility*, Oxford University Press, Oxford, 1960.

J.P. Anton and A. Preus, *Essays in Ancient Greek Philosophy II*, SUNY Press, Albany, N.Y., 1983.

J.P. Anton and A. Preus, *Essays in Ancient Greek Philosophy IV: Aristotle's Ethics*, SUNY Press, Albany, N.Y., 1991.

P. Aubenque, *La Prudence chez Aristote*, Paris, Presses Universitaires de France, 1963.

K. Baier, *The Moral Point of View*, Cornell University Press, New York, 1958.

C. Bailey, *Epicurus. The Extant Remains*, Georg Olms Verlag, Hildesheim and New York, 1970 (1st ed. 1926).

R. Bambrough (ed.), *New Essays on Plato and Aristotle*, Routledge and Kegan Paul, London, 1965.

E. Barker, *The Political Thought of Plato and Aristotle*, London, 1906.

E. Benveniste, *Le Vocabulaire des Institutions Indo-Européennes*, Paris, Les Editions de Minuit, 1969.

L.A. Blum, *Friendship, Altruism, and Morality*, Routledge and Kegan Paul, London, 1980.

M. Whitlock Blundell, *Helping Friends and Harming Enemies. A Study in Sophocles and Greek Ethics*, Cambridge University Press, Cambridge, 1989.

D. Bolotin, *Plato's Dialogue on Friendship*, Cornell University Press, Ithaca, N.Y., 1979.

S.W. Broadie, *Ethics with Aristotle*, Oxford University Press, Oxford, 1991.

F. Brentano, *The Psychology of Aristotle*, transl. by R. George, University of California Press, Berkeley and Los Angeles, 1977.

C.D. Broad, *Ethics and the History of Philosophy*, Routledge and Kegan Paul, London, 1952.

J. Butler, *Sermons on Human Nature*, 1726.

S.R.L. Clark, *Aristotle's Man*, Clarendon Press, Oxford, 1975.

J.M. Cooper, *Reason and Human Good in Aristotle*, Harvard University Press, Cambridge, Mass., 1975.

M. de Montaigne, *Essais*, 1588.

R. Descartes, *Philosophical Writings*, transl. by J. Cottingham, R. Stoothoff, D. Murdoch, Cambridge University Press, Cambridge, 1984.

I. Dilman, *Love and Human Separateness*, Blackwell, Oxford, 1987.

K.J. Dover, *Greek Popular Morality in the Time of Plato and Aristotle*, Basil Blackwell, Oxford, 1974.

R.W. Emerson, *The Selected Writings of Ralph Waldo Emerson* (ed. with a bibliographical Introduction by Brooks Atkinson), The Modern Library, New York, [Copyright 1940/1950].

T. Engberg-Pedersen, *Aristotle's Theory of Moral Insight*, Clarendon Press, Oxford, 1983.

R. Flaceliere, *L'Amour en Grèce*, Paris, Hachette, 1960.

O. Flanagan and A.O. Rorty (eds.), *Identity, Character, and Morality*, MIT Press, Cambridge, Mass., 1990.

M. Foucault, *The History of Sexuality*, translated by R. Hurley, Penguin Books, 1987.

E.M. Forster, *Two Cheers for Democracy*, Edward Arnold, London, 1951.

J.-C. Fraisse, *PHILIA: La Notion d'Amitié dans la Philosophie Ancienne*, Paris, Vrin, 1974.

W. Frankena, *Ethics*, Prentice-Hall Inc., Englewood Cliffs, N.J., 1963.

R.-A. Gauthier, *La Morale d'Aristote*, Paris, Presses Universitaires de France, 1958.

P. Gilbert, *Human Relationships*, Blackwell, Oxford, 1991.

C.L. Griswold, *Self-Knowledge in Plato's Phaedrus*, Yale University Press, New Haven, 1986.

W.F.R. Hardie, *Aristotle's Ethical Theory*, Second edition, Clarendon Press, Oxford, 1980.

E. Hartman, *Substance, Body, and Soul*, Princeton University Press, Princeton, N.J., 1977.

G. Herman, *Ritualized Friendship and the Greek City*, Cambridge University Press, Cambridge, 1987.

T. Hobbes, *Leviathan*, 1651.

P. Huby, *Greek Ethics*, Macmillan, London, 1967.

D. Hume, *A Treatise of Human Nature*, ed. by L.A. Selby-Bigge, Clarendon Press, Oxford, 1888.

T. Irwin, *Aristotle's First Principles*, Clarendon Press, Oxford, 1988.

W. Jaeger, *Aristotle. Fundamentals of the History of his Development*, transl. R. Robinson, Oxford University Press, Oxford, second ed., 1948.

W. Jaeger, *Paideia: the Ideals of Greek Culture*, transl. by G. Highet, Blackwell, Oxford, 1975.

I. Kant, *Groundwork of the Metaphysic of Morals*, transl. by H.J. Paton, Hutchinson, London, 1948.

A. Kenny, *The Aristotelian Ethics*, Clarendon Press, Oxford, 1978.

A. Kenny, *Aristotle on the Perfect Life*, Clarendon Press, Oxford, 1992.

D. Keyt and F.D. Miller, Jr. (eds.), *A Companion to Aristotle's Politics*, Blackwell, Oxford, 1991.

B. Knox, *The Oldest Dead White European Males*, W.W. Norton and Co., New York, 1993.

R. Kraut, *Aristotle on the Human Good*, Princeton University Press, Princeton, N.J., 1989.

C.E. Larmore, *Patterns of Moral Complexity*, Cambridge University Press, Cambridge, 1987.

J. Lear, *Aristotle: The Desire to Understand*, Cambridge University Press, Cambridge, 1988.

H. Lesser and A. Loizou, *Polis and Politics: Essays in Greek Moral and Political Thought*, Avebury, Aldershot, 1990.

A. MacIntyre, *After Virtue*, Duckworth, London, 2nd edition, 1985.

A. MacIntyre, *Whose Justice? Which Rationality?*, Duckworth, London, 1988.

G. Meilaender, *Friendship*, University of Notre Dame Press, Notre Dame and London, 1983.

I. Meyerson (ed.), *Problèmes de la Personne*, Mouton and Co., Paris and The Hague, 1973.

M. Midgley, *Wickedness. A Philosophical Essay*, Routledge and Kegan Paul, London, 1984.

D.K.W. Modrak, *Aristotle. The Power of Perception*, The University of Chicago Press, Chicago and London, 1987.

H. Monsacre, *Les larmes d'Achille. Le héros, la femme et la souffrance dans la poésie d'Homère*, Paris, Albin Michel, 1984.

P. Moraux, *A La Recherche de l'Aristote Perdu. Le Dialogue "Sur la Justice,"* Paris et Louvain, Editions Béatrice-Nauwelaerts, 1957.

P. Moraux (ed.), *Untersuchungen zur Eudemischen Ethik*. Akten
   des 5. Symposium Aristotelicum, 1971, Walter de Gruyter,
   Berlin, 1971.

R.G. Mulgan, *Aristotle's Political Theory*, Clarendon Press, Oxford,
   1977.

T. Nagel, *The Possibility of Altruism*, Princeton University Press,
   Princeton, 1970.

T. Nagel, *The View From Nowhere*, Oxford University Press,
   Oxford, 1986.

F. Nietzsche, *Daybreak*, translated by M. Hollingdale, Cambridge
   University Press, Cambridge, 1982.

M.C. Nussbaum, *Aristotle's De Motu Animalium*, Princeton
   University Press, Princeton, N.J., 1978.

M.C. Nussbaum, *The Fragility of Goodness. Luck and Ethics in
   Greek Tragedy and Philosophy*, Cambridge University
   Press, Cambridge, 1986.

M.C. Nussbaum, *Love's Knowledge. Essays on Philosophy and
   Literature*, Oxford University Press, Oxford, 1990.

F. Nuyens, *L'Evolution de la Psychologie d'Aristote*, Editions de
   L'Institut Supérieur de Philosophie, Louvain, 1948.

L. Olle-Laprune, *Essai sur la Morale d'Aristote*, Paris, Vve Eugène
   Belin et Fils, 1881.

D.J. O'Meara (ed.), *Studies in Aristotle*, The Catholic University of
   America Press, Washington, D.C., 1981.

J. Owens, *Aristotle: Collected Papers*, ed. by J.R. Catan, SUNY
   Press, Albany, N.Y., 1981.

B. Pascal, *Oeuvres Complètes*, Paris, éditions Louis Lafuma,
   Editions du Seuil, 1963.

J. Passmore, *The Perfectibility of Man*, Duckworth, London, 1970.

G. Patzig (ed.), *Aristotle's Politik. Akten des XI Symposium
   Aristotelicum 1987*, Vandenhoeck und Ruprecht,
   Göttingen, 1990.

A. Plomer, *Phenomenology, Geometry and Vision*, Avebury,
   Aldershot, 1991.

R. Porter and S. Tomaselli (eds.), *The Dialectics of Friendship*, Routledge, London and New York, 1989.

J.E. Powell, *A Lexicon to Herodotus*, Georg Olms Verlagsbuchhandlung, Hildesheim and New York, 2nd ed., 1960 (1st ed., 1938).

A.W. Price, *Love and Friendship in Plato and Aristotle*, Clarendon Press, Oxford, 1989.

J. Rawls, *A Theory of Justice*, Harvard University Press, Cambridge, Mass., 1971.

L. Robin, *Aristote*, Paris, Presses Universitaires de France, 1944.

A. Rorty (ed.), *Essays on Aristotle's Ethics*, University of California Press, Berkeley, 1980.

D. Ross, *Aristotle*, Methuen, London, 5th ed., 1949.

G. Ryle, *The Concept of Mind*, Hutchinson, London, 1949.

R. Scruton, *A Dictionary of Political Thought*, Macmillan, London, 1982.

N. Sherman, *The Fabric of Character. Aristotle's Theory of Virtue*, Clarendon Press, Oxford, 1989.

J.N. Shklar, *Ordinary Vices*, The Belknap Press of Harvard University Press, Cambridge, Mass., 1984.

H. Sidgwick, *Methods of Ethics*, Macmillan and Co., 1874.

H. Sidgwick, *Outlines of the History of Ethics*, Macmillan and Co., London, 1886.

B. Snell, *The Discovery of the Mind in Greek Philosophy and Literature*, Dover Publications Inc., New York, 1982.

Spinoza, *Ethics*, transl. by A. Boyle, revised by G.H.R. Parkinson, Dent, London, 1989.

G. Steiner, *Antigones*, Clarendon Press, Oxford, 1986.

R.J. Sullivan, *Morality and the Good Life. A Commentary on Aristotle's Nicomachean Ethics*, Memphis State University, Memphis, 1977.

E. Ullman-Margalit, *The Emergence of Norms*, Clarendon Press, Oxford, 1977.

220   *Select Bibliography*

J.O. Urmson, *Aristotle's Ethics*, Blackwell, Oxford, 1988.

J.-P. Vernant, *L'Individu, la Mort, l'Amour: Soi-Même et Autre en Grèce Ancienne*, Paris, Gallimard, 1989.

A.-J. Voelke, *Les Rapports avec Autrui dans la Philosophie Grecque: d'Aristote à Panetius*, Paris, Vrin, 1961.

E. Wharton, *Sanctuary*, Charles Scribner's Sons, New York, 1914.

C.H. Whitman, *Homer and the Heroic Tradition*, Harvard University Press, Cambridge Mass., 1958.

K. Wilkes, *Physicalism*, Routledge and Kegan Paul, London and Henley, 1978.

B. Williams, *Moral Luck*, Cambridge University Press, Cambridge, 1981.

B. Williams, *Shame and Necessity*, University of California Press, Berkeley, 1993.

AUTHOR INDEX

Adkins, A. W. H., 6, 17, 68-70
Allan, D. J., 71
Alpern, K. D., 38
Annas, J., 153, 190 n. 15
Aquinas, 13, 171
Aubenque, P., 166, 192 n. 53

Baier, K., 199-200 n. 66
Barker, E., 166
Benson, J. 43-45, 180 n. 2
Bentham, J., 208 n. 76
Benveniste, E., 6, 179 n. 6, 181
    n. 16
Blum, L. A., 190 n. 9, 209 n. 82
Blundell, M. Whitlock, 179 n. 9
Bodeus, R., 201 n. 22, 206 n. 32
Bonitz, H., 13-14, 55-56, 189
    n. 79, 193 n. 6
Burnet, J., 137, 138
Butler, J., 79, 96

Cicero, 12-13, 149, 165, 171,
    209 n. 87
Clark, G., 210 n. 3
Clark, S. R. L., 181 n. 12, 184
    n. 65, 185 n. 80, 191 n. 24, 200-
    1 n. 19, 204 n. 4, 209 n. 88, 210
    n. 3
Cooper, J. M., 38, 150, 152-53,
    184 n. 72, 185 n. 75, 204 n. 7

Da Ponte, L. 97
Decarie, V., 55
Descartes, R., 22-24
Dilman, I., 62, 63-64
Dirlmeier, F., 83, 180 n. 5, 194
    n. 32
Dover, K. J., 88, 109, 115

Emerson, R. W., 40
Engberg-Pedersen, T., 105-107,
    115
Epicurus, 62, 149, 167, 203 n. 71
Euripides, 17, 111

Flaceliere, R., 180 n. 1
Forster, E. M., 165-66, 209 n. 87
Foucault, M., 15
Fraisse, J.-C., 166, 193 n. 58, 201
    n. 32
Frankena, W. K., 197 n. 6

Gauthier, R.-A., and Jolif, J.-Y., 6,
    32, 83, 85, 87-88, 90, 92, 104-5,
    131, 137, 138, 199 n. 47, 202
    n. 58, 206 n. 30
Gilbert, P., 174-75, 190 n. 12
Goethe, J. W., 173

Hamlyn, D. W., 21-22, 182 n. 36
Hanfling, O., 39-40

Hardie, W. F. R., 137, 185 n. 75
Herman, G., 204 n. 3
Herodotus, 7
Hicks, R. D., 182 n. 36
Hobbes, T., 119-20
Homer, 6, 16-17, 111-12, 115
Hooker, J., 179 n. 5
Huby, P., 180 n. 1
Hume, D., 24

Irwin, T., 70, 71, 166 ff., 195 n. 52, 199 n. 56, 202 n. 43, 210 n. 102
Isaiah, 96

Jaeger, W., 83, 184 n. 65, 192 n. 55

Kahn, C. H., 53, 183 n. 46, 188 n. 73, 210 n. 101
Kant, I., 20, 39-40, 79
Kenny, A., 192 n. 54
Kerferd, G. B., 135
Knox, B. 181 n. 12
Kraut, R., 110, 184 n. 72, 193

Lear, J., 188 n. 61, 200-1 n. 19
Luke, 87, 117-18

Macintyre, A., 192 n. 40
Madigan, A., 112-13, 197 n. 14
Matthew, 100
Millgram, E., 180 n. 2
Modrack, D. K. W., 182 n. 36, 183 n. 44
Monsacre, H., 181 n. 19
Montaigne, M. de, 63, 171, 210 n. 1
Moravscik, J., 208 n. 77
Mulgan, R. G., 207 n. 57

Nagel, T., 105-6, 114
Newman, W. L., 208 n. 75
Nietzsche, F., 142
Nussbaum, M. C., 65, 73, 144-45
Nuyens, F., 32, 83, 185 n. 85

Olle-Laprune, L., 190 n. 5

Pascal, B., 60-61, 75
Passmore, J., 201 n. 30
Plato, 32, 72, 82-84, 98, 101, 112, 115, 118, 123-24, 125-28, 130, 141, 149, 165, 175, 195 n. 45, 201 n. 23
Plomer, A., 183 n. 48
Politis, V., 100-1
Powell, J. E., 179 n. 10
Preus, A., 199 n. 52
Price, A. W., 67, 166ff.

Rackham, H., 55-56, 195 n. 45
Ranke, L. von, 179 n. 1
Rawls, J., 191-92 n. 40
Ross, W. D., 34, 137, 138, 183 n. 44
Ryle, G., 24

Shakespeare, W., 95, 97, 99
Shermanb, N., 107, 186-87 n. 26
Shklar, J. N., 209 n. 88
Sidgwick, H., 62, 66, 189 n. 74
Snell, B., 181 n. 17
Sophocles, 6, 17, 130, 165-66
Spinoza, B. de, 107-9, 114-15
Steiner, G., 182 n. 22
Stern-Gillet, S. M. F., 190 n. 10, 203 n. 71
Stewart, J. A., 107, 131, 140
Stocker, M., 190 n. 8

Telfer, E., 63-64, 190 n. 7
Thucydides, 112, 115
Tricot, J., 182 n. 36, 186 n. 20

Ullman-Margalit, E., 120-21

Vernant, J.-P., 15-16, 18, 182 n. 21
Vlastos, G. 175 ff.

Wharton, E., 62
Williams, B., 142-45, 181 n. 12
Woods, M., 106

Xenophon, 7, 118, 194 n. 38, 195 n. 42

SUBJECT INDEX

Activity (*energeia*): as distinguished from process (*kinesis*),
40-1, 42-3
Actuality (*energeia*): as opposed to
potentiality (*dunamis*), 33, 49-
50, 138
Akolasia. See intemperance
Akrasia. See incontinence
Allos autos (another self), 11-5,
28-9, chapter 2 *passim*, 136-39,
188 n. 73. *See also alter ego*
and self, selfhood
Altruism, 4, 79-80, 118-20, 173-74,
Nagel's view of, 105-6; altruistic dilemma, 120-1; altruistic
suicide, 104, 110-6, 164. *See
also* egoism and self-love
Autarkeia. See self-sufficiency

Blessedness (*makaria*), 130, 133-
37

Civic friendship, 66, chapter 7
passim; as related to primary
friendship, 148-49, 163-64,
166-69; in *Politics*, 149, 153,
204-5 n. 7; and moral virtue,
152-53, 156-57; and justice,
154-60. *See also* constitution
Community (*koinōnia*), 150, 154-
55, 161-63

Competition, 68-71, 103-4, 116-20
Concord (*homonoia*), 149, 152, 158
Constitution: aristocratic, 156-58;
polity, 156, 158-59, 168-69
Contemplation (*theōria*), 30-2,
125, 131, 168

Egoism, 68-70, 79-80, 114, 173-74;
psychological vs. ethical, 104-5.
See also altruism and self-love
Ergon. See function
Eudaimonia. See happiness

Fine (*to kalon*), 70-1, 103, 105-7,
111, 113, 120-1
Function (*ergon* argument), 96,
128, 138, 173
Friendlessness, 130-31, 141, 147-48
Friendship: modern conceptions
of, 8, 14, 60, 61-4, 75, 173-77.
See also civic friendship, guest
friendship, pleasure friendship,
primary friendship, and utility
friendship

God (prime mover), 33, 34, 42, 51,
125, 129, 132
Good, 167; internal and external
goods, 125, 131-32, 191-92 n.
40; unconditional and conditional goods, 69-70, 75, 127-28

Guest friendship, 6, 7
Guilt, 87-8
Great-souled man *(ho megalopsy-chos)*, 110, 125

Happiness *(eudaimonia)*, 4, 15, 96, 104, 125, 127-28, 133, 166-67
Homonoia. *See* concord

Inclination, 8, 71-72, 74, 173. *See also* friendship
Incontinence *(akrasia)*, 26-7, 85-6, 89-95 *passim*, 97-8, 172
Intemperance *(akolasia)*, 86, 89-95 *passim*

Justice, 154-60, 162, 163, 164, 165, 169, 206-7 n. 34; universal and particular, 155-56. *See also* civic friendship and constitution

Kalon to. *See* Fine
Koinōnia. *See* community

Love, 39-42, 61-7, 173-77; as disinterested, chapter 3 *passim*. *See also* friendship

Megalopsychos ho. *See* great-souled man
Metameleia. *See* regret

Nous (understanding, intellect, practical and theoretical reason): identified with self, 25-8, 30-3; 113; active and passive, 23, 33-4, 185 n. 76; as practical reason, 25-27, 29, 35; as theoretical reason, 30-3, 35; plasticity of, 49-51, 53. *See also self-actualization*

Oikeios (one's own), 31, 133-36

Perception, 19-22, 48, 55, 183 n. 48
Philautia. *See* self-love
Philia: translation of, 5-8. *See also* friendship
Pleasure friendship, 38-9, 43, 45, 64-5, 66-7, 114, 125-26
Primary friendship, 8, 11, 39, 43, 52-3, 74-6, 126, 172; primacy of, 37, 134; cognitive benefits of, 45-6, 49-54, 56-7; presupposes moral virtue, 46; as other-regarding, chapter 3 *passim*; dissolution of, 72-3. *See also* self-awareness, self-love, self-sufficiency
Psychē. *See* soul

Regret *(metameleia)*, 85ff., 96ff., 195 n. 45
Remorse. *See* regret

Self, selfhood, 4, chapter I *passim*, 67-8, 73-4, 99, 121-22, 172-74; pre-classical concepts of, 15-18. *See also allos autos, nous*, perception, self-actualization, self-awareness, self-love, self-sacrifice, and self-sufficiency
Self-actualization, 4, 50-4, 57-8, 137-42, 173
Self-awareness: in perception, 19, 21; as distinct from Descartes' concept of, 22-3, 24-5; in primary friendship, 49-51, 53-7, 129, 132-33, 134-135, 139, 140-1
Self-love *(philautia)*, chapters 4 and 5 *passim*; two senses of, 80, 100; paradoxical aspects of, 81-82; as condition of primary friendship, 84, 99-101; as related to moral virtue, 85, 98-100; Spinoza's conception of, 107-8; and self-sacrifice, 113-14. *See also* altruism and egoism
Self-sacrifice, 103ff.; examples of, 110-12; for primary friends,

110, 112-15; for native country, 113, 115-16. *See also* altruism
Self-sufficiency *(autarkeia)*, 14-5, 54-6, chapter 6 *passim*; and happiness, 127-28; and human sociality, 128-131, 141-42; and primary friendship, 132-41, 203 n. 71; as a moral ideal, 142-45
Sensus communis, 20-1, 183 n. 48
Shame, and guilt, 87-8
Soul *(psychē)*, 17, 23, 25, 32-4; and self-love, 80-83, 98-9
State, 125, 128, 147, 149, 154-55. *See also* constitution

Theōria. See contemplation

Universality, 109, 114-15
Utility friendship, 7, 38-9, 43, 45, 61-2, 64-5, 66-7, 114, 125-6, 150-51, 208 n. 71

Virtue, moral: 25-8, 98, 109
Vice *(kakia)*, 26-7, 85-6, 93-6, 155. *See also* wickedness

Weakness of the will. *See* incontinence
Wickedness *(mochteria)*, 85-98 *passim*, 109, 172

INDEX LOCORUM

Posterior Analytics
81a38:48

Topics
145a22: 107

De Sophisticis Elenchis
176b36: 90

De Anima

II. 5
passim: 19
417b23-24: 51
417b24: 51

II. 6
418a14-15: 19
418a17-18: 20

II. 12
424a17-19: 51

III. 2
425b15-16: 19
425b20: 19¶
426a7-8: 19
426b8-12: 19
426b17-23: 20
426b18-20: 20
426b29: 20
427a9: 20

III. 4
429a13-24: 49
429b3-4: 51
429b5-9: 49-50
429b14-18: 33

III. 5
430a10-19: 33
430a12: 185, n. 76
430a15: 185, n. 85
430a22-23: 33
430a23: 34

III. 7
431a12-17: 48
431a14-16: 48
431a21-22: 20

III. 8
432a2: 51
432a7-9: 48

III. 9
432a22-b7: 81

III. 10
433a22-25: 52

De Sensu

VII
passim: 20¶

De Somno et Vigilia
455a15-17: 21

Metaphysics

V. 4
1015a3-5: 50

IX. 6
1049b18ff.: 42

IX. 8
1050a34-b2: 42

XI. 7
passim: 42

XII. 7
1072a21: 133
1072b18-24: 52

XII. 9
1075a7-9: 34

Nicomachean Ethics

I. 2
1094b7-10: 167

I. 6
1096a16-17: 165
1096a23-24: 127
1096b27-29: 127-28

I. 7
1097a18-20: 128
1097b8-11: 128
1097b14-15: 128
1097b16-20: 127
1097b24ff.: 128
1098a12-17: 25

I. 8
1099a31-b6: 125

I. 10
1101a14-16: 104

I. 13
1102b14-18: 42

II. 3
1104b3-5: 46

II. 6
1106b36-1107a2: 52
1106b36-1108a1: 47
1107a1: 29

II. 8
1109a10: 195, n. 52

III. 2
1111b13-16: 42

III. 5
1114a7: 94
1114a20-21: 94
1114b22-25: 94

IV. 3
1124b8: 110
1124b8-9: 110
1124b31-1125a1: 110
1125a12: 125

IV. 9
1128b19-21: 88

V. 1
1129b17-19: 207, n. 42
1129b25-27: 155
1130a5-8: 155

V. 2
passim: 155

V. 9
1136b6-9: 42

V. 11
1138a18-20: 81
1138b5-6: 81
1138b8-11: 81-82

VI. 2
1139a21-26: 48
1139b4-5: 52

VI. 7
1141b12-14: 52

VI. 9
1142b18-20: 95

VI. 12
1144a29-30: 52

VI. 13
1144b30-1145a2: 164

VII. 3
1147a17: 27

VII. 4
1148a29: 27

VII. 7
1150a22ff.: 85-86

VII. 8
passim: 89
1151a1: 27
1151a6: 96

VII. 11
1152b7-8: 133

VIII. 1
1155a2-6: 125
1155a3-4: 46
1155a22-23: 167
1155a23-24: 45
1155a24-26: 152
1155a26-27: 151 & 163
1155a26-28: 46
1155a29: 65

VIII. 3
1156a9-10: 64
1156a10-16: 64
1156a15: 59
1156a15-19: 66
1156a17-19: 38
1156a34-35: 43
1156b7: 59
1156b7-8: 37-38
1156b9-11: 66
1156b10: 39
1156b10-11: 59
1156b11: 66
1156b11-12: 67
1156b12-13: 72
1156b15-17: 133-34
1156b24-25: 167
1156b25-26: 177
1156b26-29: 72

VIII. 4
1157a10-11: 37-38
1157a30-32: 37
1157b3: 59

VIII. 6
1158a15-16: 72
1158b5-8: 37

VIII. 7
1158b23-28: 39

VIII. 8
1159a34-35: 41
1159b2-4: 144
1159b5: 164
1159b6-7: 164
1159b12-13: 144
1159b19-20: 203, n. 76
1159b20-21: 204, n.77

VIII. 9
passim: 150
1159b29-31: 154
1160a4-6: 154
1160a11-12: 205, n. 12
1160a14-15: 155
1160a21: 154-55
1160a22-23: 155

VIII. 10
1160b3-5: 125

VIII. 11
1161a10-11: 155
1161a16-17: 44
1161a18-20: 44
1161a30-b12: 150

VIII. 12
1161b27-29: 28
1161b28-29: 12

VIII. 13
1162b5-6: 208, n. 71
1162b8: 118
1162b16-17: 208, n. 71
1162b16-21: 65
1162b21-31: 150
1163a9-16: 65

IX. 1
1164a9-10: 37-38

IX. 3
1165b15: 73

IX. 4
passim: 98
1166a1-2: 100
1166a4: 39 & 59
1166a10-31: 80
1166a13: 100
1166a13-17: 26
1166a17-25: 100
1166a29-32: 28
1166a29-33: 99
1166a32: 12
1166a33-35: 81
1166b2-25: 84-85
1166b7: 27
1166b7-8: 89
1166b8-10: 90
1166b11-13: 90
1166b13-17: 91
1166b18-25: 91-92
1166b24-25: 86
1166b25-26: 82
1166b27-28: 82
1166b28-29: 99

IX. 6
1167a22: 152
1167a22-29: 152
1167a29-32: 152
1167b2-4: 150
1167b4-5: 152+
1167b5: 152
1167b9-16: 152

IX. 7
1168a5-9: 131
1168a19-20: 40-41

IX. 8
1168a33: 98
1168b2-3: 65
1168b7: 17¶
1168b9-10: 80 & 100
1168b15-19: 80

1168b22-23: 114
1168b28-29: 100
1168b29-35: 82
1168b34-35: 25

IX. 8
passim: 80
1169a7-8: 103
1169a8-10: 103
1169a8-13: 116
1169a11-12: 80
1169a14-15: 119
1169a17: 113
1169a17-18: 109
1169a17-22: 103
1169a18ff.: 46
1169a19: 112
1169a20: 66
1169a20-22: 70
1169a20ff.: 113¶
1169a24-25: 111
1169a28-35: 117
1169a32: 164
1169a32-34: 121
1169a32-b1: 70
1169b1: 80

IX. 9
1169b5-7: 28
1169b6-7: 12
1169b9-10: 125 & 131
1169b12: 46
1169b13: 131
1169b16-19: 200, n. 18
1169b29-30: 133
1169b33: 133
1169b33-35: 49 & 134
1169b33-1170a1: 49
1170a1: 135
1170a2-4: 136
1170a5-6: 136-37
1170a14-16: 138
1170a17: 138
1170a17-18: 138
1170a18-19: 138
1170a19-21: 138
1170a20-24: 138

1170a26-27: 138
1170a27: 138
1170a27-29: 138
1170a29-32: 139
1170a29-1170b1: 50-51
1170a31-b1: 21 & 139
1170a33: 21
1170b1-4: 139
1170b5-7: 28, 51 & 139
1170b6-7: 12
1170b7-8: 51 & 139
1170b8-14: 139
1170b11-12: 47
1170b17-20: 140

IX. 10
1170b28-29: 43
1171a17-20: 168

IX. 11
1171b22-25: 65-66

X. 5
1176a15-19: 53

X. 7
1177a12-18: 30
1177a27-28: 125
1177a32-34: 9
1177a32-b1: 200-01, n. 19
1177b26-30: 30
1177b30-31: 34
1177b31-1178a2: 30
1178a2-4: 30

X. 8
1178a22: 31

X. 9
1179b2-3: 48
1179b23-26: 48

Magna Moralia

II. 11
passim: 75

II. 15
1213a15-24: 49
1213a16-24: 134
1213a23-24: 11

Eudemian Ethics

I. 5
1216a26-27: 151
1216b21-23: 48

II. 7
1223a36-37: 93
1223b30-31: 93

VII. 1
1234b33: 147

VII. 2
passim: 37
1235b30ff.: 69
1236a39-b1: 43
1236b5-6: 72
1236b22-24: 38
1236b29-33: 59
1237a35-37: 59
1237a40-b3: 66
1237b1-5: 59
1237b4: 39
1237b10: 67
1237b10-19: 72
1237b30-35: 59
1237b32-34: 65
1237b40: 74
1238a3-4: 75
1238a4-7: 75
1238a12: 125

VII. 5
1239b11-14: 27
1239b32-34: 144
1240a1: 144
1240a2: 144

VII. 6
1240a19-21: 81
1240b3: 17
1240b14-15: 98
1240b22-24: 96
1240b23-24: 195, n. 52
1240b27-28: 98

VII. 7
1241a7-8: 65
1241a16-17: 152

VII. 7 *(continued)*
1241a22-28: 152
1241a26-27: 152
1241a30-31: 152
1241a32-33: 152

VII. 8
1241a40: 41

VII. 9
1241b24-25: 154-55

VII. 10
1242a6-8: 150
1242a25-40: 150
1242b26-27: 151
1242b35-36: 151
1242b35-37: 150
1242b35-1243a2: 160
1242b39-1243a1: 151
1243a2-b38: 65
1243a31-b14: 150
1243a32-33: 163

VII. 12
1244b7-10: 125
1244b21-1245b19: 132
1244b23-25: 56
1244b23-26: 54
1244b26-27: 55
1244b29-33: 55
1244b33-34: 55
1245a2-3: 57
1245a2-4: 53
1245a4-5: 55
1245a5-9: 50
1245a6-7: 57
1245a8-9: 57
1245a29-30: 11-12
1245a34-35: 12
1245a35-37: 50 & 57
1245b1: 57
1245b4: 57
1245b7-9: 57
1245b11: 57
1245b18-19: 129

VIII. 1
1246b32-33: 209, n. 83

VIII. 3
1248b18-23: 106
1248b20-21: 70
1249a9: 107

Politics

I. 2
1252b30-32: 45¶
1252b30-1253a1: 147
1252b32-1253a1: 124-25
1253a2-3: 45
1253a6: 128
1253a25-27: 128
1253a27-33: 130
1253a37-39: 155

II. 4
1262b7-8: 151
1262b7-9: 144, 149 & 167

II. 5
1263b1: 80

III. 1
1275b17-20: 156

III. 4
1277b18-19: 157

III. 6
1278b27-30: 139

III. 7
1279a34-35: 157-58

III. 9
passim: 156 & 157
1280a20-25: 159-160
1280a34-36: 165
1280b36-40: 115-16

III. 10
passim: 158

III. 12
1282b17: 155-56
1283a20-21: 156

III. 13
1283a38-40: 157

III. 18
1288a37-39: 157

IV. 1
passim: 158

IV. 7
1293b5-6: 157

IV. 8
passim: 158

IV. 9
passim: 158

IV. 11
passim: 158
1295b3-5: 158
1295b21-25: 159 & 204, n. 7
1295b29-32: 158-59
1295b33: 159

IV. 12
1297a6-7: 159

V. 2
passim: 160

VII. 3
passim: 157

VII. 4
1326b14-16: 158

VII. 8
1328b16-17: 125

VII. 9
passim: 157
1328b37-39: 157

VII. 13
passim: 156 & 157

VII. 14
1332a32-34: 158
1332a32-36: 156
1332b25-27: 156
1332b27-29: 156

Rhetoric

I. 5
1360b26-28: 125
1360b29: 125

II. 4
1380b36-1381a3: 59

II. 8
1386a9-10: 125

Poetics

1451b5-7: 77